AF531720

Mughal-e-Azam

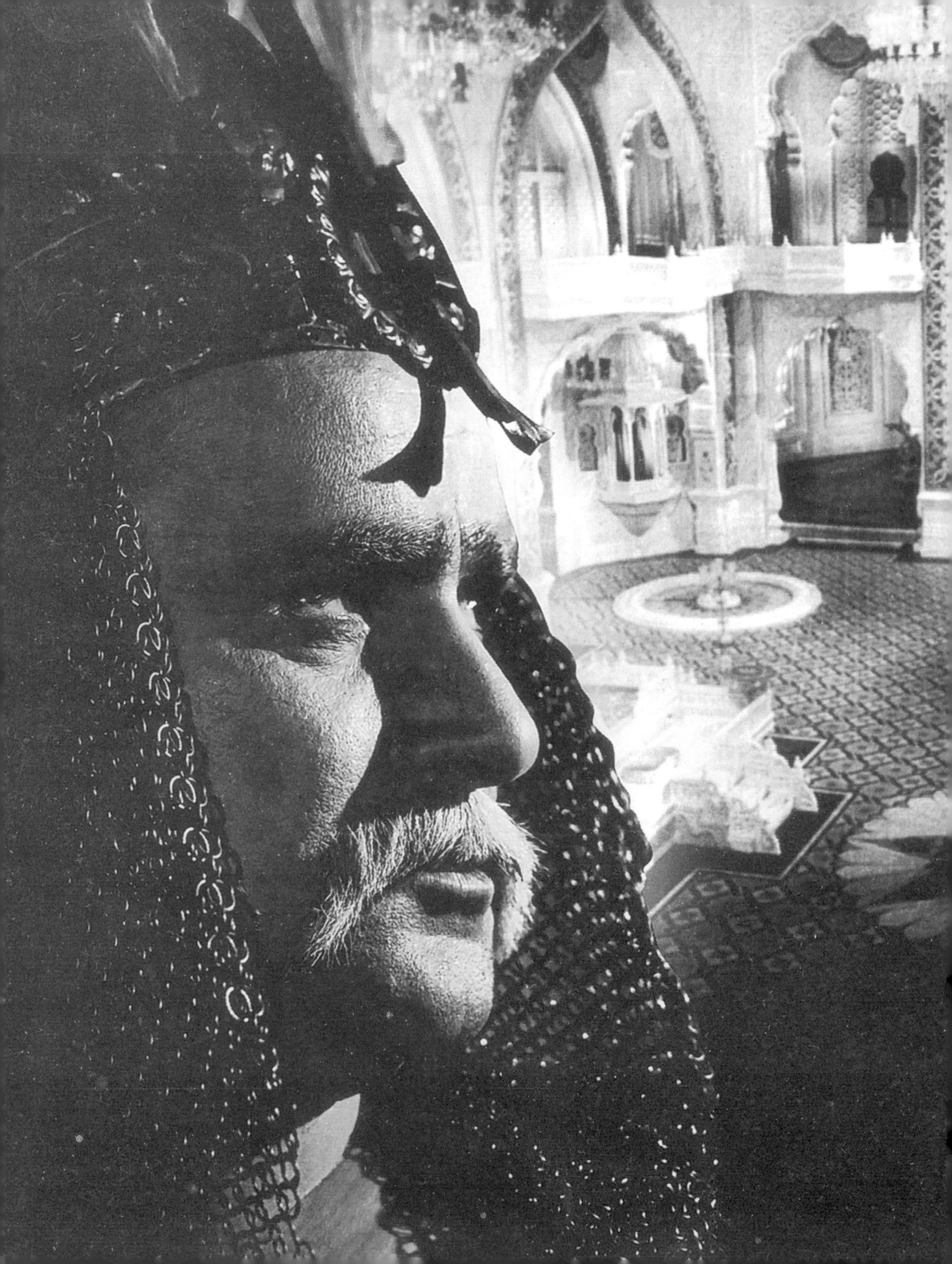

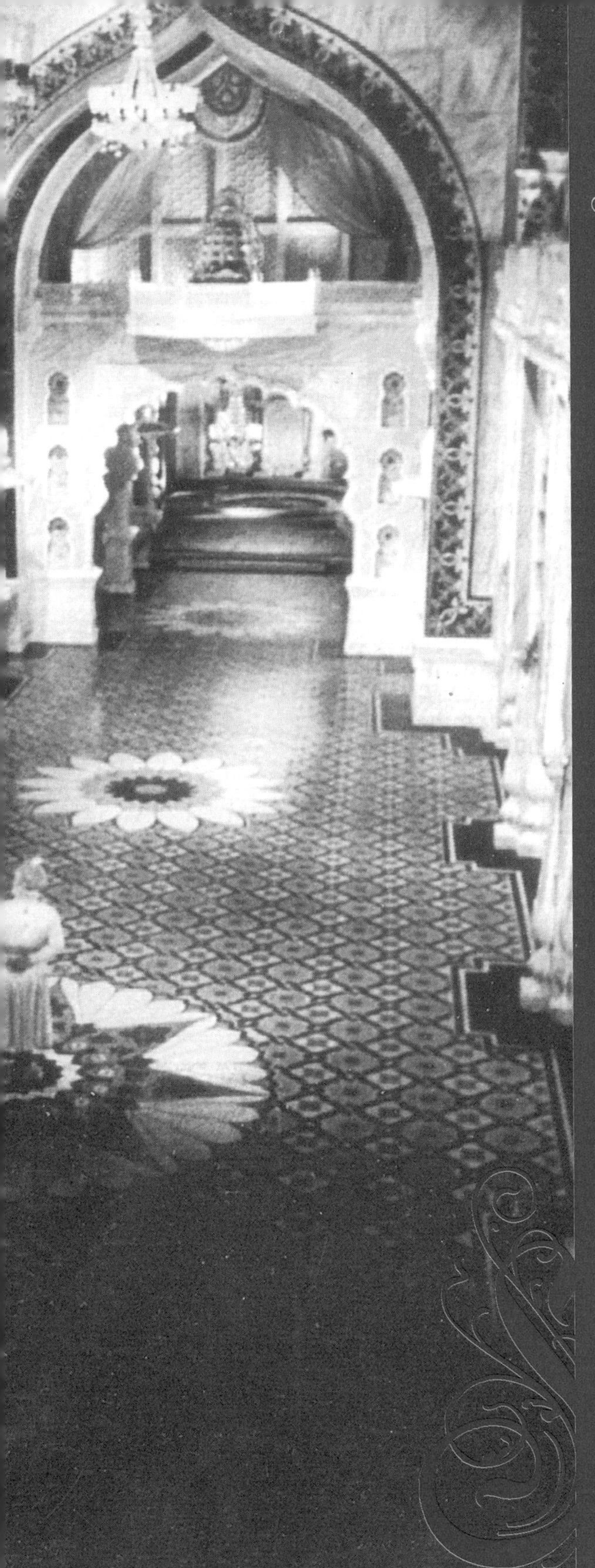

Mughal-e-Azam

An Epic Of Eternal Love

Shakil Warsi

Rupa & Co

Copyright © Shakil Warsi 2009

Published 2009 by
Rupa . Co
7/16, Ansari Road, Daryaganj,
New Delhi 110 002

Sales Centres:
Allahabad Bangalooru Chandigarh Chennai
Hyderabad Jaipur Kathmandu
Kolkata Mumbai

All rights reserved.
No part of this publication may be reproduced, stored in a retrieval system, or transmitted, in any form or by any means, electronic, mechanical, photocopying, recording or otherwise, without the prior permission of the publishers.

The author asserts the moral right to be identified as the author of this work.

Design and Typeset by
Arrt Creations
45 Nehru Apartments, Kalkaji
New Delhi 110 019

Printed in India by
Nutech Photolithographers
B-240, Okhla Industrial Area, Phase-1,
New Delhi - 110 020, INDIA

I dedicate this book
to my daughters
Zeba and Nida
who are a blessing to me from god
and my wife,
Begum Mehrunnisa Warsi,
to whom I shall remain forever indebted
for all her support and encouragement
while I spent hundreds of hours
working on it.

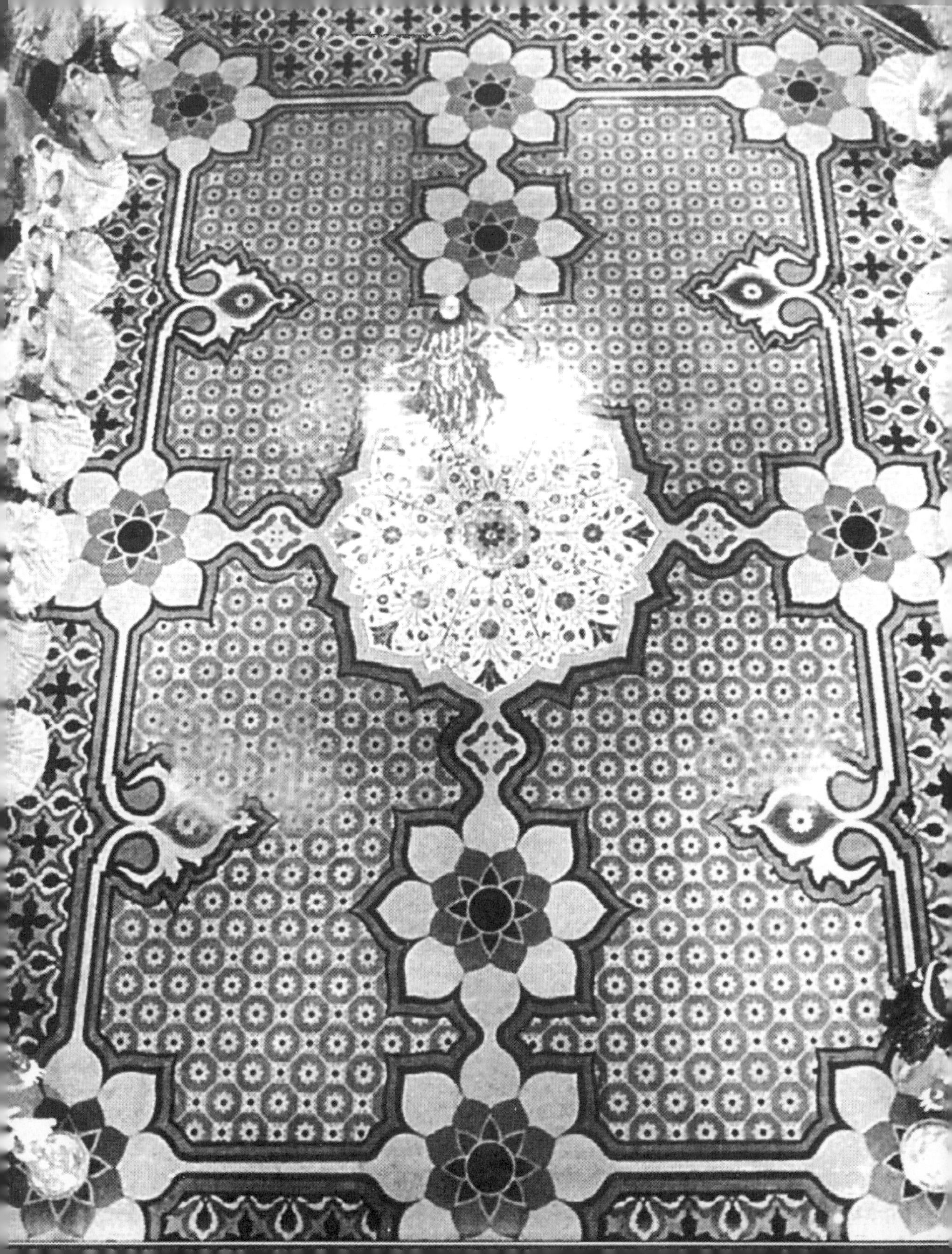

Contents

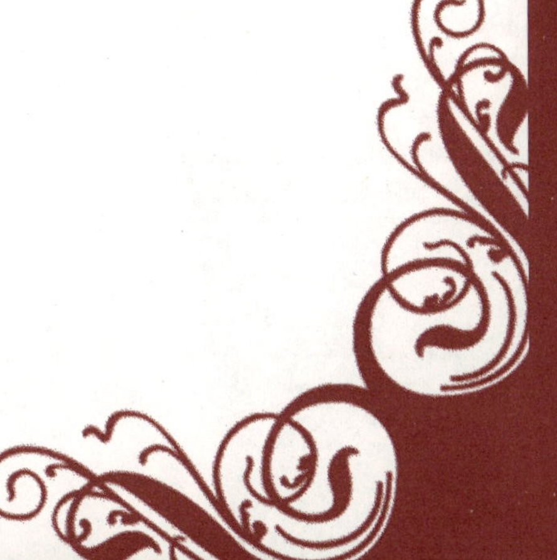

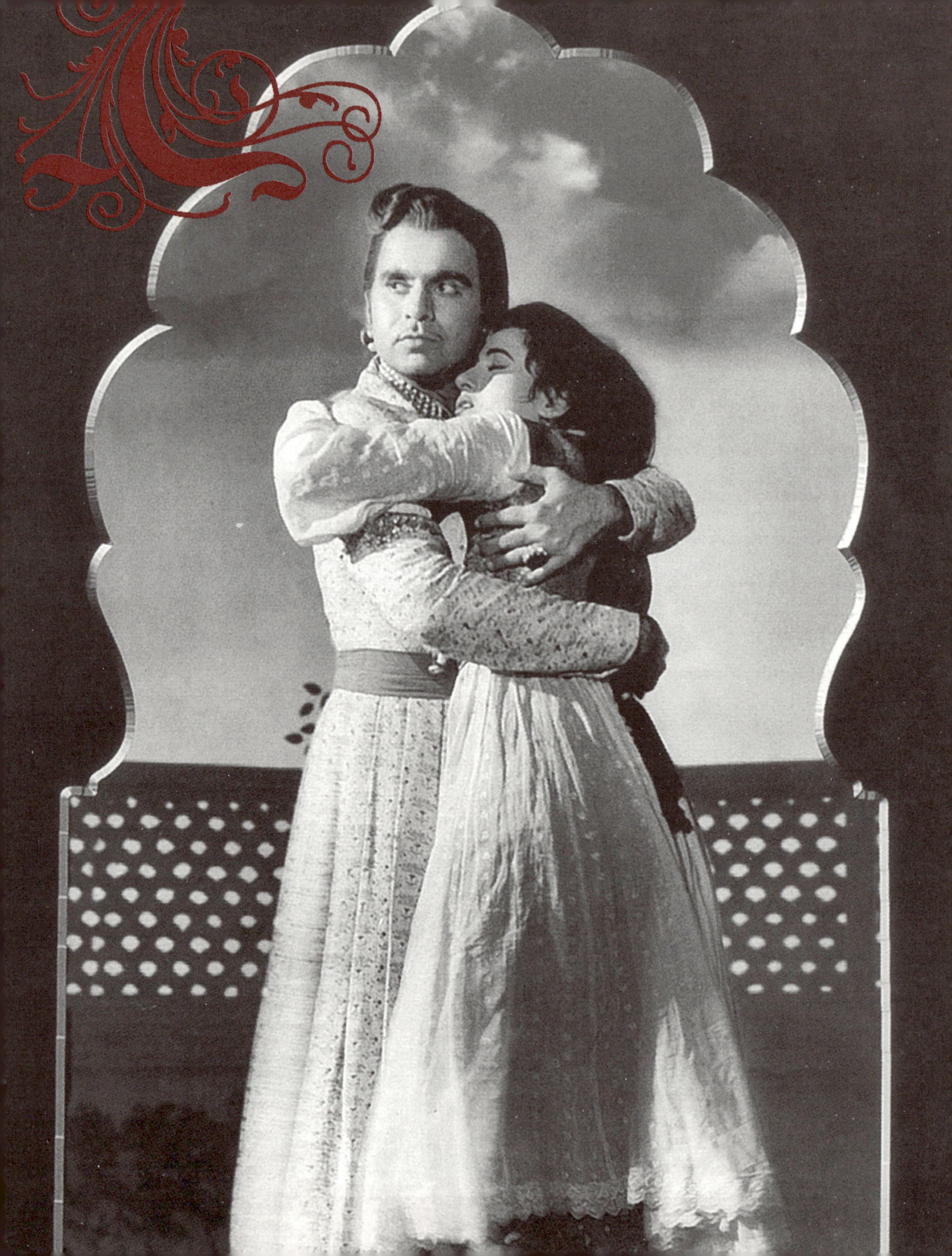

Acknowledgements

I express my gratitude to all my friends and well wishers for their help and encouragement in writing this book. I must especially mention S.M.M. Ausaja, one of India's leading collector of film memorabilia, who gave me unconditional access to his archive of research material and rare images. I am also thankful to Sunil Nair and his wife Aruna Chakravorty, both noted journalists, for their time and efforts in editing the first draft of the text. Beside, I must also name some of my friends for their valuable suggestion and information on the subject: late Suraj Sanim, well known script writer, Umar Siddiqui, managing director, Indian Academy of Arts & Animation, Sanjit Narvekar, film historian and well-known author, C.M. Desai, senior film journalist and Subhash K. Jha, business executive, Cine Advance and Viswamitra.

An overview of historical films

While the effect of seeing larger than life pictures on screen for the first time was mesmerising, the shows were accessible only to a limited, elite audience. Because of the magic quality and the potential mass appeal of cinema it came as no surprise that Indians had entered into the domain of filmmaking.

It was on 7 July 1896 that a crude hand-operated projector threw its silver rays on an improvised screen in India. The place was Watson Hotel, now Esplanade Mansion, near Kala Ghoda in Colaba, Bombay (now Mumbai). The show was a film called *Cinematograph*, made by the French Lumiere Brothers and had, as a catch line, the words, 'Marvel of the Century'. It presented scenes from everyday life in Europe — a train arriving, a structure being demolished, workers emerging from a factory in hordes — marking the advent of cinema in India.

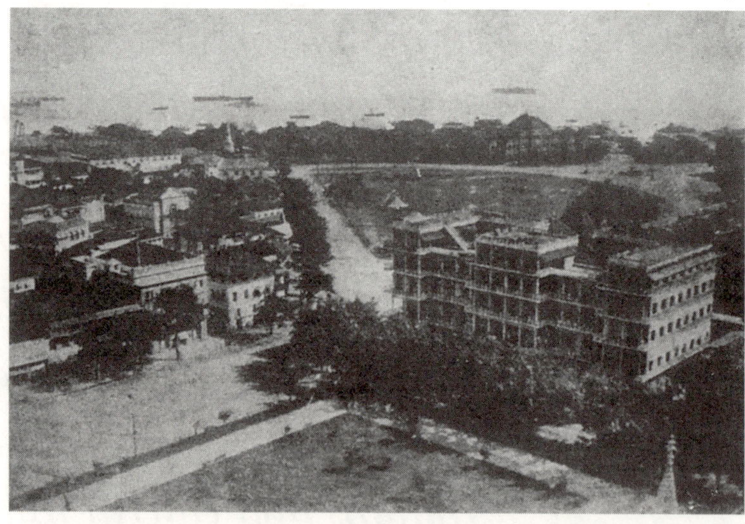

This photograph, taken in 1879 (by Raja Deendayal, first photographer in India), shows Watson's Hotel in the foreground where the Lumiere Brothers' moving pictures were shown (7 July 1896).

While the effect of seeing larger than life pictures on screen for the first time was mesmerising, the shows were accessible only to a limited, elite audience. Because of the magic quality and the potential mass appeal of cinema it came as no surprise that Indians had entered into the domain of filmmaking. The first Indian movie buff, attracted by the medium was

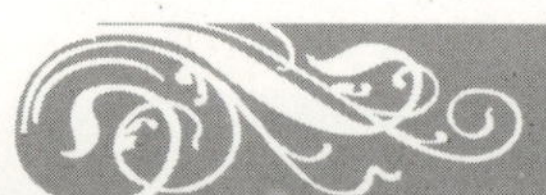

Harishchandra Sakharam Bhatvadekar, popularly known as Save Dada. He was a still photographer and a trader in photographic equipments. He filmed two scenes of three minutes' duration each by an imported camera; the first one was titled *Do Pehelwanon ki Kushti* and the second one, *Bandar ko Nachata Hua Madari*. These films were just short moving images shown in 1898. In subsequent years, many Indians entered into the art of making such movies; among them, most prominent were F.B. Thanawala and Hira Lal Sen. Thanawala made *New View of Bombay* in 1901, which showed some important landmarks of Bombay and generated great interest. Thanawala later made a short film based on Muslim religious processions and named it *Tabut*.

Heeralal Sen, a native of Calcutta (now Kolkata) made his mark as a film producer with a deep interest in Indian history and mythology. He photographed scenes from some plays at Classic Theatre in Calcutta. Such films were shown as an added attraction in the intermission and after the stage performances were over. The possibility of reaching a larger audience through recorded images which could be projected several times through mechanical gadgets, caught the fancy of peoples in the performing arts, stage and entertainment business. Thus, movie making took shape as a profit earning institution gradually, and soon it got linked with exhibition and distribution system. Jamshedji Framji Madan, popularly known as J.F. Madan, belonged to a middle class Parsi family of Bombay. He was a theatre enthusiast and could foresee imminent commercial possibilities in filmmaking in India. Along with his brother Pestonji, he laid the foundation of two theatre companies, the *Elphinston* and *Khatau Alfred*. Madan shifted base to Calcutta in 1902 and began showing films in tent bioscope. In later years, he founded the famous Madan Theatres Limited, which led him not only to build a vast production, exhibition and distribution empire on the lines of Hollywood, but he also brought in foreign actresses like 'Ermline', 'Patience Cooper'. His production company also imported many American films and appointed many experienced foreign directors like Eugelio De Liguoro and Camille Legrand.

Even though the early entrepreneurs of the film fraternity

contributed immensely in the evolution of Indian film industry, yet the approach was just amateurish and inspired by western stalwarts, focusing mostly on foreign ideas. In later years, due to strong bonds of religious faith of masses and their desire to see Indian experiences and Indian characters on screen, filmmakers got inclined to make films on mythological themes. One more reason which prompted Indian filmmakers to opt for mythologies, was the uncertain world of the new and struggling medium. They wanted to take up themes of undoubted audience appeal, and what better way of ensuring this than to rely on stories drawn straight from the scriptures already being enacted in folk dramas. The most prominent producers among those who got fascinated to make such Indian films were Dada Saheb Torne, N.G. Chitre and P.R. Tipinis. They collaborated with English cinematographer Mr. Stevenson and his technical crew Bourne & Shepherd to shoot a play based on the story of a Maharashtrian saint, written by Ramrao Kirtikar and staged by Shripad Sangeet Mandali of Nasik. The film was titled *Pundlik* which was the first 1,500 feet long film made in India. It had to compete with the then released foreign picture *The Dead Man's Child*, which was full of exciting and dramatic situations, suited to that time and atmosphere. *Pundlik* was released on 18 May 1912, and it was a matter of great gratification that people patronised this film much more than *The Dead Man's Child*.

Dhundiraj Govind Phalke, Father of Indian Cinema.

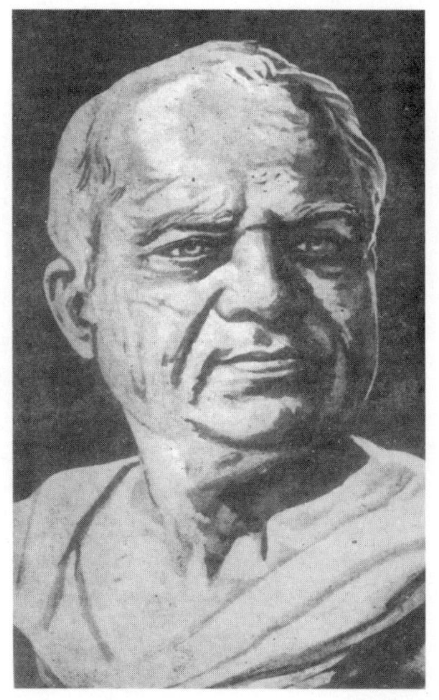

Though *Pundlik* was the first feature film to be made in India by an Indian filmmaker, it was shot by an English cameraman and was never regarded as a first independent Indian film. Moreover, the film was shot with a heavy camera, fixed on a platform, with no close ups, mid-shots and profiles. After watching the single shot recorded movie, Dada Saheb Torne was not happy with overall performance and the effect it was giving; so he decided to re-record it in parts and then join the film together. Perhaps, this was the first approach towards the concept of editing in India which later became one of the most important tasks in the field of filmmaking. Dada Saheb Torne was the original director and pioneering prodigy in the art of movie making, but not much appreciated due to his low profile nature.

People in Bombay and other parts of India waited in eagerness and curiosity for about one year after seeing *Pundlik*. It was only on 3 May 1913 that Indian audiences enjoyed the thrills of the magical world of cinema. Dhandiraj Govind Phalke alias Dada Saheb Phalke released his *Raja Harishchand*ra in Coronation Theatre, Bombay, for which the scripting, photography, processing, printing and editing were carried out in India by the director himself. He once attended screening of a foreign film *The Life of Christ* at P.B. Mehta's American Indian Cinema and was inspired to make films himself. He was convinced of the possibility of establishing an indigenous film industry by focusing on Indian themes. After seeing *The Life of Christ* Dada Saheb Phalke thought why could they not make a film on the lives of Lord Ram and Lord Krishna? After much struggle and hardship he planned *Raja Harishchandra*, the story of a honest king who, for the sake of his principles, sacrifices his kingdom and his family before God, who impressed by his honesty, restores the previous glory.

Thus, the honour of making the first original Indian feature film, by an Indian, goes to Dada Saheb Phalke, because his film was totally Indian in terms of production and as an independent, self-contained work in its own right. The 3,700 feet long celluloid (in comparison of 1,500 feet of *Pundlik)* to run for fifty minutes, was instantly successful due to the splendid special effects by trick photography done by the director. The film laid the foundation for thriving movie industry in India and vastly popular genre of mythological

Left: *Dadasaheb Phalke working with his artistes in the make-up room before filming* Raja Harishchandra.

Right: *Phalke directing his artistes in* Raja Harishchandra.

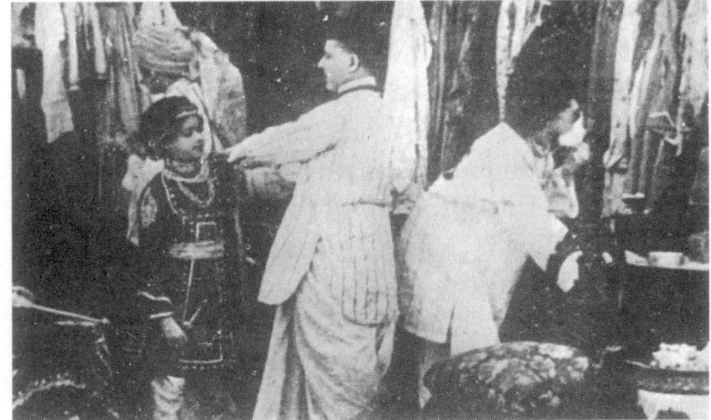

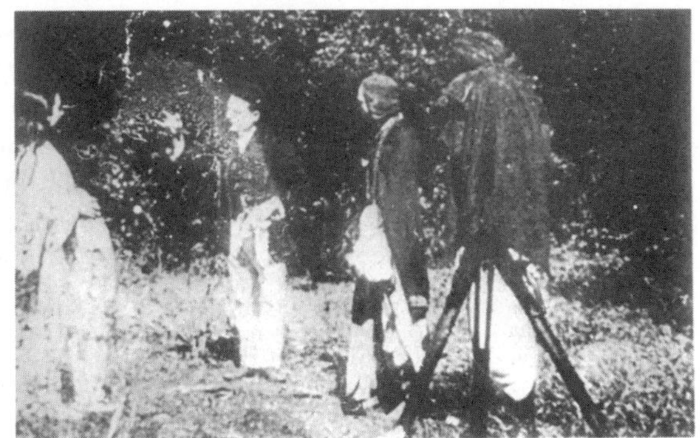

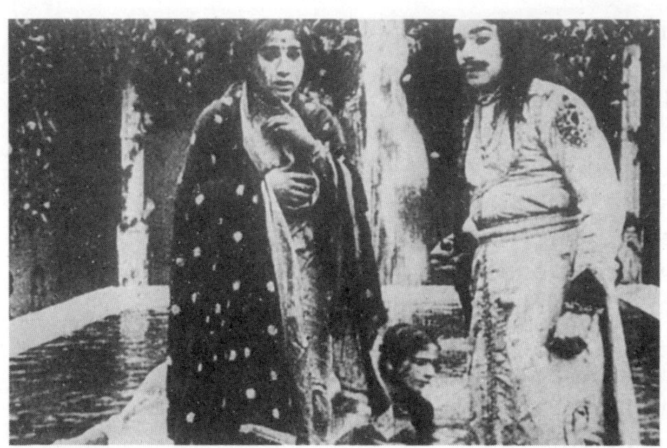

A scene from Raja Harishchandra.

films. Dada Saheb Phalke is truly regarded as the father of the Indian film industry as he fought against all odds and paved the way for present gigantic entertainment trade. He was a multidimensional personality; a skilled writer, director, cinematographer, editor, a painter and a magician. He once said that his decision to make mythologicals was not only because such subjects attracted his religious minded audience, but also allowed him 'to bring mystery and miracles'. After the success of *Raja Harishchandra*, he produced and directed about one hundred films mostly based on Hindu mythology. Some of the most successful films among them are *Mohini Bhasmasur*, *Savitri Satyavan*, *Krishna Janam*, *Kalia Mardan*, and the box office smash hit *Lanka Dehan* which was released in 1917. The first ten days' box office collection of this film was Rs. 32,000. Due to increasing demand, distributors had to screen the movie after every hour whole day at West End Cinema (where Naaz Cinema is situated now at Grant Road in Mumbai). Long queues of bullock carts outside the theatre were often seen, as people flocked to see the movie from far-off villages and towns.

The first decade of Indian cinema was an era in which viewers rushed to movie houses to see their gods perform miracles on screen, as a result, many production houses mushroomed following the runaway success of the initial films, made by Dada Saheb Phalke. Some of the stalwarts of those days who joined him in producing mythological films were Dhiren Ganguli, J.F. Madan, A.N. Bose, S.N. Patankar, N. Mudaliar, Kanjibhai Rathod, D.N. Sampat, Suchet Singh, Babu Rao Painter (Kolhapur) and R. Prakash (Madras). Some of the noted mythological films made by these filmmakers were *Keechaka Vadham* released in 1916 and *Draupadi Vastrapaharan* released in 1917, both directed by N. Mudaliar, *Satywadi Raja Harish Chandra* and *Nala Damayanti*, produced by J.F. Madan were released in 1917 and 1918, respectively. S.N. Patankar produced and directed three mythologicals: *Prahlad Charitra*

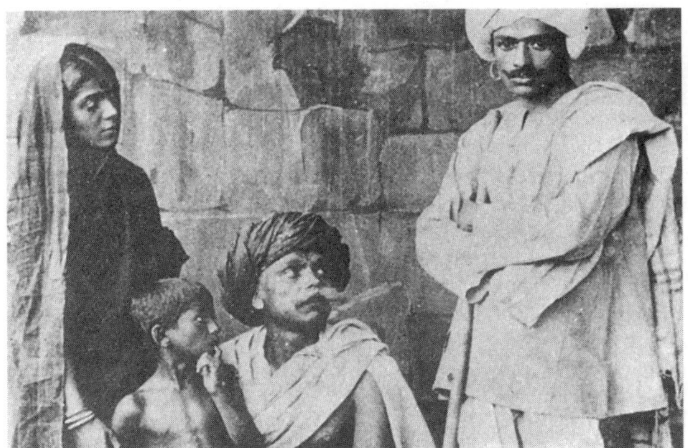

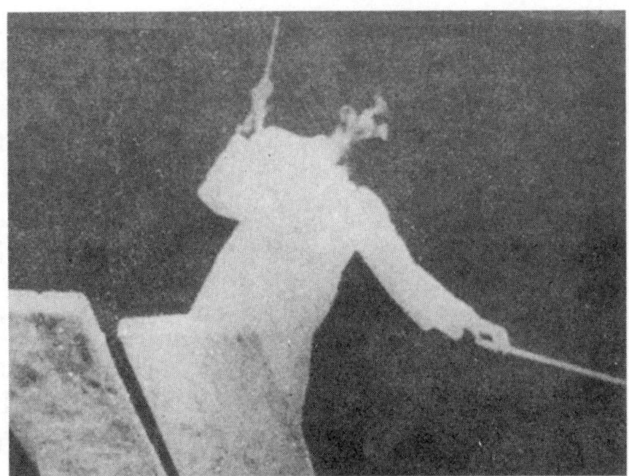

Left: *A scene from Baburao Painter's* Savkari Pash.

Right: *Baburao Painter at work.*

in 1917, *Exile of Shri Rama* in 1918 and *Kachh Devyani* in 1919; Babu Rao Painter directed *Vatsala Haran* in 1919; and Suchet Singh directed *Shakuntala* in 1920. Another mythological, *Krishna Maya* was directed by Kanjibhai Rathod in 1921. Madan made one more mythological, *Savitri* aka *Satyavan Savitri* in 1923. Thus, numerous mythologicals were made until the era of the historicals dawned in the early 1920s.

Though it is difficult to differentiate historicals from periodical costume dramas, films of such genre have always been fascinating to Indian filmmakers. 'Historical films' do not necessarily mean the depiction of history; they often provide a canvas for romantic or melodramatic stories about characters, set against a specific period. Certain facts can be argued and distortion of facts is a common allegation, yet, since they involve real characters and situations, 'historicals' have yielded many successes in the nearly nine decades from 1913 to 2008, arguably the most ambitious venture in Indian cinema.

The first historical in the history of Indian cinema was produced by M/s Patankar Union, Bombay in 1915. The film titled *Murder of Narayan Rao Peshwa* was directed by S.N. Patankar. G. Ranade, D. Joshi, and K.G. Gokhle were the main actors in the film. Since the Indian film industry was passing through its infancy period; this film was just a beginning of something significant. After a gap of seven years, the next historical *Ashoka* was produced by Madan Theatres

Ltd. in 1922 and proved nothing more than an honest effort to make a good historical. In 1923, Madan again launched a historical this time with a better script. It was based on the story of the beautiful Mughal queen and wife of emperor Jahangir. The film was titled on her name *Noorjahan,* which means *'Light of the World'*. Madan directed the film himself and cast the foreign actresses Patience Cooper, Albertina along with Indian stars of the time, namely, Azra Mir, D. Sarkari and M. Chhapqar. This film was below the mark, as regards presentation and picturisation. After this, the Kolhapur based Maharashtra Film Company came up with an important venture, titled *Sinhgadh* in the same year. Based on Hari Narayan Apte's Marathi novel *Gad Ala pan Simba Gela*, the film was directed by Baburao Painter and had a young, enthusiastic production assistant on the company's rolls acting in it, whose name was V. Shantaram. Bala Saheb Yadav, Kamla Devi, Nalini, K.P. Barve and G.R. Morey were the other actors. The film was regarded as India's first full scale (6,880 feet long) historical and Maharashtra Film Company's costliest project to date. It retold a famous episode in the military career of Maratha king Shivaji (played by Babu Rao Painter) and his lieutenant Tanaji. The film featured Tanaji's invasion of the fort of Sinhagad in the dead of night, using his pet lizard to run up the wall with a rope. This film was a trendsetter, inspiring many to exploit the dramatic episodes from medieval history.

More historicals were released in 1924 than previous years, for instance, *Chandragupt* and *Mahatma Chanakya* was released by Star Films of Bombay, Madan Theatres Ltd. produced *Misr Rani* (or *Queen of Egypt*) in which Nihar Bala, the famous actress of silent era played the female lead. Hindustan Film Company's *Shivaji's Escape from Agra* and Ashoka Pictures' *Prithvi Vallab* were also produced in the same year. *Shivaji's Escape from Agra* was a Dada Saheb Phalke film while *Prithvi Vallabh* was directed by the then famous director Mani Lal Joshi. Wagle Sandow, P.Y. Altekar, Fatima Begum, Sultana, Zubeda and Bhalji Pendharkar comprised the main star cast of the film.

Prithvi Vallabh, based on a Gujarati novel written by K.M.

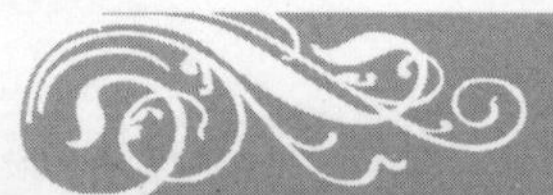

Munshi, was an important silent historical film. Just before the film's release, the story was published in a journal *Vismi Sadi* and became controversial, as Gandhiji criticised it for departing from non-violence and abstinence. The story featured King Monja, the famed warrior and patron of art, a swashbuckling young man, fond of extracting joy from every moment, under all conditions; in conquest or defeat, in prison, in love when betrayed and sentenced to death. The highlights of the film were huge sets, designed by R.S. Choudhry, imposing shoot locations, mainly around the Makkar Pura palace in Baroda and scenes featuring the elephant stampede. The film was technically weak, yet the director Mani Lal Joshi defended the same by saying in a note, published on the release of the film, ' ...all those defects would be excused when one day, my film would find a place in world cinema.'

Shahjahan, *Raziya Begum* and *Veer Durgadas*, all produced by Majestic Film Company, were also released in 1924. *Shahjahan* was jointly directed by Nawal Gandhi and Ardeshir Irani. It was Irani's first venture in historical films who later became a pioneer of talkies in Indian cinema by producing and directing the first talkie *Alam Aara* in 1931. *Razia Begum* was also directed by Ardeshir Irani. Jillobai, the famous actress of the silent era acted in the film. The Eastern Film Company

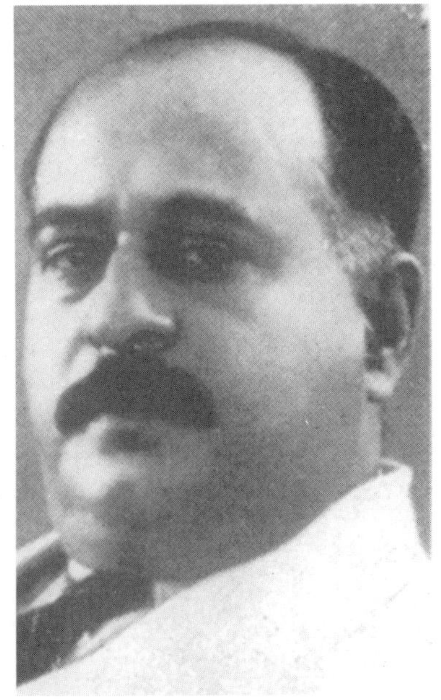

Ardeshir M. Irani, father of the Indian talkie.

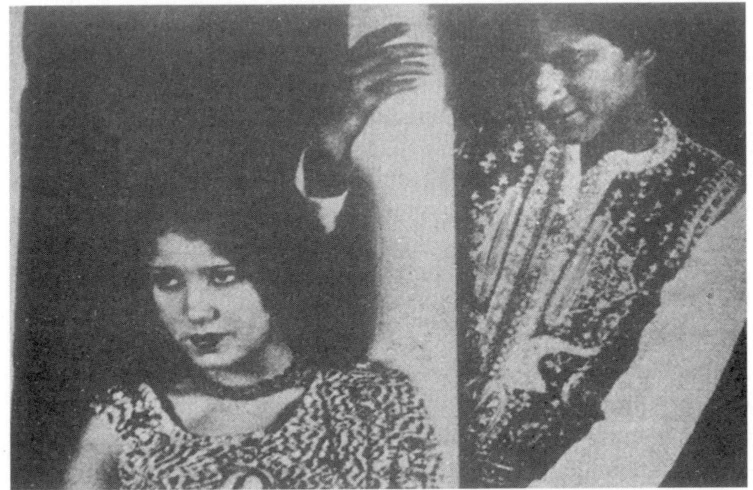

Master Vithal and Zubeida in Alam Ara, *India's first talkie (1931).*

produced the famous historical *Prithviraj Chauhan* in the same year. The Maharshtra Film Company of Kolhapur again produced two historicals in 1924: *Kalyan Khazina* (the Treasure of Kalyan) and *Sati Padmini*, both directed by Babu Rao Painter. Balasaheb Yadav, Nalini, Sultana and Master Vithhal were the actors of *Kalyan Khazina* and the film was based on the exploits of the seventeenth century when Shivaji was in confrontation with Mughal empire. The film's dramatic highlight occurs when inspecting the Mughal wealth, Shivaji is suddenly confronted with not a box full of coins but a fair maiden, emerging from one of the craters. *Sati Padmini* starred Nalini, Balasaheb Yadav, Ganpat Bakre and Shantaram as main actors of the film. It was a true story of legendary Rajput queen Padmini of Chittor, in fourteenth century when the Sultan of Delhi Alla-u-ddin Khilji caught sight of her and became so infatuated that he attacked the fort of Chittor. The Rajputs were defeated, however, Padmini committed sati by the time Khilji arrived. The film was screened at British Empire Exhibition and got some favourable reviews in the British press for its presentation.

Ranak Devi, another historical, was made in the same year by National Film Company of Bombay. The film was directed by S.N. Patankar. Deccan Pictures produced *Poona Raided* in the same year. Mama Warekar, a major Marathi playwright of the time, directed the film with the actors Qaisar, Dulari, Miss Bhawani, Krishna Rao Ketkar, Shankar Rao Sahasra, Shankar Rao Moghe, Vishnu Pant Pagnis and Sunderrao Nadkarni. *Poona Raided* was an expensive historical of that time and paralleled the scale of *Sinhagadh*. The film retold much talked about episode of the attack of Emperor Aurangzeb's army on the fort of Poona. Thus, several historical films were made in 1924; the themes of some of which continued to fascinate producers in the following years, sustaining a regular flow of historicals.

Royal Arts Studios of Bombay produced *Amarsingh Dagger* and *Devi Ahlaya Bai* in 1925. The Maharashtra Film Company of Kolhapur produced *Rana Hamir,* another historical released in the same year. The film was directed by Babu Rao Painter. The Patel Brothers' *Rana Pratap* was also released in the same

year. Balasaheb Yadav and Sushilabai were the main actors in this film. Sharda Films' *Bajirao Mastani*, and United Pictures' *Chhatrapati Sambhaji* were also produced in 1925. *Chhatrapati Sambhaji*, directed by N.D. Sarpodar, was based on the story of Maratha ruler Sambhaji, son of Shivaji. *Baji Rao Mastani*, an important historical, focused on the life of Maratha Peshwa of the eighteenth century. The film was directed by Nanubhai Desai and co-directed by Bhaji Pendharkar. Bhogi Lal, K.M. Dave, Nana Saheb Pathak, Master Vithal and Yakub were the main actors of the film. This film proved to be an uncharacteristic launch of stunt movies in the silent era.

Mani Lal Joshi directed Kohinoor Film Company's *Veer Kunal* released in the same year, with Raja Sandow, Yakbal, Miss Moti, K.B. Athavle and Bachubabu acting in the film. The film depicted the legendary character of Kunal, son of King Ashoka and Queen Padmavati. Kunal had beautiful eyes, but it was predicted that he would go blind. Tishiyaraksha, played by Yakbal, gained Ashoka's trust and conspired to have Kunal blinded and killed. The execution spared him and he left the kingdom with his beautiful wife Kanchanmala, played by Moti. He later became a talented singer. King Ashoka once happened to be in Patliputra and heard his son singing the songs. Impressed by his singing, the king realised Kunal's misfortune and brought him back to the palace and punished Tishiyaraksha.

Some other historical films with low budgets were also made in 1925, namely, *Light of Deccan* by Indian Pictures Corportion Bombay, *Suvarna* by Luxmi Pictures Bombay and *Mulraj Solanki* by Royal Art studio, directed by Ardeshir Irani.

The year 1926 too witnessed many historical film. *Abola Rani* a product of Excelsior Film Company was directed by S.N. Patankar with Zubeida in the female lead. *Dha Cha Maa* or *Murder of Narayan Rao Peshwa* was another historical produced in 1926 by United Pictures Syndicate Poona. The film was directed by N.D. Sarpodar. W. Kulkarni, Gaungoobai Durgabai and Verne were the main stars. Nanabhai B. Desai's directorial venture *Dil Aram* produced by Sharada Film Company, was also released in the same year. Dwarka and Mary Kapoor were the main actors in the film. The Saraswati

Film Company of Bombay produced *Dulari,* directed by Mani Lal Joshi starring M. Udavdia, Putli, Baburao, Jilloo, Yusuf, Elzer and M. Vakil. Another historical of 1926 was *Ra Kawat*, produced by Kohinoor Film Company and directed by M. Bhavnani. Gohar, Raja Sandow, Sulochna and Ghanshyam acted in the film. *Mumtaz Mahal* the more familiar historical of the year was also produced by the same production house with the same star cast. Homi Master was the director of this film. *Panna Ratna* or 'Jewel of Mewar', a low profile historical of the year was produced by Krishna Film Company, Bombay and directed by Harshadraj Mehta. Faiman, Nand Ram, Gangaram and Kamlakar were the main actors of the film. The more popular historical, *Lion of Mewar* (also known as Diwan Bhamashah) was also released in 1926. The film was directed by M. Bhavnani for Imperial Film Company with Jillo and Putli as the main actors.

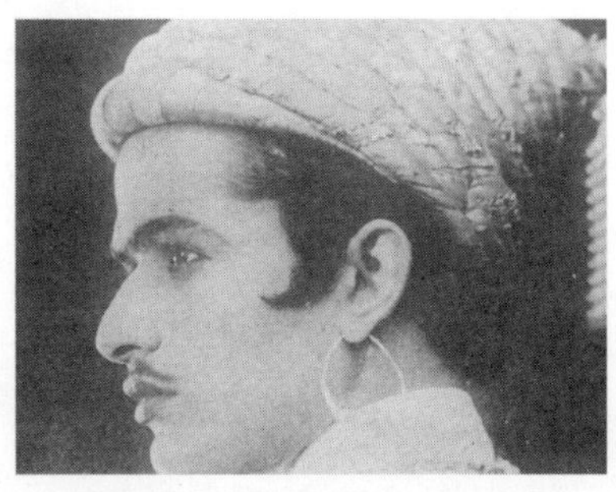

V. Shantaram as Shivaji in Udaykal.

Maharashtra Film Company's next historical in 1927 was *Netaji Palkar,* which marked V. Shantaram's debut as a director. Bala Saheb Yadav, Zunzarrow, Pawar, Ansuya, Ganpat Bekre and Sushilabai were the main actors. United Pictures Syndicate of Poona again produced two historicals in 1927: *The Fair Warrior* or *Shur Killedarin* and *Thoratanchi Kamla*. The former was directed by Vishnupant Aundhkar and the latter by N.D. Sarpodar. One more historical made in 1927 was Madan Theatre's *Durgesh Nandini,* which was directed by Priyanath Ganguli starring Sita Devi, Patience Cooper, Durgadas Banerji, P.C. Bose and Asha Bose.

The more talked about historical films followed in 1928. Among them, the most prominent were *Anarkali* aka *Monument of Tears* and *Loves of Mughal Prince.* Anarkali was produced by Imperial Film Company and directed by R.S. Choudhry while *Loves of a Mughal Prince* was an ambitious project of Great Eastern Film Corporation, directed by Prafulla Roy and Charu Roy. Both the films were based on the legendry love tale of Mughal Prince Salim and the beautiful courtesan Anarkali, which has been picturised several times.

Few more historical films were released in 1928. For instance, Lokmanya Film (Bombay) Company produced *Emperor Ashoka* or *Samrat Ashok*, with Zubeida, Putli, Vakil,

Elizer and Jiloo as the main actors. Another film with the same name was made earlier by Madan Theatre of Calcutta in 1922. *Fall of Pawagadh* and *Jai Bhavani* were also produced in 1928, by Indulal Yangik and Jagtap Picture, respectively. *Fall of Pawagadh* was directed by N. Majumdar with Iris Crawford and Navichandra as the leading actors, while K.P. Bhave directed *Jai Bhawani* with Dwarkee, Bhonsle, R. B Jagtap, Dabir and Yashwantrao More, playing the main roles in the film.

The flow of historicals continued in 1929. Himanshu Rai, founder of Bombay Talkies, produced *Shiraz* in 1929. The film was based on a fictional tale written by Niranjan Paul that narrates the story of the architect of Taj Mahal, which is contrary to popular romantic tale of Prince Khurram (who later became Shahjahan) and Arjumand Banu alias Mumtaz Mahal. Himanshu Rai himself played the title role along with Charu Roy, as Shahjahan. Sita Devi, Maya Devi, Enakshi Ramarao and Prafulla Kumar were the other actors. German director Frans Osten directed the film which had a number of passionate kissing scenes. The cinematography received favourable comments introducing a baroque camera style that became inescapably linked with the genre of Mughal romances in later films.

Among other historicals produced in 1929, notable were *Fall of Mauryas* or *Maurya Patan*, *Jai Somnath* and *Siraj-ud-Dowla*. *Fall of Mauryas* was produced by Royal Pictures Corporation, Bombay and directed by R.S. Chaudhry. Jillo, Putli, Zebunnisa, M. Vakil, Elizer, Rustom and Baburao were the actors. *Jai Somnath* was produced by Mehta Production, directed by J.S. Mehta with Kale Apte, Rampyari, Gulab, Ibrahim, Haider Shah and Shanta as the main actors. *Siraj-ud-Daula* based on the conflict with British forces and the Battle of Plassey, was produced by International Pictures Corporation. Jani Babu, Zebunnisa and Vithal starred in the film. A few more historicals released in the same year – *Jewel of Rajputana* or *Mewar nu Moti*, produced by Imperial Film Company and directed by B.P. Misra with Sulochna, Billimoria, Jillo, M. Vakil, Mazahar Khan and Jamshedji as main cast of the film; *Karuna Kumari* a Sharda Films production, was directed by H.S. Mehta. Vishnu Films

Company produced *Veer Haq* or *Triumph* which was directed by A.P. Kapoor. Bachu, Tara, Lobo, Bose and Atta Mohammad starred in the film.

The historicals that followed in 1930, were *Birth of Shivaji, Fall of Raigard* or *Jeejabai, Benevolent Bravery* or *Shurn Sangram, Glory of India* or *Noor-e-Watan, Bharat Ramani, Goddess of War* or *Ran-Chandi, Raj Sinha, Justice of Jahangir from Adle-Jahangir* and *Ranak Devi*.

Birth of Shivaji was produced by Gajanan Film Company of Bombay. *Fall of Raigadh* was made by United Pictures of Poona. Pandurang S. Taligere was the director while Gangoobai, V.S. Bapat and Jairam Desai were the actors. *Benevolent Bravery* or *Shur Sangram* was produced by Krishna Film Co. M.D. Shah directed this film with Sardar, Vishnu, Gulab and Ranibai as the main actors. Jayant Desai directed *Noor-e-Watan* for producer Ranjit Film Company, Bombay. Sultana, Inamdar, Baba, Vyas, Manilal and Shanti was the cast of this film. *Bharat Ramani,* another historical, was a Madan Theatres' product. Sita Devi, D. Sarkari, Lalita Devi and Patience Cooper starred in the film. Homi Master was the director of *Ran Chandi* which was produced by Kohinoor United Artistes, Bombay. Jamna, Khalil, Thomas and Fatima were the main actors in the film. Madan Theatre produced another historical that year titled as *Raj Sinha* with the star cast Patience Cooper, Indira Devi and Ahindra. This film was directed by Jyotish Banerji. Naval Kapoor Production made *Adl-e-Jahagir.* Nandram and Zebu were the main stars of the film. This film was re-made many times in later years. Ranjit Film Company of Bombay produced *Ranak Devi* which was a re-make of an earlier version produced by National Film Company in 1924. Ranjit's *Ranak Devi* was directed by Nanubhai Vakil with leading actors Putli, Baburao, Manilal and Ishwarilal. *Prithviraj Samyukta,* another notable historical, was also released in 1930, which was produced by Aryan Films and directed by N.D. Sarpodar; Ambu and Bhagirthi were the main actors of the film.

Ardeshir Irani was a renowned producer and director of the silent era. He began his film career in the mid-1920s. After directing several successful silent films, Irani founded his mega film production company, Imperial Film Company in 1926 in

partnership with Esoofally, Mohammad Ali and Dawoodji Rangwala, which soon became a major dream factory of the era. The company owned India's top silent stars. Sulochna, Zubeida and the young Prithviraj Kapoor were on the company's monthly pay roll. This was the first attempt for a star-oriented marketing strategy in the silent period. Irani also had a tie-up with talented directors of the era, such as R.S. Choudhury, B.P. Mishra and Mohan Bhavnani. He was far sighted enough to recognise the potential of sound tracks in films and called Wilford Deming, an American engineer to assemble equipments and the latest technique for his company's innovative plans. Irani himself learned the rudiments of recording from Wilford and soon launched his pioneering mega venture *Alam Ara,* a period fantasy based on Joseph David's popular Parsi play. The film was released as the first talkie in Indian cinema on 14 March 1931 at Majestic Theatre in Bombay, closely beating Madan Theatre's (Calcutta) ambitious and big budgeted talkie *Shirin Farhad*. Though *Shirin Farhad*, based on a legendry Persian love tale, was a bigger hit, *Alam Ara,* became a landmark in the history of Indian cinema due to its earlier release.

After directing the first talkie, Ardeshir Irani produced *Noorjahan* in 1931, as the first talkie historical directed by Azr Mir; Vimas played the title role with Nayampally (maternal uncle of actress Shobha Khote) as the hero of the film and Joseph David as the music director. Irani's *Noorjahan* was in fact a re-make of an earlier silent film made with the same title in 1923, by his competitor Madan Theatres. Beside *Noorjahan*, a few more historicals were released in 1931: *Ronaq Mahal* by Mehta Lohar Pictures, directed by H.S. Mehta with actors Navinchandra, Bapurao Apte and Sultan Alam; *Raj Bhakt* or 'Peace-Maker', produced by Aryan Film Co. and directed by Dinkar Bedekar Dattar. Sandow, Das and Meera acted in the film. *Prithviraj*, with Nandram, Promodh Bose and Balabhai as the main actors, was produced by Sharda Film Co. and directed by Vaidya. *Drums of Love* or *'Premi Jogan'* was another historical made in 1931, produced by Ranjit Films Company and directed by Nandlal Jaswantilal, starring Shanta Kumari, D. Billimoria, Putli and Ishwarlal.

Throne of Delhi aka *Afghan Abla*, was another historical produced in the same year by Kohinoor United with Jamna, Ibrahim and Mijjan playing the main roles.

More filmmakers were fascinated to produce more talkie historicals in 1932. Indian Art Productions' *Veer Kunal,* released in 1932, was directed by M. Bhavnani and G. Deune. Ashraf Khan played the title role while Mehtab was the female lead who later married Sohrab Modi. This film was also a re-make of a silent version of the same title, produced by Kohinoor Film Company in 1926. Other notable historical films released in 1932 were *Bhavani Talwar*, *Gurjar Veer*, *Hoor-e-Hind, Bibi Sultana Chand* and *Tiger of Rajputana*.

Bhawani Talwar was produced by Aryan Film Company and directed by N.D. Sarpodar with actors Dattar, Amboo, Sandow, Das, Shelke, Bala Saheb, Heerabai and Kanheri- *Gurjar Veer* was the product of Sharda Film Company, directed by Dhirubhai Desai, with Yashwant Dave, Bhim, Chandrika and Himmatlal as main actors. H.S. Mehta directed *Hoor-e-Hind* for producer Mehta Luhar Production with actors Navin Chandra, Meera, Nizamuddin and Lobo. *Sultana Chand Bibi*, another notable historical made in 1932 was directed by N.D. Sarpodar for Aryan Film Company with actors Datta, Sandow and Heera Bai. *Tiger of Rajputana* was also produced in the same year by Paramount Film Company and directed by R.N. Vadiya. Chotu Bhai, Noorjahan and Shiraz were the lead actors in the film.

There was only one historical released in 1933: *Prithviraj Sanyojita*, a love tale, produced by Maharashtra Cine Tone and directed by Nana Saheb Sarpodar. Navichandra played Prithviraj and Padma played Sanyojita. This film too was a re-make of earlier version made in 1930, titled *Prithviraj Samyukta*. *Kurukshetr*, a period drama with a historical backdrop was also produced in the same year by Chhatrapati Cine of Kolhapur. Madhav Rao and Padma Nandreka were the main actors.

East India Film Company of Calcutta re-made *Chandragupt* in 1934 with A.R. Kardar as the director and K.C. De (uncle of playback singer Manna De) as the music composer. Gul Hamid, Sabita Devi and Nazir Ahmed were

the main actors. A film on the same subject was released a decade earlier as a silent film and titled *Chandrgupt and Mahatma Chanakya. Mumtaz Begum*, another historical was also made in 1934 being produced by East India and directed by Akhtar Nawaz. Akhtari and Mazhar Khan were the main actors; Akhtari played the title role. United Artists re-made *Ad-le-Jahangir,* in 1934 which had been produced earlier by Sharada Films in 1930. The 1934 version of *Ad-le-Jahangir* was directed by K. Sardar; Ishrat Sultana composed the music. Kantilal, Pushpa, Anwari Begum and Padmawali were the main actors of the film. *Noor Mahal* another historical costume drama was also released in the same year, which was directed by Moti Gidwani with main actors, Yakub and Dulari. Shanta Kumar composed the music.

Madan Theatres of Calcutta followed with *Jahan Ara* in 1935, with F.R. Irani as the director and Kajjan in the lead role. Pirjan, Mustafa and Jagdish Sethi were the other actors. Ardeshir Irani re-made *Anarkali* in 1935 and repeated the entire star cast of his silent version made in 1928.

Although numerous historicals were made between 1915 and 1935, barring a few exceptions, most were amateurish efforts devoid of a realistic depiction of the period. In those early years of silent movies and talkies, a star-cast with histrionic capabilities, deft direction, dramatic dialogues, intelligent camerawork and enlivening music was more the exception than the rule. After a lapse of four years, since Irani's *Anarkali* had been released, the first landmark historical, *Pukar,* came in 1939, which was produced and directed by Parsi theatre's veteran Sohrab Modi, the founder of Minerva Movietone, which soon became famous for spectacular historicals in Indian cinema. The film had the strikingly handsome Chandramohan as Emperor Jahangir, while Naseem Bano, mother of actress Saira Bano, played Noorjahan. The narrative was based on the legend surrounding Jahangir's sense of fair play and his reputation as a ruler who never discriminated between the rich and the poor, Hindus and Muslims. Naseem Bano, an aristocratic and stunningly beautiful lady, was perfectly cast as Noorjahan. Although according to the critics of the time, her performance was not

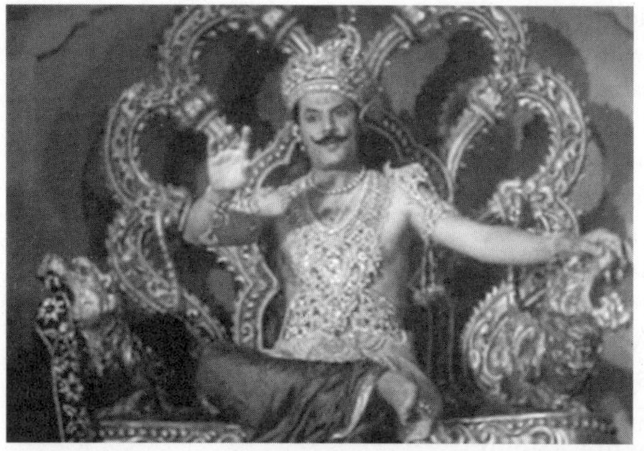

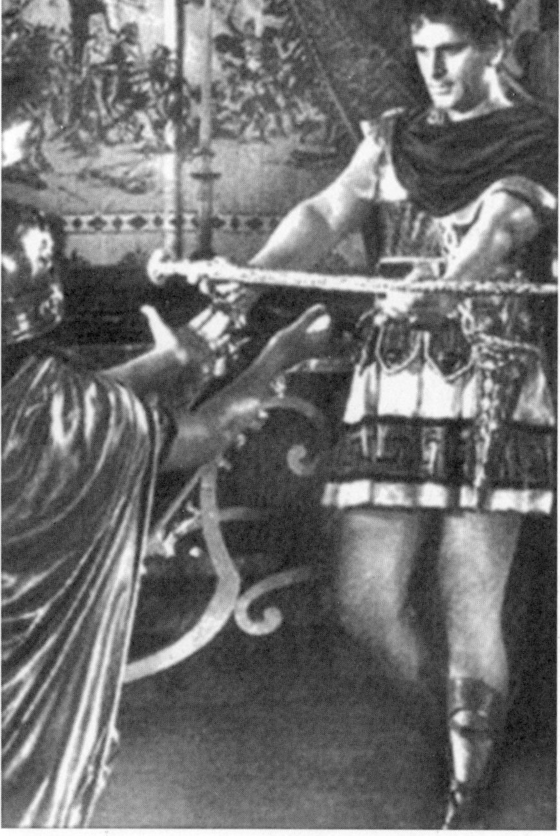

extraordinary, the ghazal *'Zindagi ka saaz bhi kya saaz hai'*, put to tune by Mir Saheb and picturised on her, became very popular.

Sohrab Modi shot portions of the film on actual locations at Fatehpur Sikri and Agra Fort which gave the film an authenticity that studio built sets could never achieve. The casting was perfect — the director himself played a key role as Sangram Singh, a prominent figure in the Mughal court. His flair for dialogues introduced a dramatic tension never seen before. Modi, who was later honoured with the Dada Saheb Phalke award in 1980, was among the first actors who made an impact with his diction and delivery. There is an interesting story in this respect; once when one of his films was being screened at Minerva Theatre in Bombay, the actor was present in the hall. Sohrab Modi noticed a man sitting in the front row with his eyes shut. Upset with such a reaction, he asked an attendant to let the viewer out and to return his money. The employee came back to say that the person was blind but had come just to hear Sohrab Modi's dialogues. The period feel of the *Pukar* too allowed him to use eloquent Urdu lines written by Kamal Amrohi and the film made box office history.

Modi's next historical mega venture, *Sikandar*, came in 1941. Though there were striking historical deviations — as was usually the case with most such films — Sohrab Modi's depiction of Sikandar as a sanguine, large-hearted general, worked. Prithviraj Kapoor, playing Sikandar with his Greek-god looks stole the show. Sohrab Modi played King Porus. The release of the film coincided with Second World War at its peak and the political atmosphere in India was tense following Gandhiji's call to

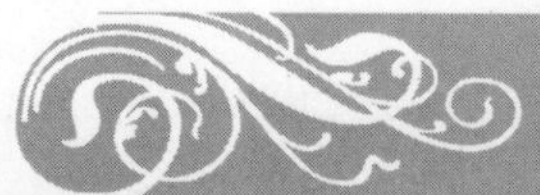

Civil Disobedience. Sikander further aroused patriotic feelings and national sentiment. Though Sikander was approved by the Bombay censor board, it was later banned from some of the theatres serving Army cantonments. However, its appeal to nationalism was so direct, it remained popular for years. It was revived in Delhi in 1961 during the Indian march into Goa. There was a high-spirited song by Rafique Ghaznavi — *'Zindagi hai pyaar mein, pyaar mein bitaye ja, husn ke huzur me, apna dil lutaye ja'.* It became so popular that the British Indian troops used the tune to coin a war-song: *'Zindagi hai war mein, war mie bitaye ja, Nazion ko kaat kaat ke giraye ja'.* Sikandar proved to be a benchmark historical. According to the critics, the movie surpassed Modi's earlier hit *Pukar* and reached the stature of Hollywood films in terms of lavish mounting, huge sets, and classic battle scenes. Sikandar was later dubbed in Persian.

After these landmark films, Sohrab Modi's third historical *Prithvi Vallabh,* was released in 1943. The film was a re-make of an earlier silent film made in 1924, and though slower in narrative, had great performances by Sohrab Modi and Durga Khote. The songs were put to tune by Saraswati Devi and the film enjoyed an average run at the box office. Modi's streak of success finally ended when his next venture *Ek Din ka Sultan,* released in 1945, became an instant failure at the box office. It was based on the life of a *bhishti* (waterman). Neither the popular romantic pair of Mehtaab and Wasti nor the music composed by the great master Ghulam Hyder could appease the audience.

Sohrab Modi's contemporaries enjoyed success to a slightly lesser degree with historicals in the 1940s, including Kedar Sharma, who made *Chitralekha* in 1941. The film had music composed by the great maestro Ustad Jhande Khan and A.S. Ghani. The film was produced by Film Corporation of India and based on a novel written by Bhagwati Charan Verma. Mehtab played the title role of Chitralekha who was a dancer in the court of Emperor Chandragupta, the founder of the Maurya Dynasty. Nandrekar, Ram Dulari, Leela Misra, A.S. Gyani, Rajendar, and Monica Desai were the other actors. This film was Kidar Sharma's first musical hit and had

Facing page above:
Sohrab Modi.
Below:
Prithviraj Kapoor, in and as Sikander, *a landmark film, produced by Minerva Movietone in 1941.*

arguably, the first erotic bathing scene in Indian cinema. Sharma re-made the film later in 1964 with Meena Kumari in the lead.

Prabhat Film Company's *Ram Shastri* and Laxmi Productions' *Mahakavi Kalidas* were released in 1944. *Mahakavi Kalidas* was directed by Sudhir Sen. Niren Lahiri had made the same film in 1942. Sen's *Mahakavi Kalidas* had music by Shridhar Pariske, while Pahadi Sanyal and Vanmala acted in the film. Prabhat's *Ram Shastri* was directed by Gajanan Jagirdar and co-directed by Raja Nene, with Lalita Pawar, Baby Shakuntala, Sudha Apte and Hansa Wadkar as the cast. The film was made in Marathi as well and G. Damle composed the music for the lyrics penned by Qamar Jalalabadi. The film was shot at an expensively mounted historical set to depict the contentious period of the Maratha empire. It was a biographical narrative of Ramshastri Prabhune (1720-89), chief justice at the court of Madhav Rao and later Nana Phandnavis.

One more historical was released in 1944 titled *Mumtaz Mahal* which was produced by Ranjit Film Company and directed by Kidar Sharma. Khemchand Prakash composed the music while Khursheed, Sulochana, Chadramohan, Kajjan and Yakub were the main actors. Historically, Mumtaz Mahal was the daughter of a Persian noble Abdul Hasan Asaf Khan and originally named as Arjumand Bano. So enthralling was her beauty that Prince 'Khurram' (who later became Emperor Shah Jahan) fell in love with her at first sight.

The story goes back to AD 1607. Once while the prince was strolling down Meena Bazaar Delhi, the then market of royal households, accompanied by a string of fawning friends, he caught a glimpse of a girl hawking silk and precious stones; and then started one of the most enticing love stories ever. After a wait of five years, their marriage was solemnised on 16 May 1612. The marriage was a success and they were so intensely in love with each other that court historians went on to document the intimate and erotic relationship the couple shared. In their nineteen years of marriage, they had thirteen children, seven of whom died at birth or at a very young age. It was during the birth of their fourteenth child (a daughter)

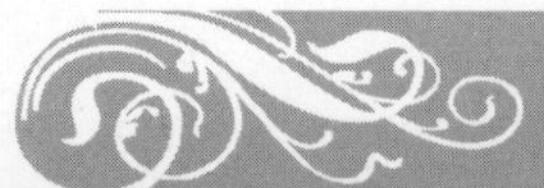

that she died. Till her death, Mumtaz Mahal remained an inseparable companion to her husband. Even during her frequent pregnancies she used to accompany him on his military endeavours and provided him with her counsel, support and comfort. As her last wish on her deathbed, the emperor promised her that he would build the world's most beautiful monument in her memory. Shahjahan was so griefstricken due to his wife's demise that he became inconsolable and went into secluded mourning for a year. When he appeared again, his hair had turned grey, his back was bent, and his face worn. It was a fairy-tale romance – one that withstood court intrigues, battles, political upheaval, plotting inside the palaces and finally the ill-fated separation that etched in stone, the Taj Mahal, living monument of love over centuries.

Back to the journey of historicals: The year 1945 saw Murti Movietone's *Amrapali* directed by Nandlal Jasvantilal, *Samrat Chandragupt*, produced and directed by Jayant Desai, Ramdik Productions' *Veer Kunal;* director: Kishore Sahu, Mehboob Khan's *Humayun*, Prakash Pictures' *Vikramaditya* directed by Vijay Bhatt and Pradeep Pictures' *Panna Dai* directed by Ram Daryani.

Amrapali (1945) had music composed by Saraswati Devi for lyrics written by (Ms) Kamal Pradeep. The cast included Prem Adeep, Savita Devi, Gulab and Jeevan. *Veer Kunal* was a re-make of two earlier versions made in 1932 and 1926. Likewise, two films had already been made on the subject of *Samrat Chadragupt* in 1924 and 1934. Jayant Desai's *Samrat Chandragupt* (1945) had the stunning star cast of the time including Renuka Devi, Surraya, Nayampalli, Mubarak and Sulochna. The music was composed by veteran C. Ramchandra. Another maestro Ghulam Haider scored the music for Mehboob Khan's *Humayun*, starring Ashok Kumar, Veena, Nargis and Chandr Mohan. Vijay Bhatt's *Vikramaditya* had also big stars like Prithviraj Kapoor, Baburao Pendekar, Jillo, Ranjan and Prem Adeeb. Shankar Ramviyas gave the music for this film. *Panna Dai*, another

Durga Khote in a scene from Amar Jyoti.

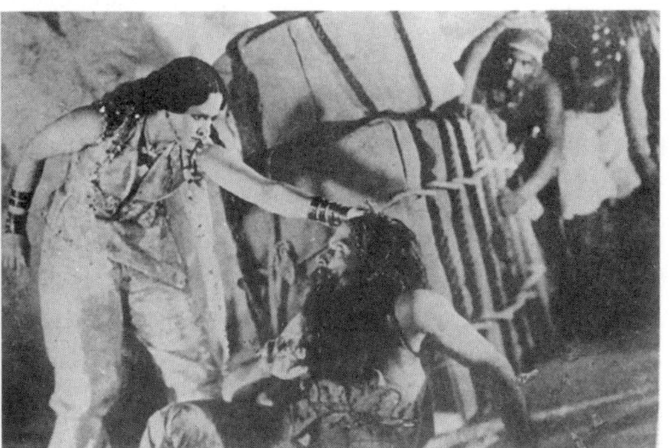

historical released in 1945 too had big stars like Durga Khote, Chandra Mohan, Meenakshi, Mubarak, Gope, Gulab and Leela Misra playing the main roles in the film.

A.R. Kardar produced and directed *Shahjahan* in 1946. A film with the same title had been produced in 1924, Naushad composed the music for Kardar's *Shahjahan* staring K.L. Saigal, Ragini, Sulochna Chatterji and Jairaj. Azoorie, Anwari and Rehaman were the other actors while the script was written by Kamal Amrohi. Standard Pictures' *Bairam Khan* made in 1946 was directed by Gajanan Jagirdar with Lalita Pawar in the lead role. Another historical released in 1946 was *Maharani Minal Devi*, produced by Luxmi Productions and directed by Chimanlal Trivedi. Saraswati Devi was the music director while the cast included Prem Adeeb, Leela Desai, Durga Khote, and Jagdish Sethi.

Bombay Cinetone's *Samrat Ashok* released in 1947, was directed by K.B. Lal. Gyan Dutt was the music composer. The lyrics were by Shams Lucknavi and the main actors included Sapru, Veena, Shakir, Himalyawala, Shamim and Husn Bano. Two films on the same subject and the same titles were made in 1922 and 1928. *Matwala Shayer Ram Joshi* produced by Ram Kamal, was another historical released in 1947. The music was composed by Vasan Desai and Baburao Painter along with V. Shantaram directed the film. It was Manmohan Krishna's debut film in the title role as 'Matwala Shayer'. Murari Pictures' *Chittor Vijay* too was released in 1947. It was a Raj Kapoor–Madhubala starrer, directed by Mohan Sinha. Monica Desai, Gulnar, Madan Puri, Wasti, Leela Pandey, Suryakant, Munshi Khunjar, Sutindra and Urvashi were the other actors.

Likewise, the 1950s saw a spate of historicals. Sohrab Modi produced *Sheesh Mahal* in 1950, co-starring Naseem Bano. Other films with a historical backdrop, were *Chhatrapati Shivaji* from Prabhakar Pictures, *Maharani Jhansi* from Subhash Pictures, and *Baiju Bawra* from Prakash Pictures, all released in 1952. *Chattrapati Shivaji* was directed by Bhalji G. Pendekar while the music was composed by C. Ramchandra. Chandrakant played the title role of Shivaji and Gajanan Jagirdar played Emperor Aurangzeb. Raja Jai

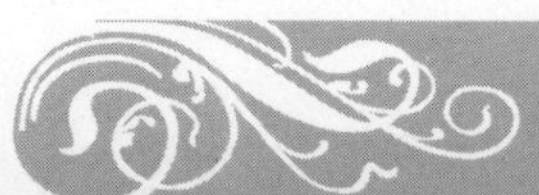

Singh was played by Prithviraj Kapoor. Lalita Pawar and Master Vithal were the other actors of the film. Jagdish Gautam directed *Maharani Jhansi* and the music was composed by Lachiram for this film.

Vijay Bhatt directed *Baiju Bawra* for Prakash Pictures. Historically, Baiju was a renowned musician like Tansen at the court of Mughal Emperor Akbar. Born as Baijnath Prasad or Baijnath Mishra in Chanderi Gwalior in 1542, he was a contemporary of Amir Khusro and a disciple of Swami Haridas. He got the name 'Bawra' meaning crazy, because he was crazily in love with a dancer of Chanderi. According to popular history books preserved in Jai Vilas Mahal in Gwalior, his rendition of *Raga Deepak* would light oil lamps, *Raga Megh Malhar* would bring on the rain and flowers would bloom when he would sing *Raga Bahar*. A creator of the Dhrupad style of music, Baiju was appointed musician at the court of Raja of Chanderi (now in Guna district of Madhya Pradesh). Later, he became musician at the court of Raja Mansingh of Gwalher, now Gwalior. Abul Fazal and Fagirullah, both renowned historians of Mughal courts, have written that Baiju defeated Tansen in a singing competition at the court of Akbar.

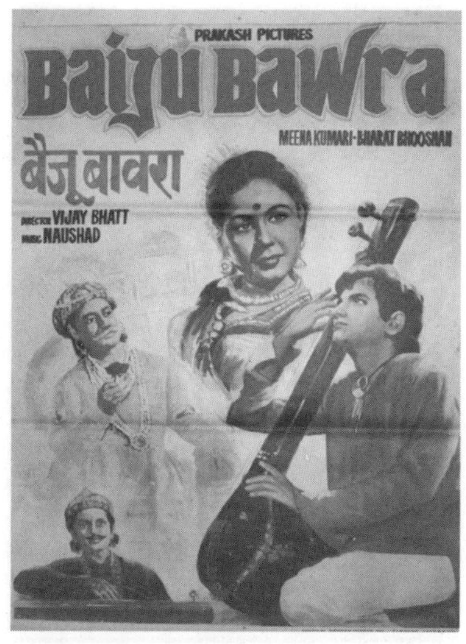

A poster of Baiju Bawra *released in 1952.*

Below: *Bharat Bhushan as* Baiju Bawra.

According to the script of *Baiju Bawra* Baiju believed, Tansen was responsible for the death of his father and he avenged his father's death by challenging Tansen to a musical duel in Akbar's court. Bharat Bhushan played the title role while Meena Kumari played Gauri, the character which was a turning point in her career and which made her a star. Interestingly, Vijay Bhatt gave her break in 1939 in his *Leatherface* as 'Baby Meena'; it was in 1952 when he gave her the first important break as 'Gauri' in *Baiju Bawra* and viewers fell in love with her captivating beauty. Surinder played Tansen and Bipin Gupta played Akbar. Kuldip Kaur, Manmohan Krishna, B.M. Vyas and Baby Tabassum were the other important actors. R.S. Choudhury wrote

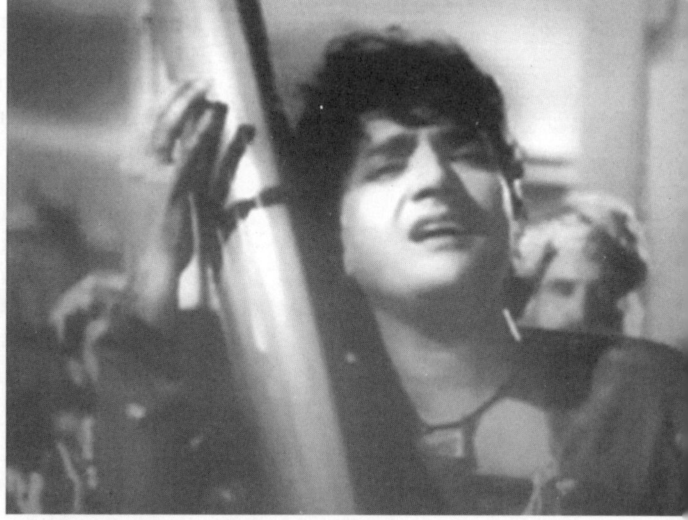

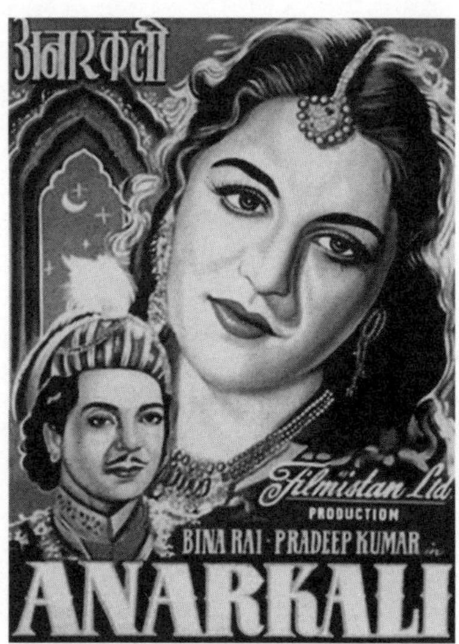

Poster of Filmistan's Anarkali *in 1953.*

the screenplay while maestro Naushad composed music for lyrics written by Shakeel Badyuni. The film was a landmark and won two *Filmfare* awards in 1954 — Meena Kumari for Best Actress and Naushad for Best Music. It was said that only a genius like Naushad had been able to do justice to the ragas sung by Baiju. One of the greatest bhajans put to music by him, to the lyrics of Shakeel Badayuni, *'Man Tarapat Hari Darashan ko Aaj'* shows that the only religion of artists is their art.

Filmistan's *Anarkali* and Minerva Movietone's *Jhansi ki Rani* followed in 1953. *Anarkali* was directed by Nandlal Jaswantilal with Pradeep Kumar and Bina Rai in the lead roles; more about this film follows in next chapter titled 'The Legendary Love Tale.'

Subhash Pictures had earlier released *Rani Jhansi* in 1952, which was an insignificant attempt, but Minerva Movietone's *Jhansi ki Raani* was Sohrab Modi's ambitious project made on a grand scale with a lavish historical backdrop of India's struggle for freedom in 1857. The story revolves around the Queen of Jhansi, known to her family and childhood friends as 'Manu'. As an eight-year-old spunky girl she was married off in her childhood to Gangadhar Rao Newalka, the Maharaja of the sovereign state of Jhansi in northwest India. She was taught by Rajguru, the Maharaja's trusted adviser, all the arts of the court, including the art of war. Circumstances led her to take up arms to defend her state from the British. She was truly an embodiment of patriotism, self-respect and heroism. Though a queen of a small state, she soon became the empress of a limitless empire of glory

L. Bijlani and Pandit S.R. Dubey wrote the script of *Jhansi ki Raani.* Mehtaab, actress-wife of Sohrab Modi played the young Rani Lakshmibai of Jhansi while her childhood role was enacted by Baby Sakina. Sohrab Modi played Rajguru and Mubarak played Gangadhar Rao, the king of Jhansi. *Jhansi ki Raani* was an unusual film with a big budget, and regarded by many to be the first colour film, though Mehboob Khan's coloured venture *Aan* had released a year earlier in 1952.

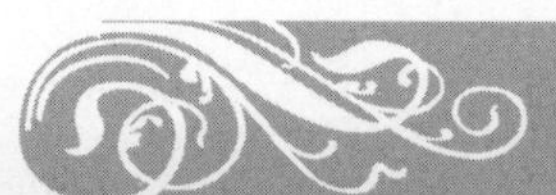

Sohrab Modi produced *Mirza Ghalib* another historical in 1954. Bharat Bhushan played the title role of the legendary Urdu poet Mirza Asadulla Khan Ghalib, who lived during the tumultuous regime of the last Mughal king, Bahadur Shah Zafar. The film revolves around his trials, his intellectual zenith, his successes, failures, fame and ultimate descent into poverty. Suraiya played 'Choudhvin' the famous dancer of that time and a hardcore fan of Ghalib's poetry. Nigar Sultana, Durga Khote, Murad, Mukri, Ulhas, Kumkum and Iftikhar were the other stars of the film. *Mirza Ghalib* won the National Award for Best Film and Best Music in 1955.

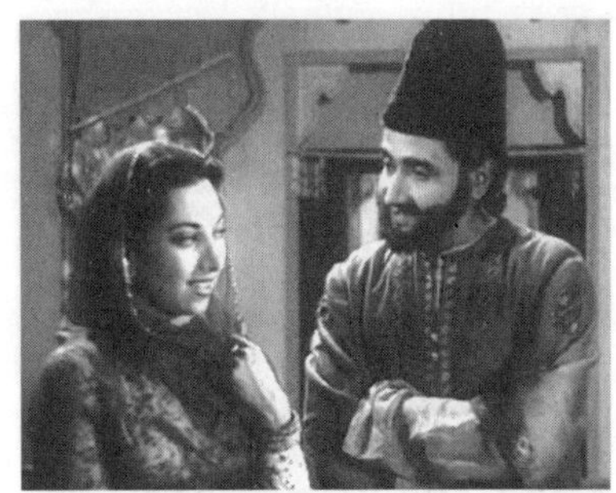

Bharat Bhushan and Suraiya in a still from Mirza Ghalib *released in 1952.*

G.P. Sippy produced and directed *Adl-e-Jahangir* in 1955, which was a re-make of earlier versions made in 1930 (silent), 1934 and 1936 *Adl-e-Jahangir* (1955), starring Pradeep Kumar as Emperor Jahangir and Meena Kumari as Noorjahan. Husanlal Bhagat Singh scored the music for lyrics written by Qmar Jalalabadi. The velvet voice of Talat Mehmood created the feeling of pathos among music lovers of the time. The songs '*Ai meri zindagi tujhe dhoondoo kahan*' and '*Chand sitare tujhe karte ishare*', became instant hits. Another historical was released in 1955: *Veer Rajputani*, starring Shakila, Manhar and Luxmi Desai which was produced by Wadia Brothers and Basant Pictures, Bombay. The story of the chivalry of Rajput women was well picturised in this seldom seen epic directed by J.B.H. Wadia. With a cast of characters that included Maharana Pratap, Emperor Akbar, Mansingh, Kavi Prithviraj, the story gallops along to a rousing climax.

Pran played title role in Halaku, *released in 1956.*

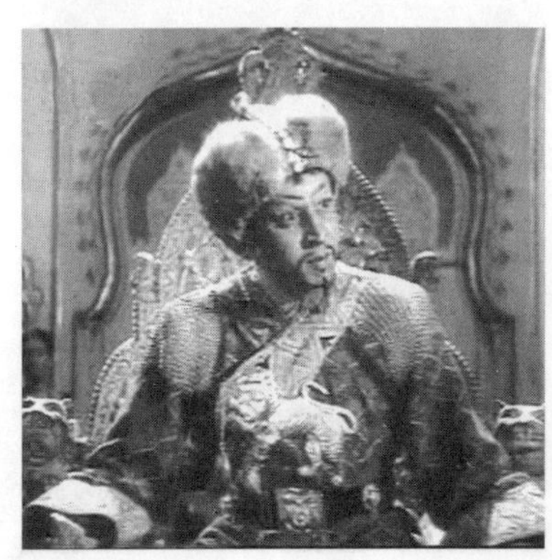

All India Pictures' *Halaku* was released in 1956 with Ajit, Meena Kumari and Pran. The film was directed by D.D. Kashyap and Shankar Jaikishan scored the immortal music. '*Aaja ke intizar mein, jaane ko hai bahar bhi, tere bager zindagi, dard ban ke reh gaie*', sung by Mohammad Rafi is still remembered by music lovers. Historically, Halaku Khan was a Mongol king and the grandson of Chengiz Khan. He was very ruthless and barbaric and lived up to his name — Halaku, meaning, one who kills. He attacked Baghdad, the capital of Iraq in AD 1258 and destroyed the city completely which was a major Islamic centre of learning. All of Baghdad was burned to ashes, its world-renowned libraries burned,

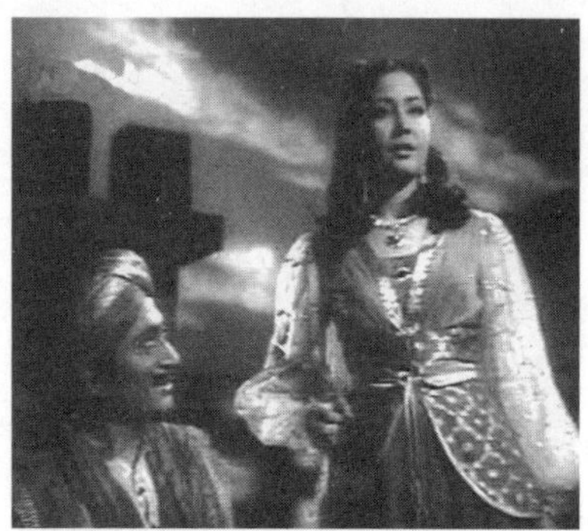

Meena Kumari in Halaku *released in 1956.*

all the books thrown in the river that flowed through Baghdad, and it created huge piles of human skulls (as a symbol of 'achievements') everywhere. Pran played the title role of Halaku, Meena Kumari played Niloufer who was in love with Parvez played by Ajit. Halaku stakes his claim on her and wants her to be his wife, in spite of his wife (played by Minoo Mumtaz), opposing his marriage plans. Niloufer refuses to submit to Halaku and invites his wrath on all: Niloufer, Pervez, and his wife.

More historicals followed in 1957. Dinesh Films' *Amar Singh Rathod* and Ravi Kalachitra's *Rani Roopmati* were two major releases. The former was directed by Jaswant Javeri and Shanmukh Babu composed the music. Jairaj and Nirupa Roy played the lead roles. *Rani Roopmati* was a successful film, mainly because of its melodious music composed by R.N. Tripathy, in particular, the song sung by Mukesh, '*Aa lout ke aaje mere meet, tujhe mere geet bulatey hein*' was very popular. S.N. Tripathy was the director with Bharat Bhushan playing Baaz Bahadar, the king of Malwa (in Madhya Pradesh) and Nirupa Roy as Rani Roopmati, daughter of a noble of Sarangpur dystrict in the same state. The story was set during the period of Emperor Akbar when he besieged almost every state except the State of Malwa, which was ruled by a Pathan king 'Sultan Shuja.' Sultan Shuja did not surrender; instead, he fought and retained his kingdom. His son Bayazid, though a brave warrior was a peace-loving person and an admirer of fine arts. After the death of Sultan, he inherited the throne and acquired title 'Baaz Bahadur'. Roopmati was stunningly beautiful and a mellifluous singer. Baaz and Roop fell in love with each other and got married according to Hindu and Muslim rituals. Baaz built a palace for his wife from where she could view her favourite river, the Narmada and perform puja. Akbar's stepbrother and commander-in-chief of Mughal forces, Adham Khan attacked Mandu which was the capital of Malwa. The small army of Baaz Bahadur was defeated and Roopmati was captured. Due to her profound love for Baaz, she did not surrender to Adham Khan's evil designs and swallowed poison. Such was the end of the magical love story, steeped in music, poetry, romance, war and death! Even

Nirupa Roy and Bharat Bhushan in Rani Roopmati *(1957).*

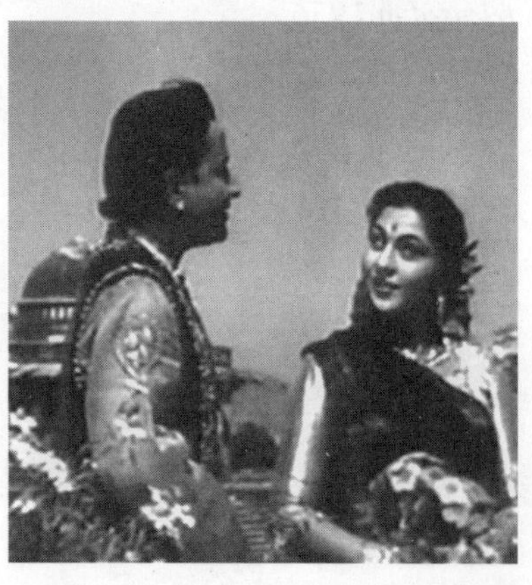

today, when tourists visit the palaces of Mandu, guides narrate this tale of eternal love.

Other historical films that followed in 1957 were Nigam Films *Mumtaz Mahal*, and N.C. Films' *Changez Khan*. *Mumtaz Mahal* had been produced twice earlier: Homi Master directed first one in 1926 and Kedar Sharma directed the second one in 1946. Nigam Film's *Mumtaz Mahal* was directed by Ram Daryani, Sheelaramani, with Jairaj and Veena as the main actors. Sohrab Modi again got tempted to make historical and produced *Nousherwan-e-Adil* (aka *Farz aur Mohabbat*) starring Raj Kumar, Mala Sinha and Naseem Bano in the main leads. Sohrab Modi himself played the title role of Nousherwan, the king of Persia who upholds the law even at the cost of his personal loss. C. Ramchandra composed his exquisite music for the lyrics penned by Parvez Shamsi. *Changez Khan* was directed by Kedar Kapoor and Hansraj Behl composed the music. Premnath and Beena Rai played the leading pair in the film.

Babubhai Mistry directed *Samrat Chandragupt* in 1958 for Mukti Films, which was a re-make of earlier versions made in 1924, 1934 and 1945. Bharat Bhushan and Nirupa Roy played the main lead while music was composed by Kalyanji Verji. Screen Arts filmed the story of *Rani Roopmati* once again with the title *Baaz Bahadur* in 1959. The film was directed by Kuldeep Sharma and the music scored by Sumant Raj. This was just an unnoticed release and soon forgotten. Another historical made in 1959 was Dinesh Films *Samrat Prithviraj Chauhan* which was again a re-make of a silent film made in 1924. Jai Raj, Anita Guha, Ulhas and Sapru acting in this film, direction by Harshukh Bhatt. The music was composed by Vasant Desai.

During the 1950s only a few made a mark while most lacked authenticity, good music, and convincing performances. Manmohan Krishna as Matwala Shayer Ram Joshi did full justice. Similarly, Pran as Halaku gave a memorable performance. *Mirza Ghalib* and *Baiju Bawra* turned out to be superhits, mainly because of the music composed by Ghulam Mohammed and Naushad, respectively. Bharat Bhushan was perfectly cast in both the films. Ghalib's ghazals in *Mirza*

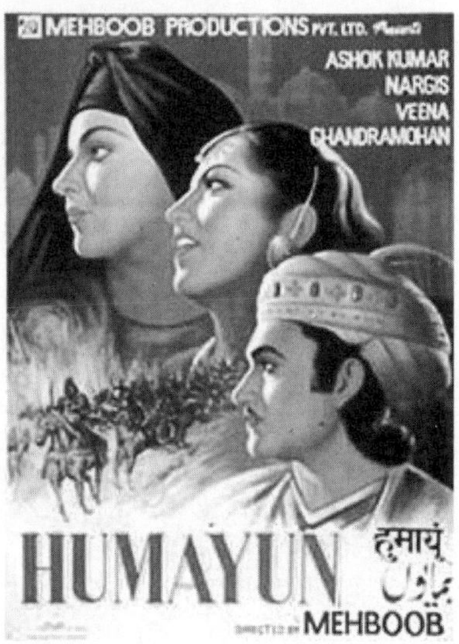

Poster of Humayun *produced by Mehboob.*

Ghalib, sung by Suraiya and Talat Mehmood, were highly appreciated and helped resurrect Modi's career as a filmmaker. Similarly, Durga Khote in *Panna Dai* and Gajan Jagirdar in *Bairam Khan* were impressive.

Among the notables, Mehboob Khan failed with *Humayun*. So did Sohrab Modi, who despite the success of *Mirza Ghalib*, was weighed down by the grand *Jhansi ki Raani,* a huge failure that landed him in a financial mess. Mehtab, many thought, was not suited to play the main role. Moreover, the friendship between the English general and the queen, shown in the film, ran contrary to popular history. *Jhansi ki Raani,* in a way, was the beginning of the end of a prestigious production company that had dominated the scene for nearly two decades. Minerva Productions' subsequent films *Nausherwan-e-Adil* and *Sheeshmahal* were also wash outs.

Finally, 1960 was the year that broke the mould. Never before had historicals been made on such a lavish scale. None of the erstwhile success stories, including those by Minerva Productions, were a match for the technical polish, drama, and presentation of the epic *Mughal-e-Azam.* Since the present book encapsulates the making of the said film and the endeavour of the great men behind the epic, the journey of historical sagas continues.

Many producers launched similar projects in its wake. In fact, more than fifteen such films were made in the 1960s, but none could hold a candle to K. Asif's magum opus. Vijay Bhatt directed *Angulimal* for producer Prakash Veramal; the music was scored by renowned music director of the time, Anil Biswas. Filmistan's *Babar,* directed by Hemen Gupta also released in 1960, but was bardly noticed, barring its soundtrack. '*Salaam-e-hasrat qabool kar lo*' by Sudha Malhotra and '*Tum ek bar meri mohabat ka imtehan to lo*' by Mohammad Rafi, set to the music of Roshan, were particularly popular. Movie India's *Razia Sultan* a Nirupa Roy–Jairaj starrer released in 1961, too, bombed, while Pushpa Pictures' *Taj Mahal* directed by M. Sadiq, was a big hit. Sahir Ludhianvi's lyrics, sung to Roshan's melodious music, were the highlight of the film. '*Jo vaada kiya*', '*Jo baat tujhme hai*', '*Paon chhuu lene do*', and the qawwali number '*Chandi ka badan*', still enthrall the music

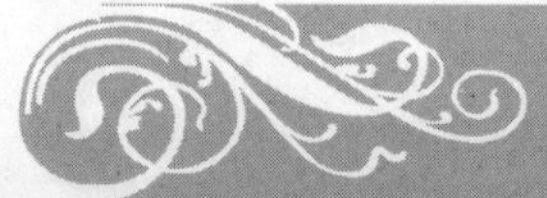

buffs. Moreover, Pradeep Kumar as Shahzada Khurram (later, Emperor Shahjahan) and Bina Rai as his charming beloved wife Mumtaz Mahal did full justice to their roles.

Most other historicals made in the same decade were mediocre attempts: For example Ramsay Production's *Rustom–Sohrab* directed by Vishram Bedekar and written by Kumar Ramsay with Prithviraj Kapoor–Suraiya as the main stars. The film was based on the story of a powerful and mighty Rustom Zabuli (Prithviraj Kapoor) of Iran and Shehzadi Tehmina (Suraiya).

Kidar Sharma directed *Chitralekha* in 1964 for producer Pushpa Kumar with Pradeep Kumar and Meena Kumari in the lead roles with music composed by Roshan. This film, too, has been made earlier with the same title in 1941. Delight Movies' *Maharani Padmini,* starring Anita Guha and Sajjan, also released in 1964, was directed by Jaswant Jhaveri while Sardar Malik composed the music. *Jahan Ara,* another historical also released in 1964, was produced by Light and Shade and directed by Vinod Kumar starring Prithviraj Kapoor, Mala Sinha and Om Prakash. Rajroop Productions' *Maharaja Vikram* released in 1965 with Anita Guha, Mahipal and Bela Bose as main stars and music being composed by S.N. Tripathi. M. Sadiq re-made *Noorjahan* for Zenith Production, in 1967 with Meena Kumari in the lead role, while Pradeep Kumar played Emperor Jahangir. Rehman and Shaikh Mukhtar were the other actors and Roshan composed the music. The earlier versions with same titles have been made in 1923 as a silent film and in 1931 as a talkie.

The 1970s saw the end of the genre, except for Satyajit Ray's *Shatranj ke Khiladi* (1977), which was based on the Urdu novel *Shatranj ki Baazi* written by Munshi Premchand. The story revolves around two local aristocrats, played by Sanjeev Kumar and Saeed Jafri. The fondness for the game of chess (*shatranj*) makes them irresponsible in their duties

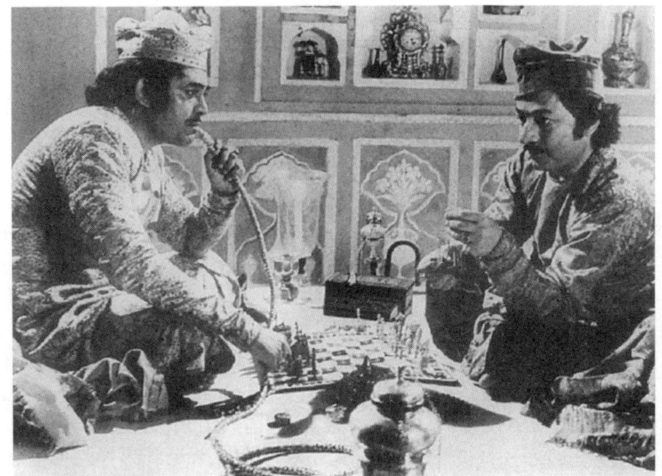

Sanjeev Kumar and Saeed Jafri in Shatranj ke Khilari.

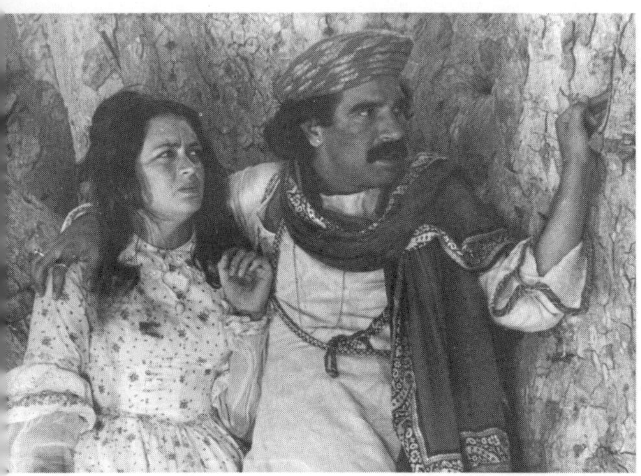

Kulbhushan Kharbanda and Nafisa Ali in Shyam Benegal's Junoon.

towards their families and society. They derive immense pleasure in developing chess strategies and ignore the real life invasion by the British army in 1856, the first freedom struggle in India (Mutiny of 1857 as the British called it). *Shatranj ke Khiladi* was Satyajit Ray's most expensive directorial venture and his only film in Hindi/Urdu. Amjad Khan played Nawab Wajid Ali Shah, an indifferent feudal Nawab who was bound by the so called 'Treaty of Friendship' designed by the East India Company.

Shyam Benegal directed *Junoon* in 1978 for producer Shashi Kapoor. Shashi Kapoor, Nafisa Ali, Tom Alter, Shabana Azmi, Jennifer Kendal, Kulbhushan Kharbanda, Naseeruddin Shah, Deepti Naval, Pearl Padamsee and Sushma Seth were the main actors of the film. The story was penned by Ruskin Bond while Ismat Chughtai and Satyadev Dube wrote dialogues for the screenplay written by the director himself. The movie depicted the period of 1857 to 1858 when Indian soldiers of the East India Company revolted. The film depicted the sufferings of a British family during the violent struggle of 1857. Some Mughals, led by Sarfaraz Khan, (played by Naseeruddin Shah) decided to rebel against their British masters, killing many, and forcing others to flee. The film won many Filmfare awards in 1979, including the National Award for Best Feature Film, Best Cinematography and Best Audiography for the same year.

Meena Kumari in Pakeezah *Produced and directed by Kamal Amrohi (1971).*

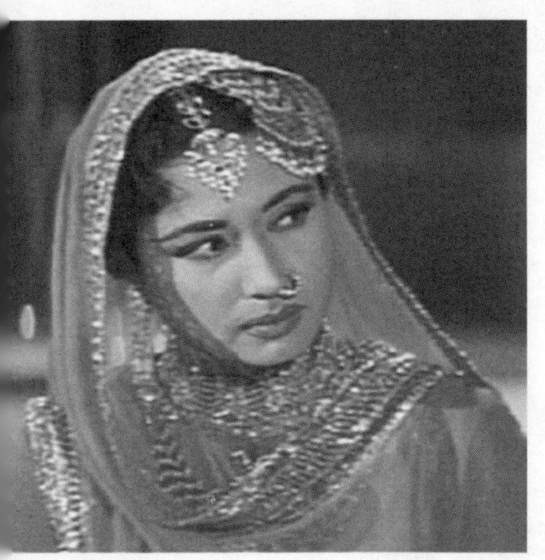

Kamal Amrohi's *Pakeezah*, released in 1971 was a love story of a nautch girl set in pre-Independence Avadh. Meena Kumari's outstanding performance, the lavish sets, and the melodious music by Ghulam Mohammed with Naushad made the film successful, but it was at best a period film, not a historical.

The 1980s, too, did not see any significant addition to the roll call. The government of Maharashtra produced *Sher Shivaji* in 1981, but it proved a letdown. Muzaffar Ali's *Umrao Jaan* in 1981 was also a period film rather than a historical.

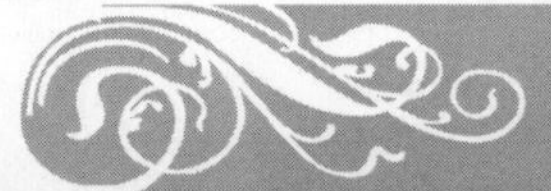

Based on the famous Urdu novel *Umrao Jaan Ada* written by Mirza Hadi Ruswa, it was a true story of a young girl abducted in her childhood, who grew up to be the famous poetess and dancer in Lucknow. Rekha, in the title role, surpassed all her previous performances and won a National Award in 1982.

Manoj Kumar made *Kranti* in 1981, with a pseudo-historical backdrop of the freedom struggle. This was Dilip Kumar's comeback film and became an instant success.

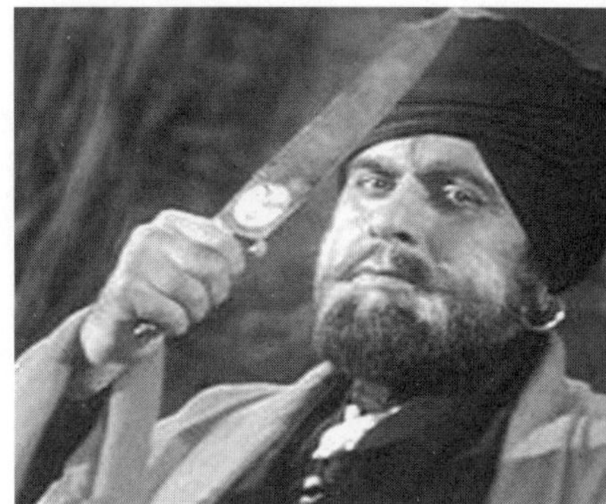

Diip Kumar played a freedom fighter in his come back film Kranti *(1981), after a gap of five years.*

Kamal Amrohi returned with the much-delayed *Razia Sultan*, which was released in 1983. Despite its grand scale, the film flopped. Dharmendra played Yakut while Hema Malini was Razia Sultan. Her gracious personality and exquisite features perfectly suited the title role. She made great effort to learn the correct diction of a queen of Turkish descent, yet, it is believed that the use of high-flown Urdu and Arabic were the main reasons for its failure. Interestingly, Kamal Amrohi was one of the four dialogue writers for *Mughal-e-Azam*. The most eloquent lines, including the confrontation of Akbar and Salim, were written in chaste Urdu by Amrohi himself.

So what made *Mughal-e-Azam* a commercial hit despite the use of literary Urdu? The reason is that it did not digress from its theme. Essentially, it remains a tale of love set against the backdrop of tumultuous historical events. However, these never intrude on the central plot unlike *Razia Sultan,* which presented a romance interspersed with political intrigue.

The 1990s saw a few noteworthy historicals: Ravi Gupta's *Train to Pakistan* in 1997, Iqbal Dhillon's *Shaheed Udhamsingh Singh*, in 1999. Though it was a Punjabi and a low profiled film, yet it successfully made its mark. Udham Singh was born and brought up in a Sikh family in Punjab during British ruled India. He portrayed a character in the film who swears vengeance as he was enraged at the massacre of over 2,000 men, women, and children at the hands of Brigadier General Edward Harry Dwyer in Jallianwalla Bagh, played by Tom Alter. The Hindustani version received the Screen–Videocon special jury award. A film that aimed to redefine history, itself created history when many multicrore extravaganzas of that time flopped miserably. Shahrukh Khan produced *Asoka* in 2001, which was a disastrous failure. Akbar Khan released

Hema Malini in Razia Sultan.

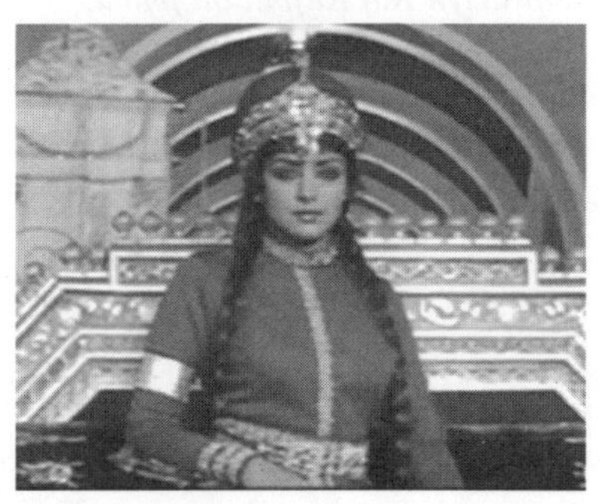

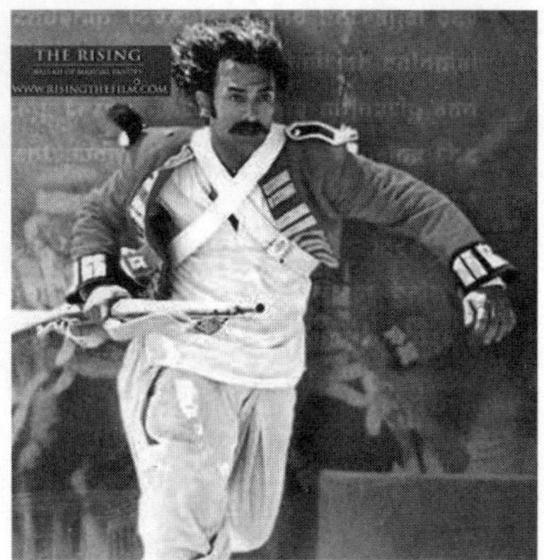

Amir Khan played Mangal Pandey in The Rising.. Mangal Pandey.

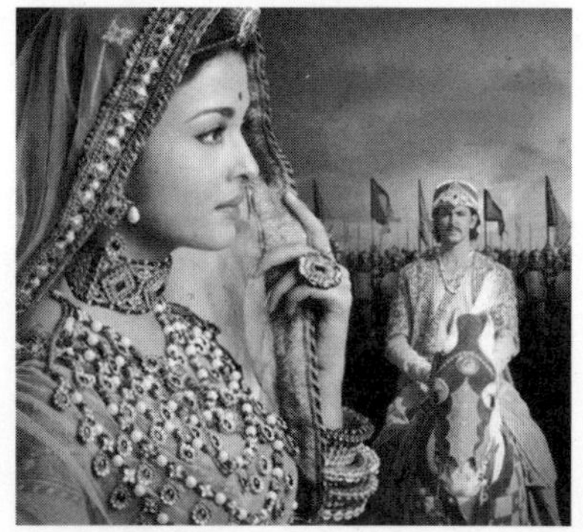

A still from Jodha Akbar, *Hritik Roshan played young Akbar and Ashwariya Rai Rajputani Jodha.*

his ambitious mega-venture, *Taj Mahal* in December 2005. The film reportedly consumed approximately Rs 70 crore. Though acclaimed by critics as good cinema, the film could not meet the box office expectations and turned out to be a commercial disaster.

Aamir Khan produced the much publicised venture *The Rising, Mangal Pandey* in which Aamir played the title role. Rani Mukherji played the role of a prostitute who lures British soldiers and later falls in love with Mangal Pandey. The film was embroiled in a controversy wherein it was believed that the character of Mangal Pandey had been distorted. It flopped at the box office. UTV Motion Picture produced their mega project *Jodha Akbar* which was released on 15 February 2008. The film was directed by Ashutosh Gowarikar starring Hrithik Roshan as young Akbar and Aishwarya Rai as Jodhabai. The film was technically extraordinary with some sequences filmed with cinematic excellence. Though *Jodha Akbar* was critically acclaimed and had a successful run at the box office, this too got victimised by some social groups and was accused for distortion of history.

In the eighty-five years from 1915 to 2008, hundreds of historical films were made, but none could parallel the towering achievement of K. Asif's magnum opus, *Mughal-e-Azam.* The film undoubtedly is a tribute to what imagination, hard work and determination can achieve. Its maker spent fifteen long years with untiring grit and unshaken confidence to craft a classic. The film has virtually become a point of reference for its grandeur and deft direction in the genre of historical sagas in Indian cinema.

The legendary love story

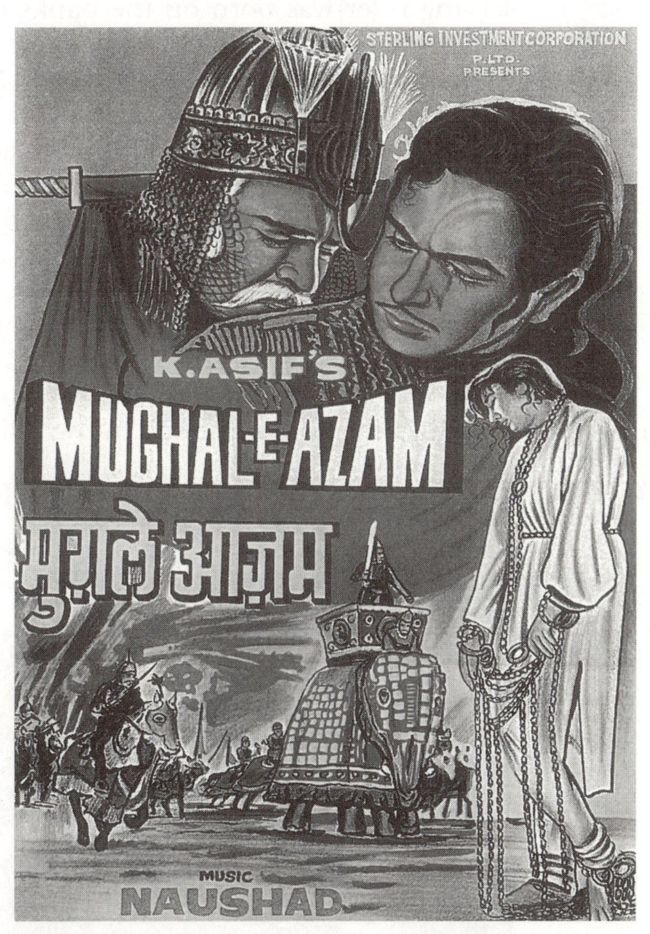

...the lovelorn prince isn't the same Salim when he returns after his apprenticeship under Man Singh. He has a will and a mind of his own...

Nearly five hundred years ago, the subcontinent's longest serving ruler was born on the banks of the Ganges in the Himalayan foothills. His name was Jalaluddin Mohammed Akbar. Son of the second Mughal emperor, Humayun, he was placed on the throne at the tender age of twelve after his father died in an accident while climbing down the steps of the library. Akbar proved to be a brave warrior and an able, progressive administrator, who oversaw the expansion of the Empire over the next fifty years. He was a connoisseur of the fine arts and a patriot at heart, a king whose love for his subjects transcended sectarian and geographical divisions. The opening commentry of *Mughal-e-Azam* describes this son of the soil in the following words:

Akbar proved to be a brave warrior and an able, progressive administrator, who oversaw the expansion of the empire over the next fifty years.

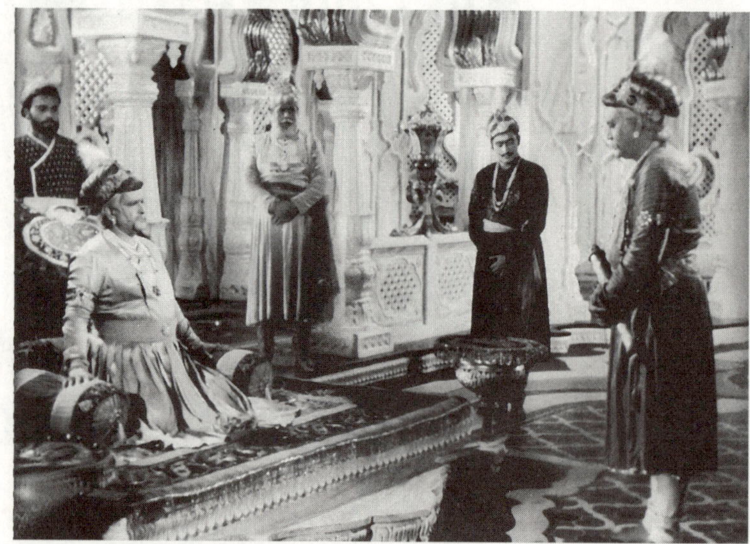

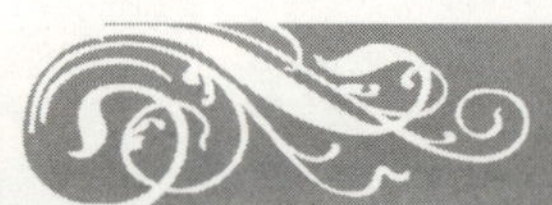

> '*Main Hindostan hun*, Himalaya *meri sarhadon ka nigehbaan hai….*Ganga *meri pavitrta ki saugandh. Tareekh ki ibtida se main andheron aur ujalon ka sathi hun….Meri khak par, sang-e-mar mar ki safed chaadron mein lipti hui yeh imartein duniya se keh rahi hain ke zaalimon ne mujhe loota aur meharbanon ne mujhe sanwara….Nadanon ne mujhe zanjeerein pahna din aur mere chahne walon ne unhein kaat phenka…..Mere in chahne walon mein ek insaan ka naam* Jalaluddin Mohammad Akbar *tha…* Akbar *ne mujh se pyaar kiya, mazhab aur rasm-o-riwayat ki deewaar se buland hokar insaan ko insaan se mohabbat karna sikhaya aur hamesha ke liye mujhe seene se lagaliya.*'
>
> (I am Hindustan … The Himalayas guard my borders and Ganga vows for my sanctity. From time immemorial, I have witnessed many ups and downs. The grand marbled structures, built on my sand, are telling the world that the wicked robbed me, yet my well-wishers resurrected me …. fools chained me; patriots unshackled me…. One among such men was Jalaluddin Mohammad Akbar. Akbar loved me; he embraced me and transcended religious and cultural boundaries to extend universal love among all human beings.)

Akbar's greatest worry, though, was the fact that none of his wives could bear him a male heir. Finally, the Rajput queen, Jodhabai bore him a son after he went on a pilgrimage to the shrine of the Sufi saint Sheikh Salim Chishti. The prince was named Nooruddin Mohammad Salim after the saint.

When the pampered prince grew up, his father realised that Salim was spoilt, flippant and given to amorous pursuits. To discipline his son and expose him to the hardships of the battlefield, the emperor placed him under the tutelage of a key general, Raja Man Singh.

This was the historical basis of the story of *Mughal-e-Azam*. Though it is a fictionalised romance, the legendary drama blurs the dividing line between fact and fiction. The lovelorn prince is not the same Salim when he returns after his apprenticeship under Man Singh. He has a will and a mind of his own. He falls in love with the stunningly beautiful courtesan Anarkali, opening the floodgates of a conflict between the defiant son and his imperial father.

Dilip Kumar as 'Sahib-e-alam' alias Shahzada Salim.

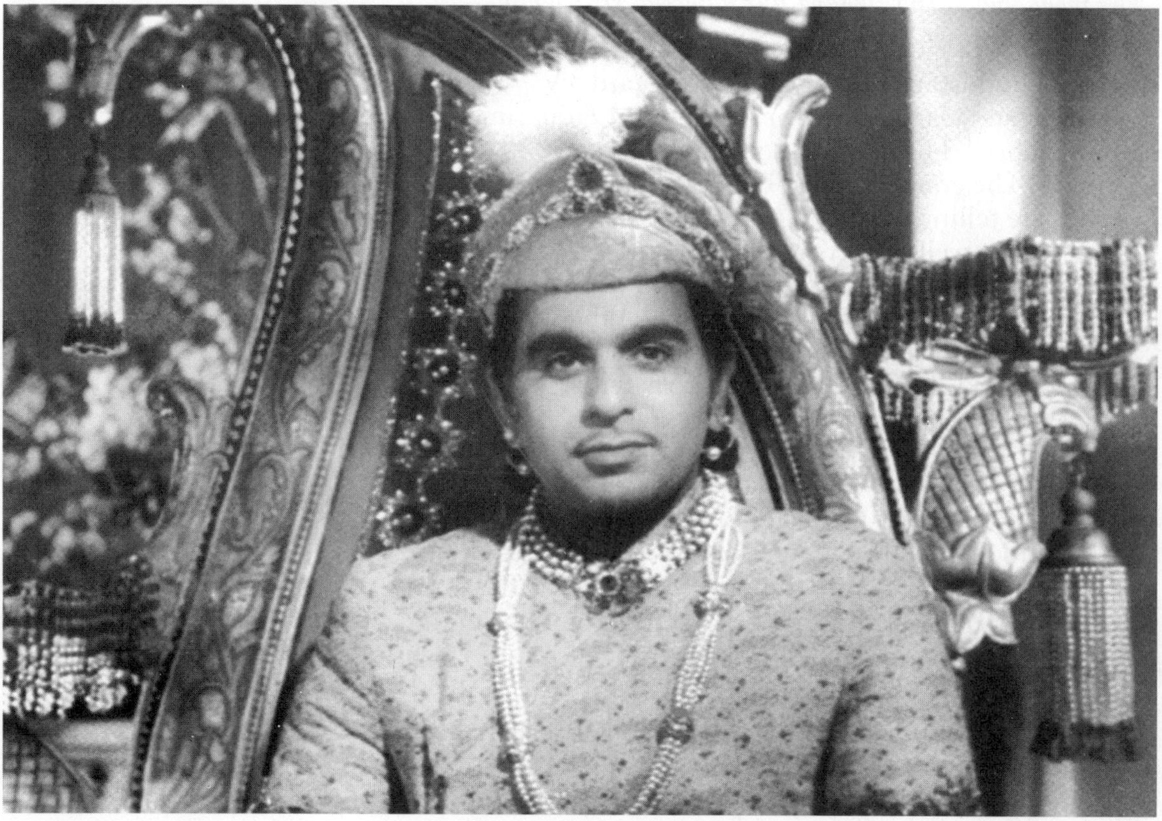

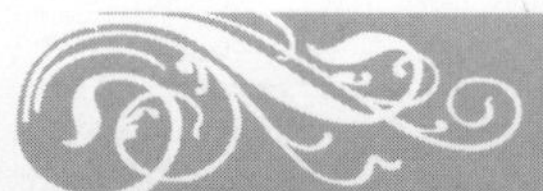

On the one hand, there was the emperor's responsibility towards his subjects and his political ambitions for his son; on the other, was Salim's personal desire. Not just the emperor, court officials, too, disapproved of the liaison and dismissed the idea of accepting an ordinary courtesan as their empress-to-be. Yet the intensity of love could not be denied. The conflict shattered Akbar's self-esteem and he roared:

> *'Hum ek ladle Betey ke shafique baap zaroor hain, lekin hum shahanshah ke farz ko nazar andaaz nahin kar sakte.'*
>
> (I am certainly a loving father of a pampered son, but I cannot ignore my obligation as an emperor of the country.)
>
> *'Apne bete ke dharakte huye dil ke liye hum* Hindustaan *ki taqdeer nahin badal saktey.'*
>
> (I can't change the course of destiny of my country for the sake of my son's pulsating heart.)
>
> Salim replied: *'Taqdeerein badal jati hain, zamana badal jata hai, mulkon ki tareekh badal jati hai, Shahanshah badal jate hain, magar is badalti huyee duniya mei, mohabbat jis insaan ka daaman tham leti hai, woh insan nahin badalta!'*
>
> (Destinies do change ... times change, the history of nations changes, kings, too, change, but those who are in love never change in this transitory world.)

Salim rebelled and lead an army against the emperor. He lost and was taken captive. In a highly dramatic courtroom scene, Akbar pronounced the death sentence against the rebellious son. The love affair, though not backed by historical evidence, has a monument to its

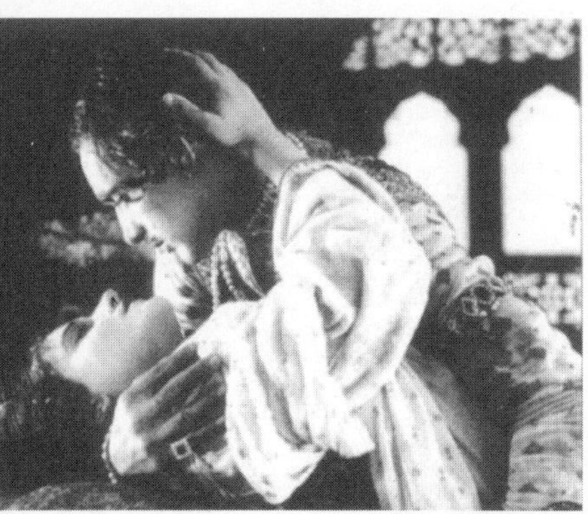

D. Billimoria and Sulochna (Ruby Myers) as Saleem and Anarkali in Ardeshir Irani's silent film Anarkali *released in 1928.*

name which may bear testimony to its reality. A mausoleum of Anarkali is situated at Lahore, and a famed shopping area is named after her — the Anarkali Bazaar.

The Urdu novelist Imtiyaz Ali Taaj had written a novel based on the love story, and later staged a theatrical version titled *Anarkali*. The show was immensely popular. Those were the days when film producers sought out plays for material. Anarkali, too, attracted many producers for its mass appeal. Thus, the first time this fascinating tale was brought to the screen was in 1928 — the pioneering Ardeshir Irani made a film named *Anarkali,* directed by R.S. Choudhary. Sulochana (Ruby Myers) played the title role, while D. Billimoria enacted Salim. At around the same time, Great Eastern Film Corporation (Delhi) started a movie on the same theme. They named it *Loves of a Mughal Prince (*Ref: *Light of Asia: Indian Silent Films 1912-1913*, published by Wiley Eastern Limited, New Delhi*)*. An Anglo-Indian actress Renee Smith, screen-named Sita Devi, played Anarkali, while Charu Roy, Sawan Singh, Maya Devi and Raj Kumari were the other actors of the film. Interestingly, Imtiyaz Ali Taj, who conceived the original idea of the legendry love tale, also played a role in this film. This film was directed by Charu Roy and Prafull Roy, and was made on a more lavish scale than Ardeshir Irani's *Anarkali*. But the latter was the first to be released in 1928, and hence became a huge hit.

Encouraged by *Anarkali*'s success, Irani re-made it in 1935 as a talkie. The entire star-cast of the silent *Anarkali* was repeated. Anna Saheb Mayankar was the music director. Zillu, who acted in both the versions, was later cast by Asif in *Mughal-e-Azam* as Anarkali's mother. And Sulochana (Ruby Myers), who played the

title role in both the silent and talkie versions of *Anarkali,* went on to be cast by Filmistan as Rani Jodhabai in their version released in 1953.

Ruby Myers was a much sought-after actress of the silent era. She was introduced in 1925 by Mohan Bhavnani in Kohinoor Film Company's *Veer Bala,* in which she acted opposite a popular hero of the era, Khaleel. She starred in many silent films such as *Cinema Queen, Wild Cats of Bombay, Telephone Girl* and the much-talked-about *Our India,* where she created a scandal by planting a full-mouthed kiss on her hero Jal Merchant; it made headlines in 1935. Ruby Myers commanded an astronomical fee of Rs 7,500 per month after the success of *Anarkali.* This was almost double the salary paid to popular male leads back then.

However, the tide turned for cinema's first Anarkali, when she ran into huge losses with a home production *Prem ki Jyot.* The actress went on to do supporting roles and even worked as an extra to make ends meet. Soon she went into oblivion, living in a ground floor house under the flyover near Kemps Corner in Bombay. Suffering from physical ailments, poverty and loneliness, Ruby Myers, once mobbed and idolised, died on 9 April 1983. Only a few neighbours and close friends attended the funeral.

The tale of Anarkali had fascinated yet another enterprising producer, the builder of Cine Laboratory, Shiraz Ali Hakeem, who joined hands with a young director, Karim Asif. They christened the project *Mughal-e-Azam* and Asif engaged four top Urdu writers of the time to put together a script: Aman (father of Zeenat Aman), Wajahat Mirza, Ahsan Rizvi and Kamal Amrohi.

Meanwhile, Amrohi had also planned a film titled *Anarkali.* The lead pair — again coincidentally —

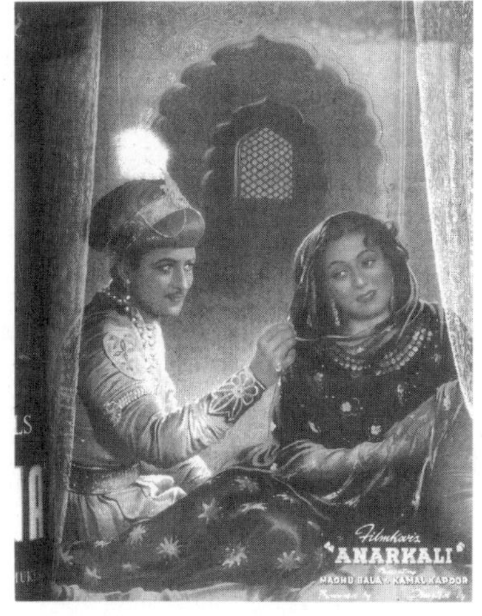

Kamal Kapoor and Madhubala as 'Salim' and 'Anarkali' on Film India *cover May 1951.*

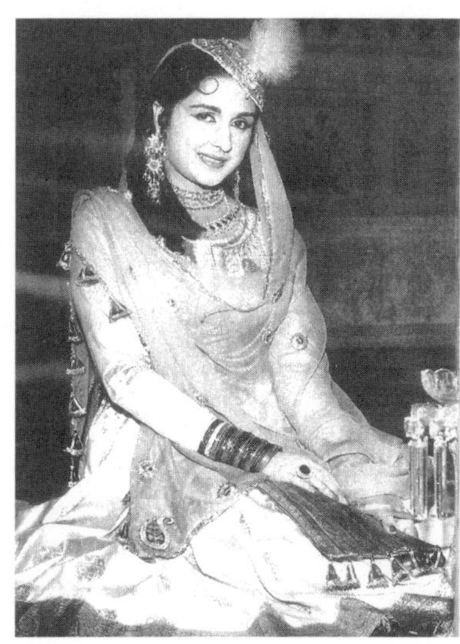

Bina Rai played the title role in Filmistan's Anarkali.

Madhubala as Anarkali and Kamal Kapoor as Salim even adorned the cover of May 1951 issue of the popular *Film India* magazine. Approximately, seven lakh rupees were spent on costumes and properties, but due to financial problems the film was shelved. The same was later re-launched with Ajit as Salim and Meena Kumari as Anarkali, and Amrohi was supposed to direct it for producer Makhanlal. It was, however, aborted following a confrontation between Asif and Amrohi. With the latter on board as scriptwriter for *Mughal-e-Azam*, Asif was concerned about a conflict of interest. He insisted that Amrohi either shelve his *Anarkali* or walk out of *Mughal-e-Azam*. Amrohi decided to sacrifice his *Anarkali* so that he could remain associated with Asif's prestigious project.

Around the same time, S. Mukherjee of Filmistan Studios also launched his version of *Anarkali*, with Pradeep Kumar as Salim and Bina Rai in the title role. Asif tried to talk Mukherjee, too, out of it, but failed. The movie was made under the direction of Nandlal Jaswantilal, with C. Ramchandra providing the music. Released in 1953, it became a huge success mainly due to Ramchandra's melodies — *Yeh zindagi ussi ki hai...*, *Duwa kar gham-e-dil* and *Mohabbhat aisi dhadkan hai*. It stirred up panic in the Asif camp, but music director Naushad assured the unit that he would come up with superior compositions.

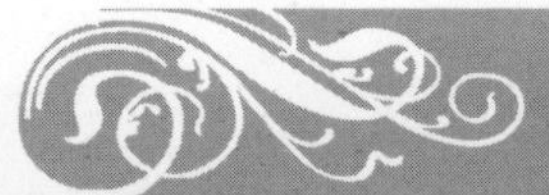

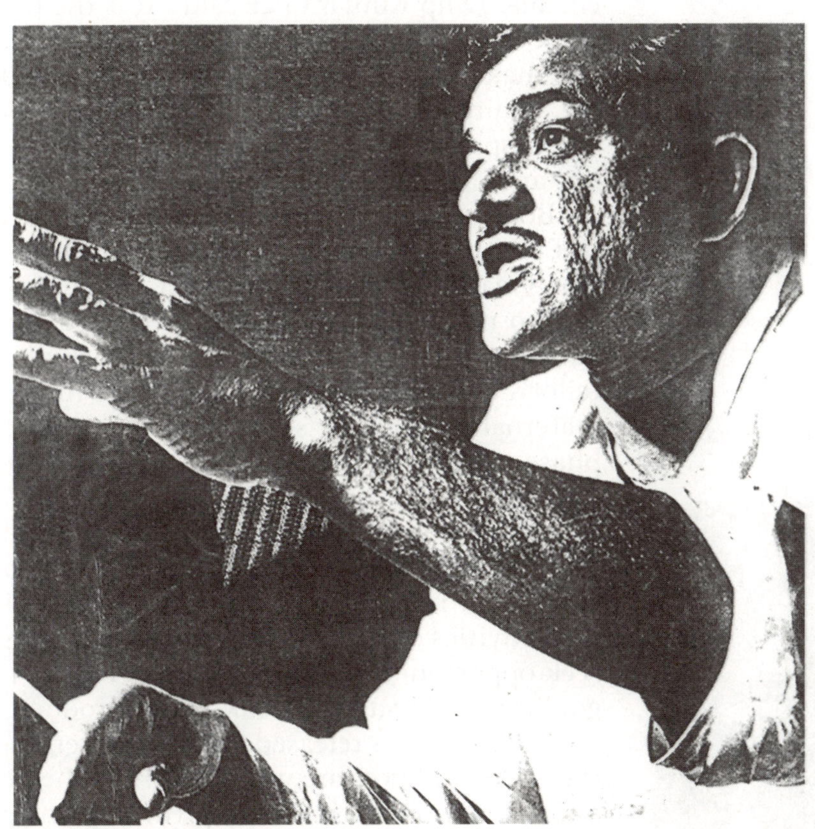

...Asif remained unmoved by the trappings of stardom. He wore simple clothes, and in an industry where imported luxury automobiles were a status symbol, he did not own a car...

Despite his limited body of work, Karim Asif is counted among the legendary directors of Hindi cinema. Dilip Kumar once said, 'It is the merit of your work by which you are judged, not the quantum of noise you make.' Asif directed all of two and a half films and left behind a string of unrealised projects through a career spanning over three decades. But the man stood out among his contemporaries.

Born on 14 June 1924, K. Asif spent his early years in Etawah, Uttar Pradesh. It was a childhood marked by a great fascination for cinema, which eventually led him to move to Bombay in his teens. Over the years, struggling through a series of jobs, including that of a tailor's assistant, he began to involve himself with his maternal uncle Nazir's film society; it was a significant phase that brought him in contact with people of the film industry.

Prithviraj Kapoor and Veena in Phool *(1943).*

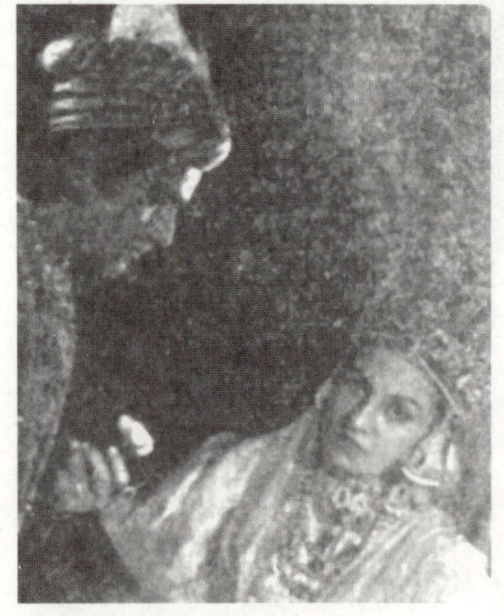

His first break came with Shaukat Hussain's *Zeenat,* for which he wrote the script. Asif was hooked. From then on, although he continued to involve himself with the activities of the film society, his primary goal was to seek opportunities to make movies. Finally in 1943, he got his first directorial break, *Phool,* produced by Shiraz Ali Hakim. It was released two years later, and although the movie did not fare well, it marked the beginning of an association with at least three principal figures involved with *Mughal-e-Azam: Phool*'s writer Kamal Amrohi, one of the four who scripted the epic, the film's villain Prithviraj Kapoor, who went on to portray Asif's Akbar, and Durga Khote, another key actress, playing

Rani Jodhabai. Veena, Yaqub, Suraiya, Zillu, and Agha comprised the other members of the big-budget cast. And among the director's assistants were comedian Mukri and S.K. Ojha.

Phool starred the famous kathak dancer Sitara, who was then his uncle's wife. *Phool* did not do well at the box office, but Asif was far from disheartened. He knew he could make a better movie; besides, *Phool* had drawn him closer to the glamorous Sitara. She was then a big star and an influential figure, and they were soon married. Partition had taken place, and Nazir had migrated to Pakistan.

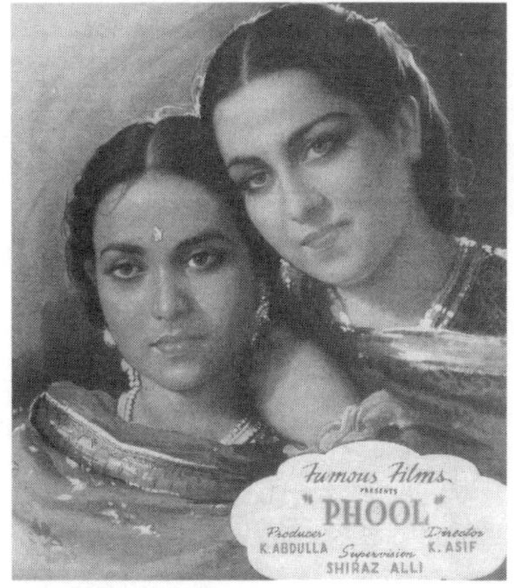

Poster of Phool, *K. Asif's directorial debut.*

Faced with limited resources, Asif had to unfortunately set aside his dream project and instead launch *Hulchul* as his first home production in 1948. The film was a Dilip Kumar–Nargis starrer, with Asif's star–wife as the vamp. It was released in 1951.

In the early fifties, as circumstances grew more favourable, Asif revived the *Mughal-e-Azam* project. The decision proved momentous, consuming the next ten years of his life, bringing him fame and laying the foundation of a lifelong relationship with Dilip Kumar.

Hulchul *(1951) directed by S.K. Ojha.*

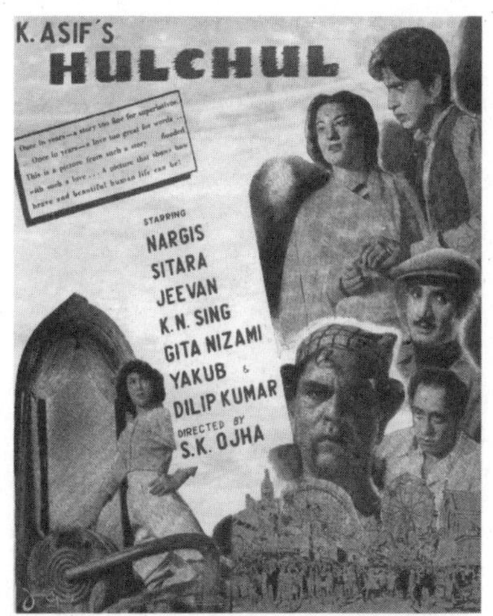

Through all this, Asif remained unmoved by the trappings of stardom. He wore simple clothes, and in an industry where imported luxurious automobiles were considered a status symbol, he did not even own a car. He lived in a two-bedroom house, moved around in a taxi, and preferred to reserve the grandeur for the screen. Although an outspoken person, Asif did not like to discuss or publicise the cost of his movies, even if his outward exuberance barely hid the tension of dealing with a grand project like *Mughal-e-Azam*. His unique strength lay in the scale of his ideas and the grand settings in which he projected them. For instance, in the case of *Mughal-e-Azam*, every frame of the film depicts his thought process. Asif's painstaking pursuit of perfection and an eye for detail ensured that he never compromised on the quality of his projects, even though he took a long time to complete them. And this was a common complaint against him. But he was not shaken. In fact, he left behind a trail of incomplete projects, including one that was extensively shot: *Sasta Khoon Mahenga Paani*. He planned, began work on, and shelved as many as six films during the making of *Mughal-e-Azam*, including *Mahabharata, Taj Mahal, Janwar.* The announcement of *Janwar* was the talk of the town those days as 'Suraiya' the lady love of Dev Anad, was to act with Dilip Kumar for the first time. The advertisement of the film showed a bare leg of a woman (Suraiya in all probability) and Dilip Kumar's mouth kissing it. Something went wrong and the film did not see the light of the day. Gossip journalists wrote stories of Dilip Kumar biting the bare leg vehemently, which infuriated Suraiya and she rejected the project altogether. In later years Suraiya herself revealed to a film journal, 'Mr Kumar was being over romantic those days.'

Asif's quest and impatience for quality gave him the reputation of being a difficult man. He was a merciless critic of his own work and constantly re-shot scenes, discarding miles of celluloid footage. Consider, for instance, that he recorded twenty songs for *Mughal-e-Azam*, ten of which were never heard, including a classical number by the three melody queens, Shamshad Begum, Mubarak Begum and Lata Mangeshkar. They were left out on the editing table along with countless other scenes.

Asif's vision was not in the slightest bit influenced by western filmmakers. His aesthetics and sensibility always remained Indian. *Mughal-e-Azam*, for instance, had an intelligent blend of Hindu–Muslim culture, a

'*sangam* of Ganga–Jamuni *sanskriti*', through which Akbar's respect for liberal values is well-established. The film underlines the emperor's passion for justice and his endeavour for communal harmony. The script had nationwide appeal. If Anarkali sings a *naat* (a poem praising the Prophet) *'Bekas pe karam ki jiye sarkare madina'*, she also sings a bhajan, *'Mohe panghat pe nandlal chedgayore'* on Krishna Janmashtami. A *moulvi* (muslim priest) ties a taweez on his arm, reciting the 'victory verse' from Quran; at the same time a Hindu pandit applies tilak on his forehead, reading a Sanskirt shloka of victory. Moreover, the rich Urdu is balanced with polished Hindi spoken by Raja Mansingh, Durjan Singh and Maharani Jodhabai. Asif also believed that the West emphasised on sex in romantic relations because it failed to understand love. To him love was a relation both material and abstract. His technique was greatly influenced by this belief, and he experimented with the same in all his romantic scenes.

After the rift healed, Dilip Kumar with sister Akhtar and brother-in-law K. Asif.

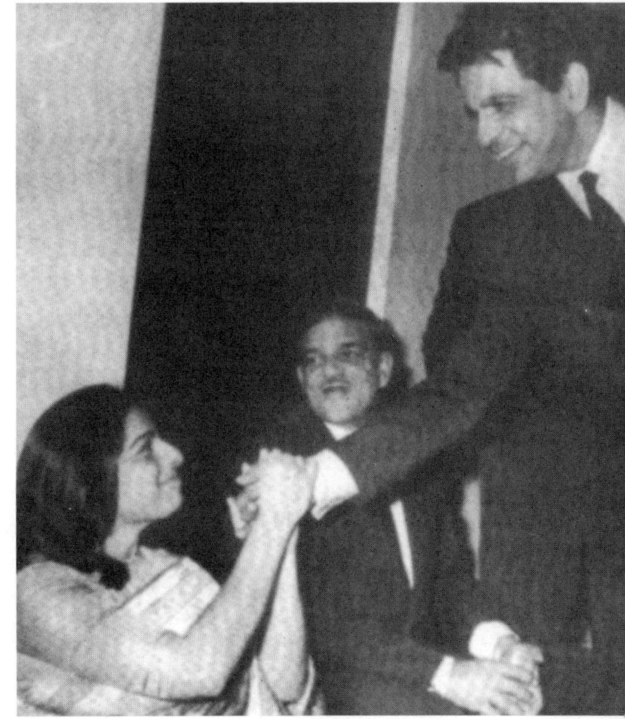

A cigarette held in a clenched fist in the right hand, Asif made for an imposing presence on the sets. Dilip Kumar once recalled an incident when the director lost his temper and picked up his shoe to hit an actor, who was faltering with his lines. The poor man was shaken. Dilip Kumar intervened and requested Asif to be more sensitive. He was in fact very sensitive in day-to-day life. Arjun Dev Rashk, a well-known writer of the industry, recalls an incidence which he wrote about in *Filmfare* on 9 April 1971. Asif once acted as an arbitrator between Rashk and a

The movie fostered a strong bond of friendship between Asif and Dilip Kumar ... until the day he became a family member in a very real sense.

well-established person in the industry. He happened to be Asif's close friend, while Rashk was just a mere acquaintance. This person owed some money to the writer and was looking for grounds to evade payments. After hearing both sides, Asif decided that the poor writer genuinely deserved his dues. Asif gave the verdict in the writer's favour and requested his friend to pay the dues. But to his astonishment, he flatly refused. Asif then said in a tone that carried with it the explosion of unhostile decision, 'There goes with you a friendship which began so many years ago ... goodbye.' Arjun Rashk was naturally sorry for the unpleasant break up of the two friends. But Asif smiled and said, 'Haven't we both gained something today? You have a big man in the dock as a defaulter, and I am rid forever of a petty friendship.'

There is another incidence that summarises Asif's scale of thinking. After the grand success of *Mughal-e-Azam*, there was a queue of financiers outside his office. But he was choosy. Despite his constant refusal, an old-time financier insisted on financing his next project. One day, he called Asif for a drink to discuss the project. Asif agreed. He kept on drinking and talked about everything except the new project. The impatient financier said, 'You have had six pegs and yet not discussed the project. Asif replied, 'You have even counted the number of pegs I had. You can't finance my film.'

During the making of *Mughal-e-Azam,* his day would normally begin at 8 a.m. If there was no shooting, he would be busy exchanging ideas and notes with writers, technicians, exhibitors and a wide circle of well-wishers and friends. These activities would usually keep him up till 2 a.m, sometimes even 4 a.m! Next morning he would be ready again for the grind. Very often, he

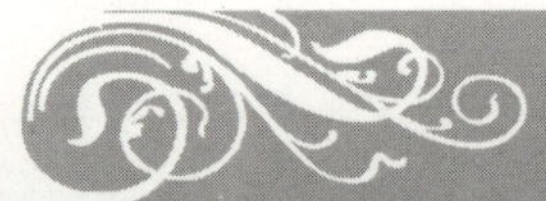

skipped shaving to save time on his hectic schedules.

The movie fostered a strong bond of friendship between Asif and Dilip Kumar. Their passion for cinema cemented it. They were always together, at work or away from it. Asif was like a family member at the actor's home, until the day he became a family member in a very real sense and their friendship soured: Asif married Akhtar, Dilip Kumar's sister. The marriage had taken place outside India without the actor's consent or knowledge. He was thoroughly annoyed. Though he kept his professional commitments to *Mughal-e-Azam*, Dilip Kumar showed his displeasure by keeping away from the premiere. The reasons were obvious: Asif was a much married man with no formal education, while Dilip Kumar's sister was a sophisticated young woman educated in the US. Dilip Kumar might have thought Asif unsuitable for his pampered little sister. But the marriage was a success! Asif's house became a home, perhaps for the first time, where he would long to return to. The couple stayed in a house at Juhu and, the rapprochement with Dilip Kumar came about under unusual circumstances. An armed robbery took place at Asif's house, in which the couple suffered severe injuries at the hands of unidentified dacoits. They were hospitalised in a Warden Road nursing home, where the actor visited them.

'A little relaxation during hectic schedules', K. Asif with wife Nigar Sultana.

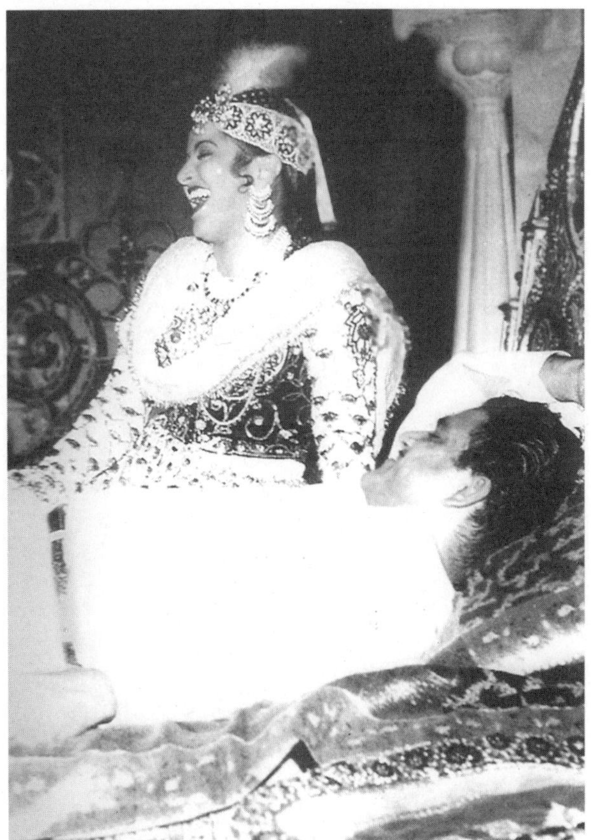

Asif had become a complete family man, with Akhtar having borne him two daughters whom he missed sorely while

K. Asif's grand vision made him visualise the tale of Laila Majnu in an altogether unique manner.

shooting outdoors. Akhtar had changed the man. He turned mellow, and she took on the role of his manager. When Asif went on various outdoor locations, the kids missed him terribly as it was a custom for papa to sleep with his arms around them. This was the softer side of the tough Asif. Once when he had to go to Delhi to attend an important meeting, his schedule extended and he had to stay for four days. Four days to Asif were like four centuries. One of his colleagues on the trip recollected that Asif Saab made few trunk calls to some of his friends in Bombay and after few hours they all were at the airport to receive his wife and kids. The educated and enlightened wife would often accompany him to the sets. She occasionally wrote scenes for Asif's films. She a good poet, and her work was often published in various periodicals.

A still from Love and God, *an incomplete masterpiece from the maker of* Mughal-e-Azam.

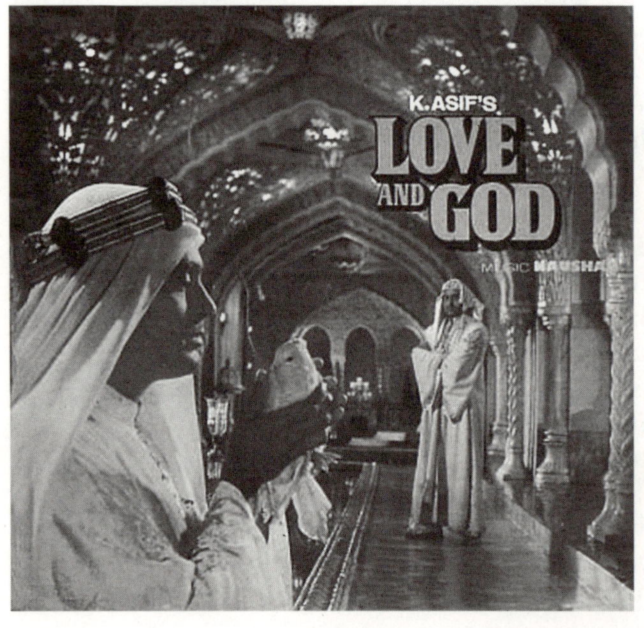

It was during the making of *Mughal-e-Azam* that Asif launched *Laila Majnu,* yet another story of star-crossed lovers, with Bharat Bhushan and Nimmi in the lead roles. Bharat Bhushan was later replaced with Guru Dutt in what clearly appeared to be a jinxed project. Planned on a magnificent scale, the film was suspended due to the untimely death of Guru Dutt on 10 October 1964. However, this did not deter the director. He replaced Guru Dutt with Sanjeev Kumar and re-launched the film. This time he planned it in colour and re-named it *Love and God*. The financiers wanted to change the female lead too, but Asif stuck to his earlier choice and Nimmi stayed on as Laila.

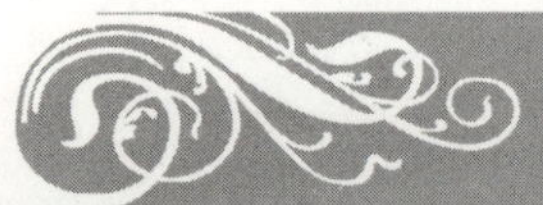

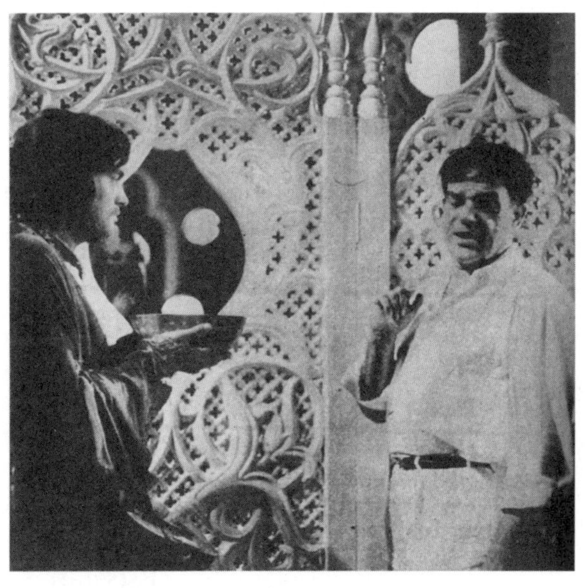

K. Asif directing Sanjeev Kumar *in* Love and God.

K. Asif's grand vision made him visualise the tale of *Laila Majnu* in an altogether unique manner. He conceived a grand set of *jannat* (paradise) where Qais (Majnu to the world) and Laila would live in eternity, beyond the reach of the material world.

He always believed in raising the bar. He knew the desert sequences of *Love and God* could be shot in Rajasthan; but the sand dunes of Jordan, he thought, had a special shade to them. So he wanted to import the same. He knew a fantasy sequence of heaven (*jannat*) could be shot in a Bombay studio with ammonia and dry ice but it could be better faked in London. So that was where he would go.

Clearly, Asif aspired to bring an unforgettable dimension to *Love and God.* His demise in 1971 terminated the work on this movie, which many say, would have been another milestone in Indian cinema. After his death, it was Akhtar, a co-writer on the film, who managed to complete the story, using voice-overs and commentaries. With the help of her brother Dilip Kumar, she got it released in collaboration with K.C. Bokadia. The final product did not appeal to audiences, though.

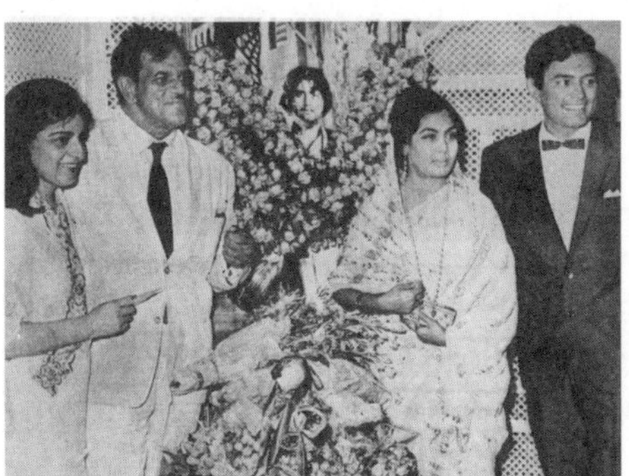

K. Asif with wife Akhtar, Sanjeev Kumar and Nimmi at the re-launch of Love and God.

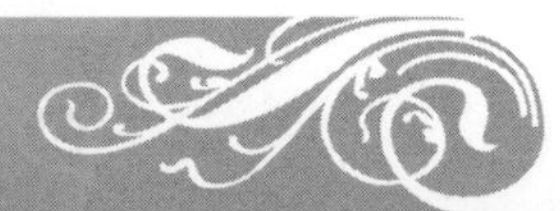

The Writers

Shiraz Ali Hakeem was the man who conceived *Mughal-e-Azam,* along with K. Asif, to bring alive a golden era in Indian history and showcase Akbar's greatness on celluloid. He hailed from Ratnagiri, Maharashtra, and was the one who built the Famous Cine Lab at Tardeo in Bombay. In the pre-Partition days, Hakeem played a significant role in the development of the Bombay film industry. He produced several Marathi films in association with the legendary filmmaker Bhai G. Pendarkar, including *Chandrarao More, Thorantan Chi Aaie, Kamla* and *Sunbai*.

Shiraz Ali purchased shares of Bombay Talkies that were surrendered by actress Devika Rani. She quit the business in 1945 and settled in Bangalore with her Russian painter husband Dr Svetslav Roerich. Ali became a partner of Bombay Talkies and a constant presence at board meetings.

Hiten Choudhary was the production controller of the company, and responsible for its day-to-day operations. He was the first person Shiraz Ali and Asif discussed their dream project with, in the early 1940s. Choudhary suggested that they make the film under a different banner. He even suggested Dilip Kumar's name for the role of Prince Salim. The actor was just a few films old then, and on the payroll of the company.

Asif and Ali gave the suggestion a serious thought and even screen-tested the young actor. It is interesting that Asif rejected Dilip Kumar, a relatively lesser-known actor then. Dilip Kumar was doing the third film of his career at that time — *Milan*, directed by Nitin Bose. Asif chose Sapru instead to play Salim, Chandramohan as Emperor Akbar, and Nargis for the role of Anarkali. Veena, was to play Bahar. K. Asif remembered the 'Heer Ranjha' episode and replaced her with his wife Sitara

Devi. For Durjan Singh, the Rajput friend of Prince Salim, Asif opted for Himalaywala, a popular actor who had played several negative roles impressively in the 1940s. Himalaywala had also worked in a few historicals like *Humayun* (1945) and *Samrat Ashok* (1947). His portrayal of a suave villain in *Jagbiti* (1947) drew lavish praise from Baburao Patel in the popular *Film India* magazine. Asif then selected some eminent Urdu writers, who had a vast knowledge of Indian history and an able experience of writing for films, to craft the dialogues.

Kamal Amrohi, his principal writer, was well read and adept at handling subjects like *Mughal-e-Azam*. Asif had already worked with him on his directorial debut, *Phool*. Moreover, Amrohi had built a formidable reputation with the dialogues while working for Sohrab Modi's *Jailor* and *Pukar*. A young man in his twenties, Amrohi was at that point a restless, brooding soul, in constant search of challenges. Amrohi's creativity was further brought into focus with Bombay Talkies' *Mahal*, a film he wrote and directed. His first home production *Daayera,* although a commercial failure, again confirmed his abilities. *Dil Apna aur Preet Paraiye* and *Pakeezah* were also scripted by Amrohi, where drama blended beautifully with poetry. K. Asif was aware of Amrohi's capacity to depict human nature in all its complexity through a convincing narrative.

A good screenplay usually has two or three characters in direct conflict with each other. As *Mughal-e-Azam*'s plot underscored the conflicts between each and every one, Asif thought he would need more than one eminent writer for his masterpiece.

Kamal Amrohi, the principal dialogue writer of Mughal-e-azam.

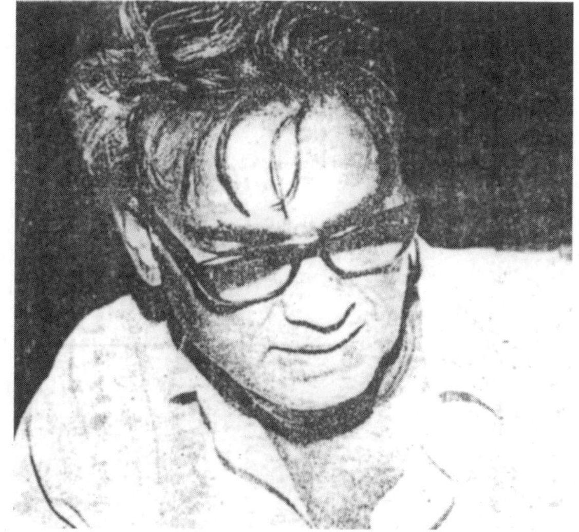

Therefore, besides Kamal Amrohi, Asif engaged **Vajahat Mirza, Ehsan Rizvi and Aman** as co-writers of the epic. Vajahat Mirza worked on many successful films, including the Dilip Kumar starrers *Ganga Jamuna, Kohinoor* and *Yahudi.* His third writer, Ehsan Rizvi, was also a well-known figure associated with several successful films, including *Victoria No.203*. Aman, the fourth writer, was primarily associated with the writing of screenplays. An impressive looking man, Aman had acted in many films including A.R. Kardar's *Jadoo* released in 1951.

Armed with a perfect script and Shiraz Ali Hakeem's war chest, Asif began shooting the film in around 1946 at Bombay Talkies. But destiny had other things in store. Jawaharlal Nehru, Mohammad Ali Jinnah and other leaders of the Congress and Muslim League had negotiated Partition. When Pakistan was created, communal carnage ravaged the country. Soon, Himalayawala and Shiraz Ali Hakeem left for Pakistan, and Asif's dream project grounded to a halt.

Shapoorji Pallonji

Before leaving for Pakistan, Shiraz Ali Hakeem had motivated a Parsi businessman, Shapoorji Pallonji, to invest in the project. Shapoorji was a merchant prince with a vast construction business. He had built Churchgate station and was involved in the development of the stretch along Marine Drive.

The sprawling business is now in the hands of Shapoorji's son, Pallonji Mistry who is counted among the wealthiest men in India. He is the chairman of the Shapoorji Pallonji group of companies, which has widespread interests in construction and textiles. He lives in Pune with his wife and two sons, Shapoor Mistry and Cyrus. The family has consolidated the businesses

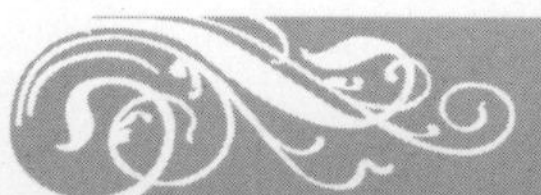

set up by Shapoorji, having developed a large chunk of Mumbai's buzzing skyline. They are also sizeable stakeholders in the Tata group. Shapoor Mistry is now the chairman of the Rs 436-crore Forbes Gokak Ltd., and is a director on the board of Indian Hotels Company. As a tribute to his grandfather's dream, he re-released *Mughal-e-Azam* in the colourised and digital version.

When K. Asif approached Shapoorji Pallonji to finance *Mughal-e-Azam,* he had little interest in show business. However, he was a great admirer of Emperor Akbar. Asif, known for his persuasive skills, exploited this very quality to convince him to bankroll the project. After much discussion and negotiations, he finally received the go-ahead in 1950. Aware that he was entering a domain he had no knowledge about, Shapoorji at the very outset asked Asif to present a detailed break-up of the budget. The director, a quintessentially creative and quirky man given to impulsive spending, had no knowledge or appreciation of such things. He would put up a budget but never stick to it. Not surprisingly, from day one, problems cropped up between the director and the producer.

There was an incident when Asif wanted to prepare a curtain of pearls and beads for the Krishna Janmashthami scene in the film. Maharani Jodhabai was supposed to give it away on Salim's arrival from the battlefield. The curtain needed rare beads, and Shapoorji's office could not arrange those in as large a quantity as Asif required. So he stopped the shoot midway and announced that it would be resumed only when the beads were made available. Shapoorji refused to yield. However, when Shapoorji sent a four-figure amount as *eidi* (a gift given on the festival of Eid), the director accepted a rupee and returned the balance to

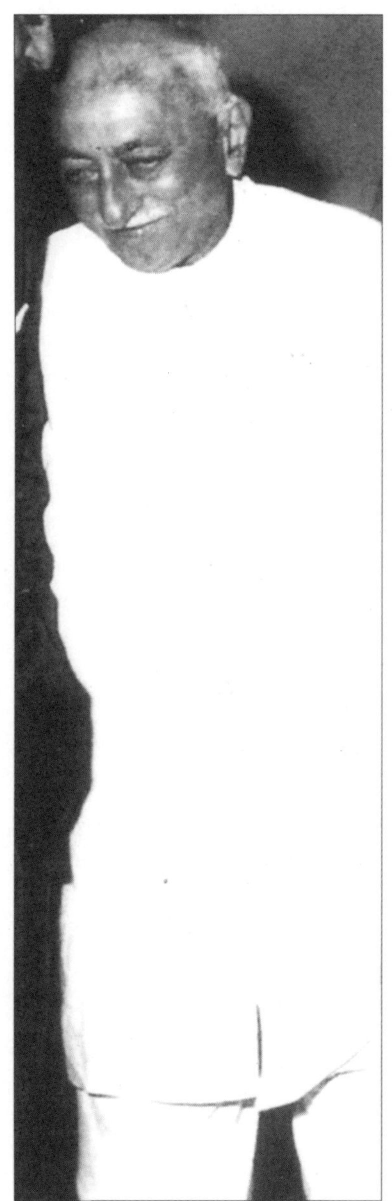

Shapoorji Pallonji, financer of the magnum opus.

his financier, requesting him to use it for purchasing the beads for the curtain.

The two admired each other. Shapoorji, for one, was impressed with his director's dedication to work. Asif's own salary was Rs 2,000 per month, all of which he would spend on his dream project. Unmindful of the discomfort, Asif often spent the night on the sets, sleeping on an ordinary *chatai* after hectic schedules.

Asif's perfectionism and passion for detail was a huge drain on Shapoorji's coffers. At some stage, the producer was prejudiced against Asif by those who claimed that the filmmaker was taking him for granted and that the project would be a complete disaster. Even his son Pallonji Mistry would tell him, 'Let this film go to hell, your health is more important'.

At a time when even a big budget production did not need more than Rs 10-15 lakh, *Mughal-e-Azam's* budget swelled to more than one crore and fifty lakh. This sum would certainly be equivalent to more than Rs 250 crore, today. Asif used about ten lakh feet of film; back then, it was considered wasteful if a director used even one lakh feet. (Even today, big production houses consume a maximum of four to five lakh feet). Out of the ten lakh feet he shot, Asif retained only twenty thousand. But his courage and integrity, and Shapoorji's patience and faith, finally bore fruit. *Mughal-e-Azam* went on to be an unparalleled achievement in Indian cinema. It not only broke box office records but also set a standard for other movies that followed.

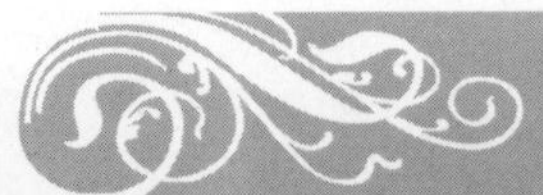

Making of the epic

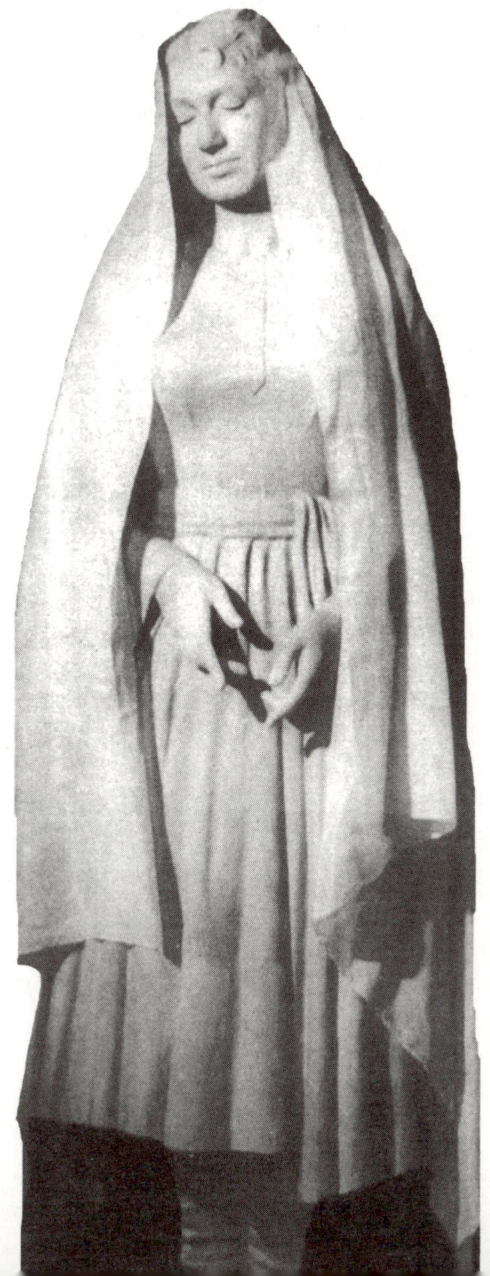

...Asif wanted real marble for Anarkali's entombment. Shapoorji, exasperated by his endless indulgences, suggested the use of Plaster of Paris, instead. 'Do you want real marble to make Anarkali's tomb or mine?' he asked...

Saleem: 'Beshak, is be-panah husn ki taab pathar hi la sakta hai!'

K. Asif was equipped with an impressive star-cast and a talented team of technicians. He signed R.D. Mathur for cinematography and A.K. Sayyad for art direction. Mathur had earlier photographed Dilip Kumar's debut film *Jwar Bhaata* in 1944.

The morning shift would start around 2 p.m. It was always noon by the time Dilip Kumar woke up and reported to the shoot. It took another six hours before he was on the set, ready with his make-up and costume. Around 8 p.m. rehearsals would begin, and then Asif would examine the lighting and camera angles. At midnight Asif would announce a dinner break, and thereafter take another couple of hours to okay the first shot. A shot was rarely approved without ten to twenty re-takes.

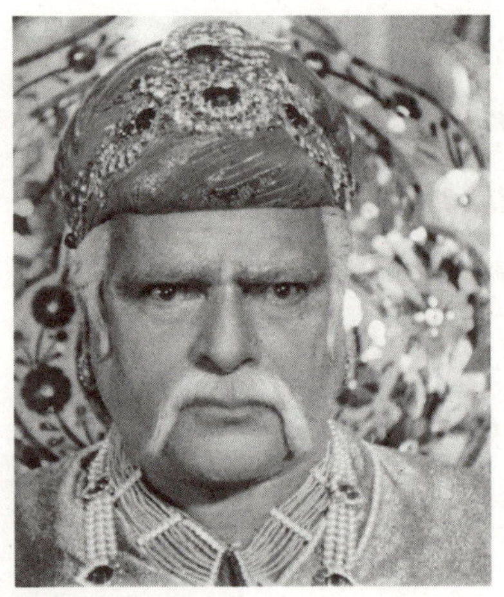

Prithviraj Kapoor as 'Akbar' enraged by 'Pyaar kiya to darna kya!'

Prithviraj Kapoor would also take a few hours to get into the skin of the character, and the unit would wait for the stalwart till he emerged as Emperor Akbar-incarnate. The actor's dedication was legendary. The veteran actor walked barefoot through the scorching desert sand while shooting for the scene where Akbar, along with his wife Jodhabai, visits the dargah of the Sufi saint Salim Chisti in Fatehpur Seekri, near Agra, to pray for a son. Asif promised Kapoor that he too would stand barefoot on the burning sand while Kapoor did the scene. Prithviraj was deeply moved by this gesture, but he stopped the director from doing so. Recounting this, Shashi Kapoor told NDTV on 12 November 2004 that 'Papaji' was even offered sandals that would have created an illusion of walking

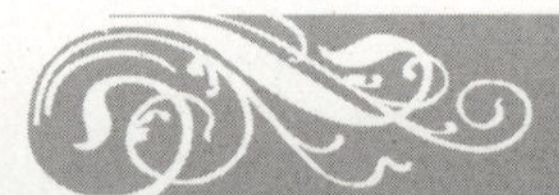

barefoot, but Prithviraj would have none of it. The pain was evident on his face as he walked on the sand like a common man to Chisti's *mazaar*. According to Shashi Kapoor, his father's feet were bruised up to his ankles. It took a long time for the injuries to heal, and the actor had to keep his feet bandaged all the time.

Kapoor's affection for his co-stars, too, was admirable. Once, Dilip Kumar fell ill during the shoot and retired to his make-up room to rest. Feverish and indisposed, he fell asleep there. When he woke up, he saw, to his astonishment, that Prithviraj Kapoor was sitting by his bedside massaging his head and shoulders. Such was the love and affection between the actors of that era!

Once, Dilip Kumar fell ill during the shoot and retired to his make-up room to rest... When he woke up, he saw, to his astonishment, that Prithviraj Kapoor was sitting by his bedside massaging his head and shoulders.

Asif exceeded the budget when the film was only halfway through. But every time a furious Shapoorji would demand to know when the film would be complete, he would resort to a clever ruse. He knew his producer's fascination for Akbar. Asif would arrange for a screening of the latest scenes shot with Prithviraj Kapoor at Mohan Studios. '*Arrey Dharamveer, Sethji ko woh scene to dikhana,*' (Dharamveer! Please show that scene to Sethji), he would say. A curious Shapoorji would protest a bit, but go away impressed after assuring him more money.

Asif wanted to shoot the famous song '*Pyaar kiya toh darna kya*' in colour. He planned to erect a magnificent set of Sheesh Mahal at Mohan Studio. The set was 30 feet high, 80 feet wide and 150 feet long. Asif wanted lakhs of small circular mirrors to be inlaid on the walls, pillars, and the ceiling. For this tedious work, he called in artisans from Ferozabad (U.P.), a town famous for glass handicrafts. It took two years to build the set, with hundreds of craftsmen working day and night. More than Rs 15 lakh of rupees were spent

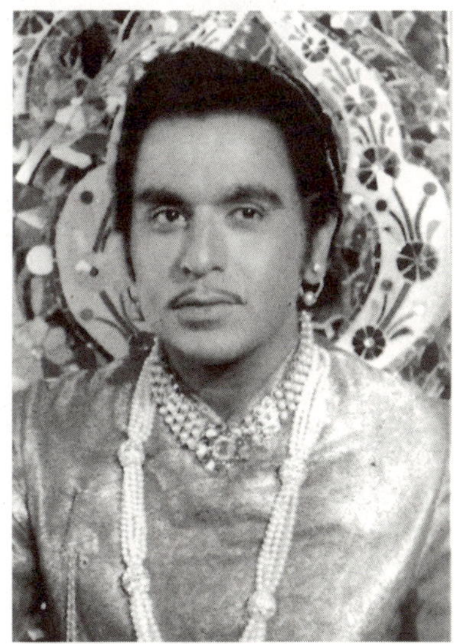

Dilip Kumar as Prince Salim.

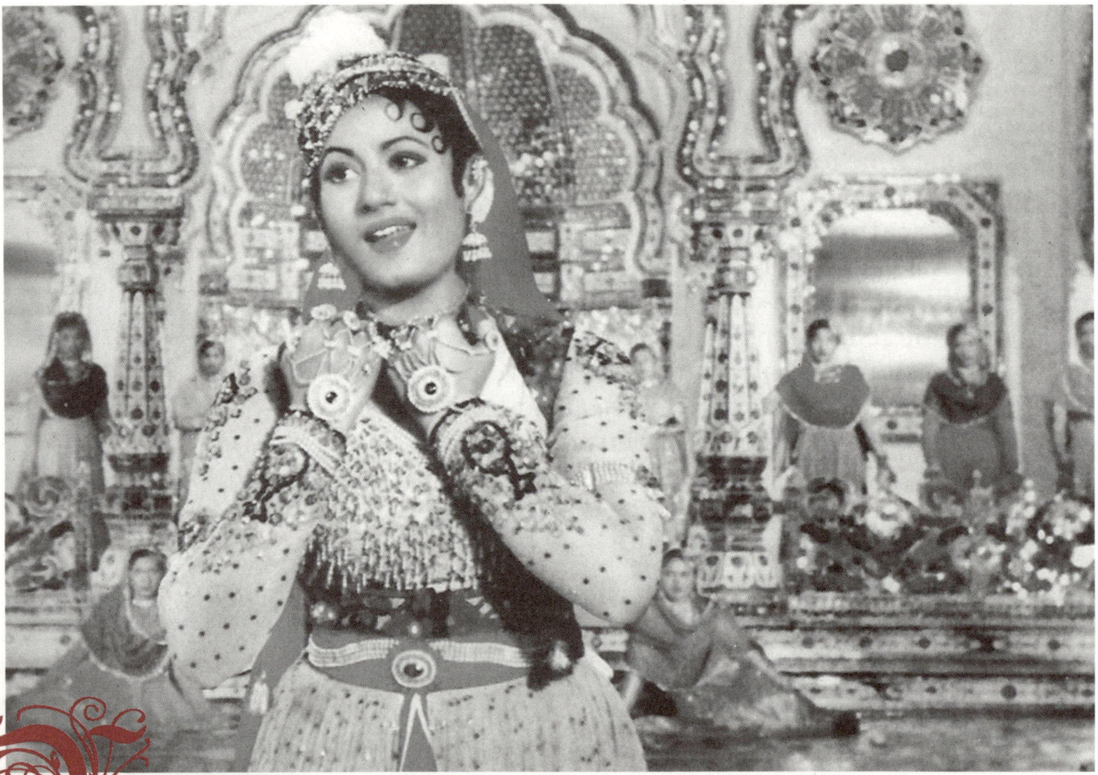

'Aaj kahengey dil ka fasana, jaan bhi leley charey zamana!'

...art director A.K. Sayyad, successfully recaptured the splendour of the Mughal era on screen.

on it. This was an enormous sum and would be equivalent to more than Rs. 3 crore today. Shapoorji was already neck-deep in trouble. *'Mera* director *pagal ho gaya hai, kanch ka pura karkhana lagaya hai* (My director has gone mad; he has set up a glass factory),' he would lament.

Credit goes to art director A.K. Sayyad, whose laborious efforts transformed Asif's imagination into reality. He successfully recaptured the splendour of the Mughal era on screen.

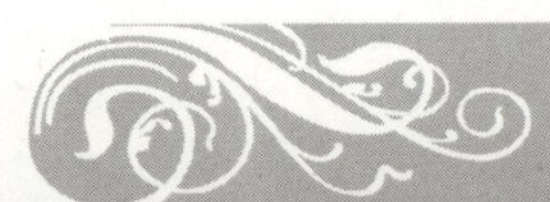

The Mahal set required a large amount of lighting equipment; the maximum portion of this sequence was shot at night as the lights were borrowed from other studios. Each morning they had to be returned to the owners. Cameraman Mathur often took eight hours to light up the set for a single shot.

When the Sheesh Mahal set was ready, came the news that almost gave Shapoorji a heart attack. Eminent European experts, including filmmakers David Lean and Roberto Rosellini, informed that it would be impossible for Asif to shoot as the coloured mirrors inlaid on the walls and pillars would reflect light. This was a serious technical problem. Shapoorji was naturally worried. Besides, he had heard rumours that Asif was taking him for a ride. Annoyed and disturbed, Shapoorji rushed to Sohrab Modi, who said it was possible to wrap the film up within two months. Asif was furious when he heard this.

One day, Shapoorji brought Sohrab Modi to the sets. It was dark when the two entered. Suddenly, Akbar's throne lit up. Asif was sitting on it with the authority of a Mughal king. He announced grimly that if anybody stepped in, he would break his leg. '*Ye* set *maine lagaya hai, ispe kam bhi mein hi karoonga* (I built this set and I will be the one to use it)'. A rattled Sohrab Modi

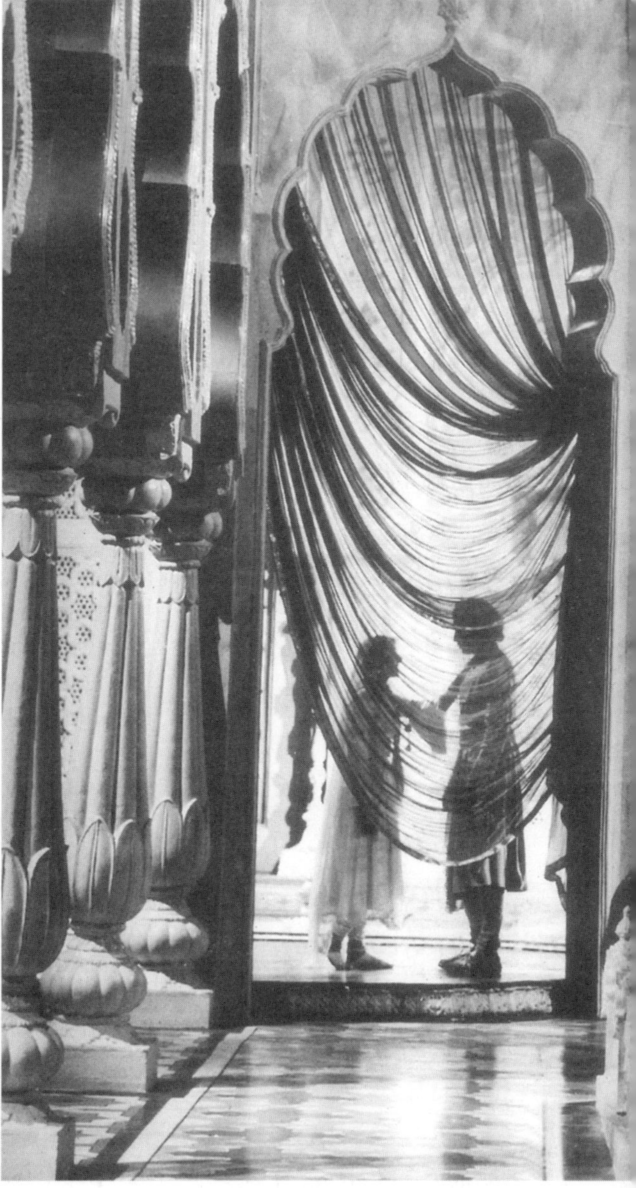

Dilip Kumar and Madhubala in a still from the film.

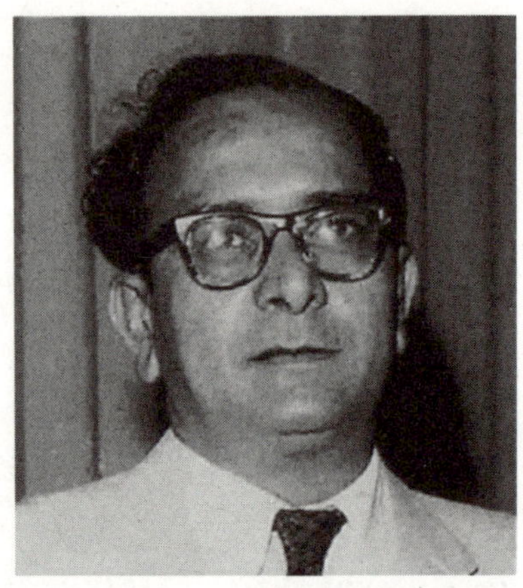

R.D. Mathur's technical virtuosity as a cinematographer ensured that the song 'pyaar kiya to darna kya' became a watershed in the history of Indian cinema.

Facing Page:
The rebellious proclamation
'Pyaar kiya to darna kya!'

made a hasty exit. Asif apologised later and requested his financier to allow him to shoot at least a few shots and examine the results.

Shapoorji granted permission on the condition that the sample rushes would be sent to a London technicolour lab for inspection. Only after they had approved the shots would Asif be allowed to shoot further. Asif discussed the problem with cinematographer R.D. Mathur in detail and sought the advice of various technical experts. Mathur would come every day and examine the Sheesh Mahal set through the eye of the camera. He would desperately try to find some solution to the problem of reflected lights. One day, he happened to see a particular spot in the frame not reflecting light, and the image of that portion was absolutely clear. Mathur's heart jumped in anticipation. On further observation, he discovered that light was in fact being bounced back on that particular portion from some object kept uselessly on the set. R.D. Mathur was thrilled; he found the solution and informed Asif that they would be able to shoot on the set. Asif then decided to send Mathur to London to study the complications of such lighting in details. After studying the technique well and interacting with experts on the subject, Mathur returned after six months. He used reflectors to bounce back lights on the inlayed mirrors and Asif shot a few close-ups, long and mid-range shots of the sets using appropriate lighting. These rushes were then sent to London for processing. After a few weeks, a cable from London announced that the results were fantastic and the work was recognised as wonderful photography!

Asif was ecstatic when the London laboratory certified his work. Shapoorji gladly permitted him to continue with the project. Thus, R.D. Mathur's

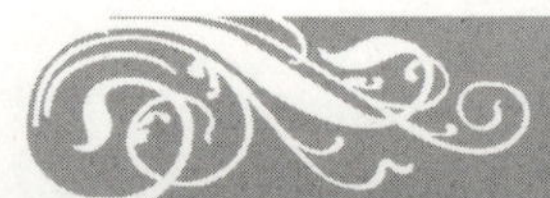

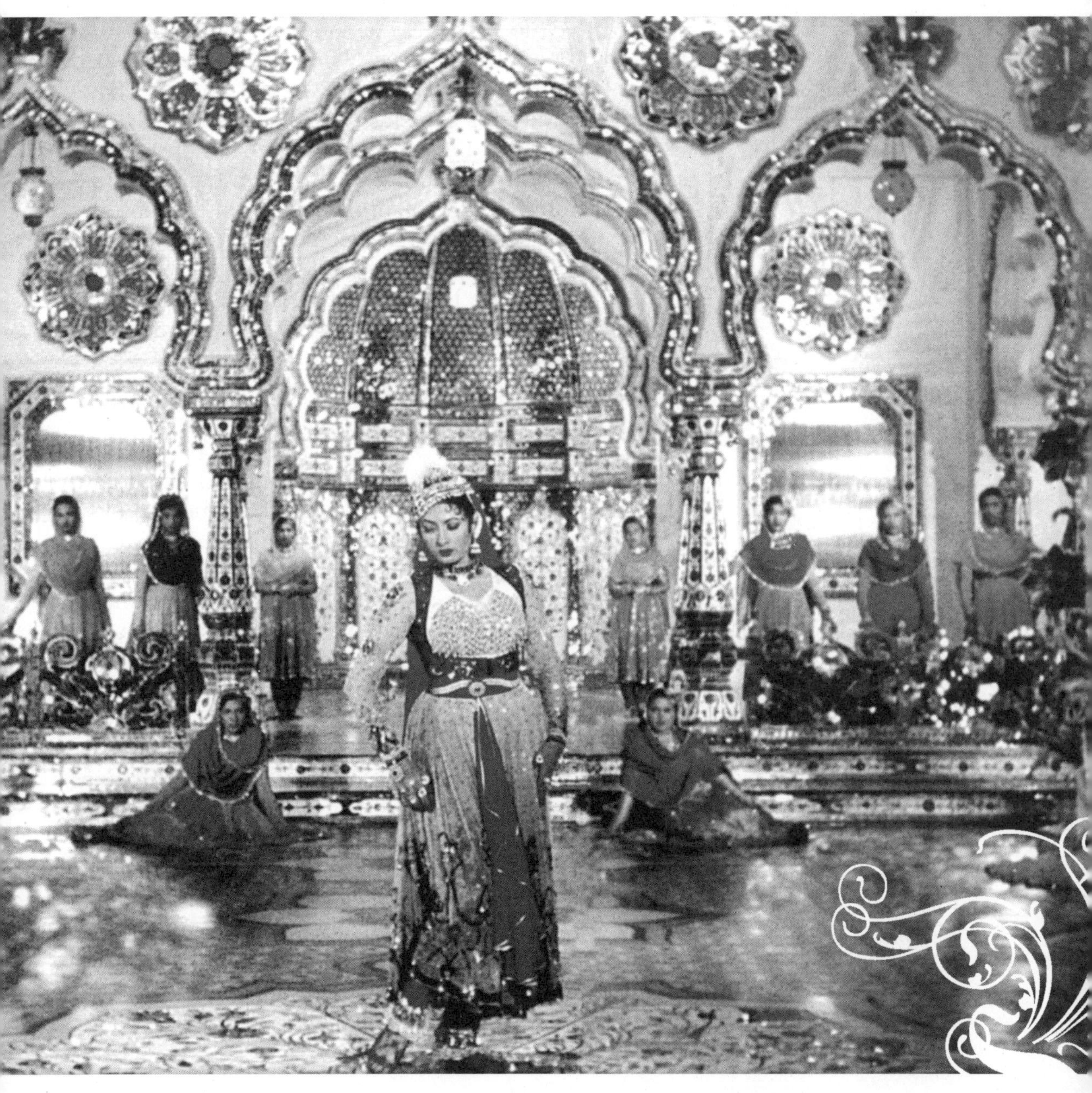

technical virtuosity as a cinematographer ensured that the song *'pyaar kiya to darna kya'* became a watershed in the history of Indian cinema. In the Sheesh Mahal dance sequence, his cameras were placed in such a way that they did not reflect on any of the thousands of small convex mirrors all over the frame! Yet, one could see Madhubala's dance movements in each of the mirrors! The sequence has become a reference point for cinematography in the country. Lighting was done with such precision that it did not dazzle the frame. A tough job, yet rendered beautifully, with Anarkali's song as the high point:

'Chhup na sakega ishq hamara,
Chaaron taraf hai unka nazaara.'

The Sheesh Mahal set was maintained at Mohan Studios for over three years. People streamed in from every corner of India and abroad to have a look at the wonder and magic of cinema.

Asif's quest for perfection had compelled him to launch a countrywide search for skilled artisans for various departments. Tailors were brought from Delhi to stitch the Mughal costume; real zardozi embroidery was used for royal robes and armours. Skilled goldsmiths from Hyderabad were called to craft ornaments, artisans from Kolhapur made crowns, and Rajasthani blacksmiths fabricated the shields, swords and armoury. Asif appointed the famous dress designers Makhanlal & Co. to take care of the costumes. The company had to increase the number of its employees from 50 to 250 during the making of the film.

Yet another time, Asif insisted on gold shoes for Prince Salim. Shapoorji blew his top. The production team had provided beautifully hand-crafted shoes with zari work, which looked perfectly suitable. Asif rejected

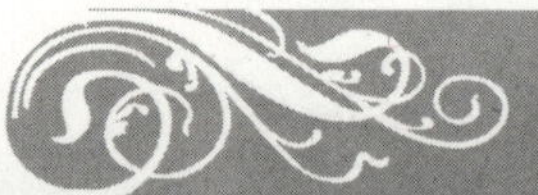

them and ordered the shoot to be cancelled unless the gold shoes were arranged. A fuming Shapoorji, submitting to his director's obstinacy, ordered the gold shoes. But these were not as beautiful as those provided earlier. Even the unit hands questioned the director's wisdom. Asif calmly replied, 'When my hero will walk with these shoes, his gait would be that of Prince Salim, not Dilip Kumar...'

'The armour and zarra bakhtar were so heavy that it was difficult to walk even a few steps.'

Madhubala once had to stand still to pose as a statue. To meet Asif's standards, she had to look like she was carved out of stone. The actress had to rehearse for months on end after smearing her body with special make-up and chemicals, which had an abrasive effect on her tender skin. Like everything else, nothing could be faked in the film. The entire process had to be undergone a number of times before the shot was canned.

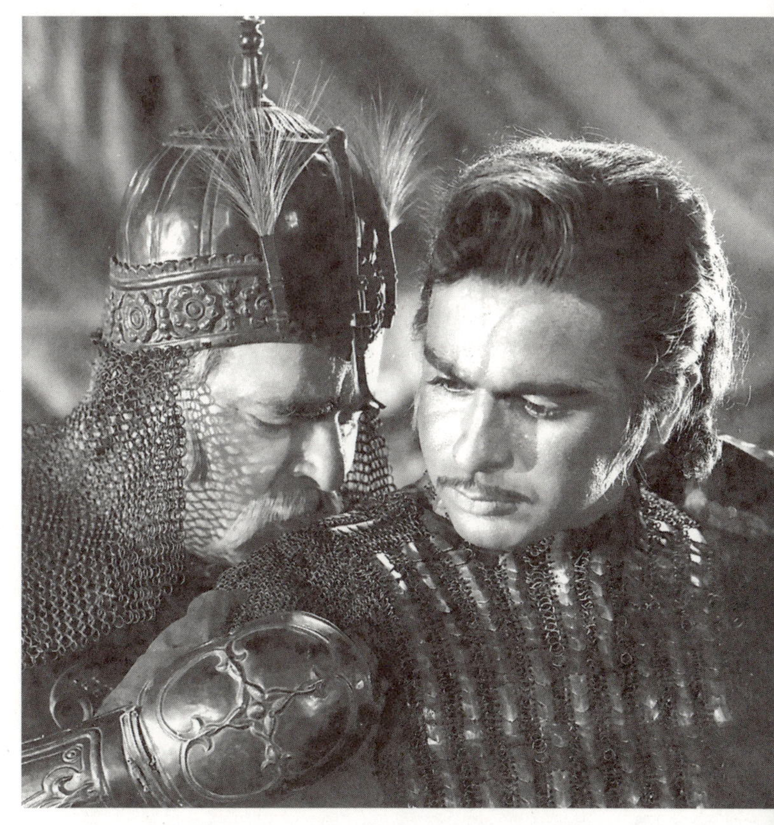

Approximately Rs 1 crore had already been spent, and the budget had doubled when Asif demanded an additional sum of Rs 15 lakh to shoot the war sequence at Jaipur. Shapoorji couldn't believe what he was hearing. But since the movie was at a critical stage, he had to relent.

In an interview, recounting the war scenes, Dilip Kumar said, 'The armour and *zarra bakhtar* were so heavy that it was difficult to walk even a few

Approximately Rs 1 crore had already been spent, and the budget had doubled when Asif demanded an additional sum of Rs 15 lakh to shoot the war sequence at Jaipur.

steps.' There were boils all over his back after the sequence was complete. The heat of the desert in Rajasthan made the whole unit miserable. There were no air conditioners, and fans were useless. Many technicians, make-up men and other crew fainted and fell ill due to the tough working conditions.

Asif wanted to shoot the sequence with real soldiers. He requested the then defence minister V.K. Krishna Menon to provide him with an infantry division. Through his contacts, he also got permission to use the Jaipur cavalry, 56 Regiment. Asif thus built a battalion of 2,000 soldiers — there were altogether 8,000 troops, 400 horses and 2,000 camels in use. For some reason, the camels were eventually dropped from the shooting sequences.

Close-ups of Dilip Kumar and Prithviraj Kapoor were shot separately in a studio later as it was impossible to shoot them on elephants and horses with the cameras available then.

Asif picturised one of the most realistic war sequences in the history of Indian cinema. It was reported that Rs 20 lakh was spent on these sequences. Though it was a

'The battle scenes are the grandest and most thrilling ever seen in Indian Cinema'.

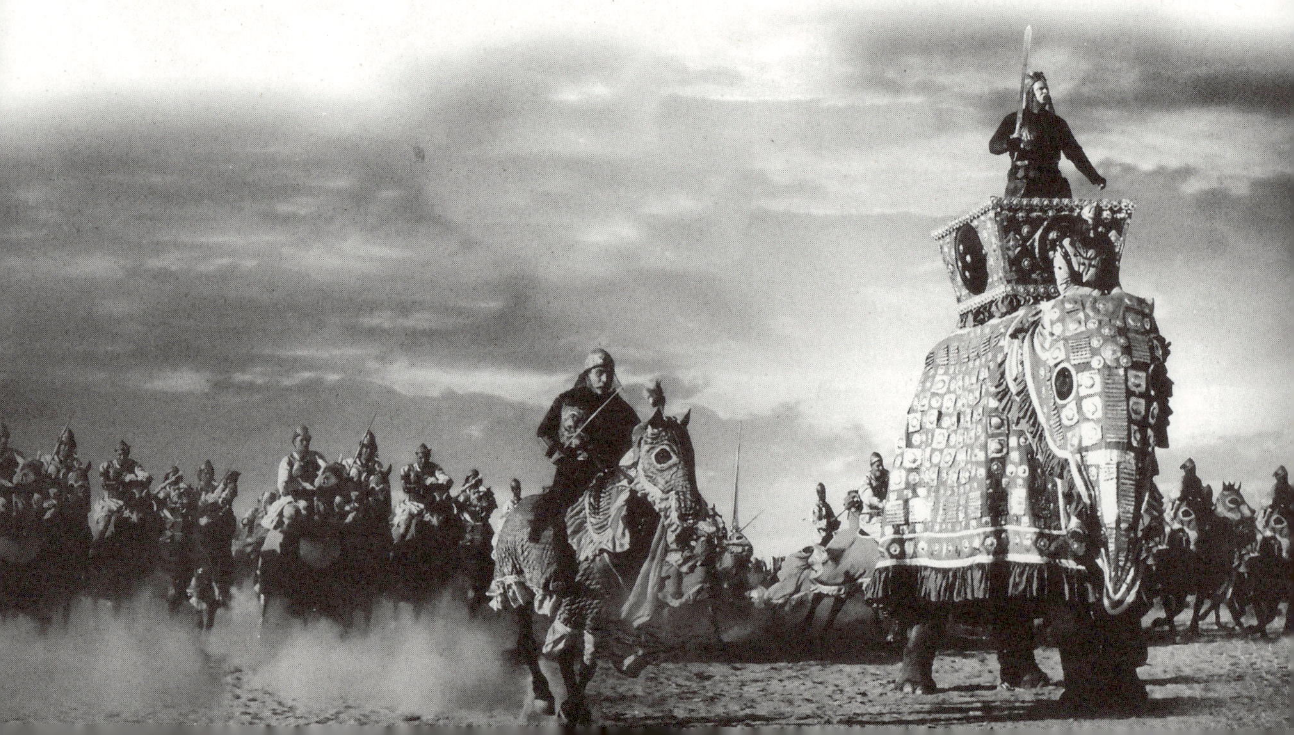

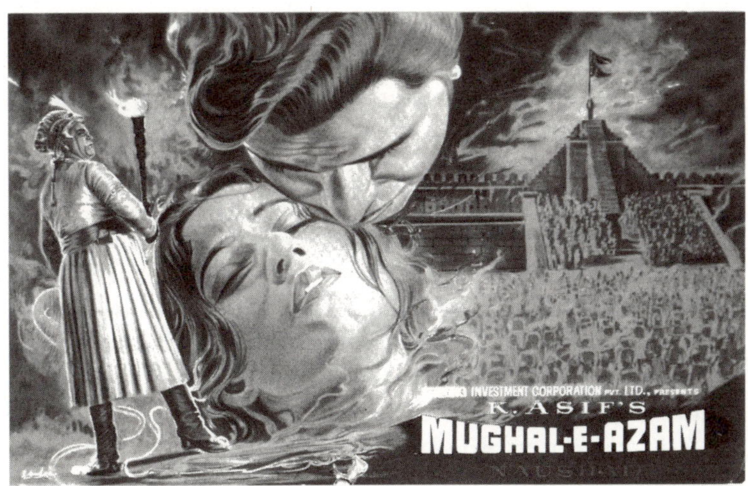

fake war, there were casualties. A jawan on horseback was blown to pieces when a cannon was fired accidentally. Some days later, another soldier lost his life. The Indian Army then filed a legal suit claiming damages. These unforeseen accidents slowed down proceedings considerably, spinning schedules out of control.

It was under such circumstances that Asif asked for the final instalment to finish the last schedules at Jaipur. Shapoorji flatly refused to invest anymore. Asif was in a fix, but Dilip Kumar swung into action. The producer owed him his dues, so he went to Shapoorji and asked him to give the money to Asif instead for the last schedule.

Dilip Kumar also assured Shapoorji that all talk about Asif cheating him was baseless, and that the film had shaped up so well that he need not worry. Shapoorji was touched by Dilip Kumar's gesture and calmed by his assurance. He embraced the actor and agreed to finance the film till its completion. Dilip Kumar, though busy producing his own film *Ganga Jamuna* at that time,

'Mughal-e-Azam' took nearly fifteen years. Normally, about hundred shifts of shooting were sufficient for a big film; this one required more than five hundred!

also went out of his way to allot the required dates for *Mughal-e-Azam*.

Mughal-e-Azam took nearly fifteen years. Normally, about hundred shifts of shooting were sufficient for a big film; this one required more than five hundred! A maximum of two cameras were used those days to shoot a film; some scenes of *Mughal-e-Azam* were shot using fourteen cameras. The film was simultaneously released in more than 150 cinema halls. It was also dubbed in Tamil and English. The dialogue writer of the Tamil version was P. Ramchandran and T.S. Vasan, while Ramesh Thapar wrote the English version.

Asif was determined to get a price of Rs 15 lakh per territory when the usual turnover in those days was a maximum of Rs 2-3 lakh per territory — and this was considered a handsome return for a black and white film! Asif eventually managed to sell the film at his price, that too without showing a single frame to his distributors!

Prithviraj Kapoor

Emperor Akbar

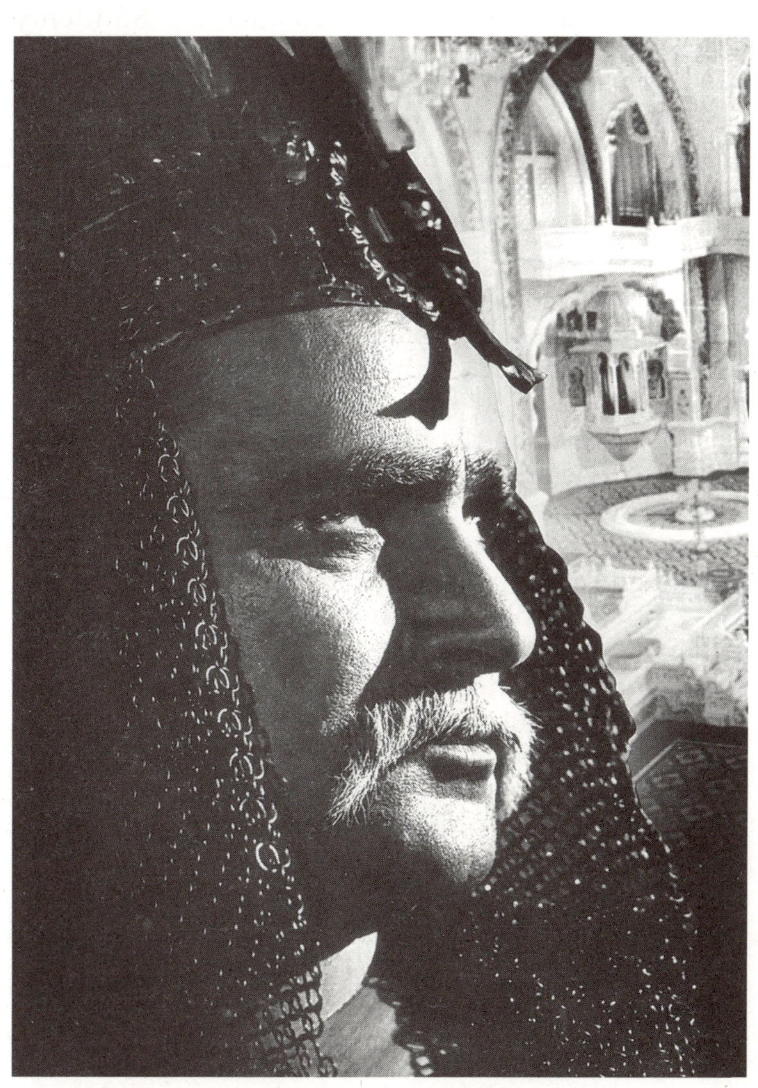

...He worked hard to develop a particular manner of speech and gait. His royal baritone and declamatory style was just what Asif needed....

Asif began his movie with Sapru, Nargis, Chandramohan and Ajit. Work progressed smoothly and a few reels were shot to the master's satisfaction. Suddenly Chandramohan, who played Akbar, suffered a fatal heart attack. The shooting had to be stopped immediately.

Shapoorji was naturally upset and his family suggested that the project be abandoned. But Asif managed to convince him to stay on board, promising to complete the film with a more impressive and commanding Akbar. He then set out to find an actor with a majestic personality, sound commercial credentials, and one whose choice would enthuse Shapoorji.

Prithviraj's royal baritone and declamatory style made the emperor come alive!

Asif was impressed with Prithviraj Kapoor's portrayal of *Sikander*. His regal personality and deep baritone had worked wonders in the film. Hence, it took no time to take the decision.

Kapoor was a father figure for the film industry. He was treated with paternal reverence. Born in Peshawar in a prosperous Punjabi family on 3 November 1906, Prithviraj had his early education in a local school at Samudri in the Lyallpur district. He was a brilliant student and graduated from Edward College in Peshawar. During his second year at college he was married, and the following year on 14 December 1924, his eldest son Raj was born.

Prithviraj was one of the leading lights of the dramatic societies in his school and college, thanks to the unflagging encouragement of his professors. He looked up to Hollywood — Douglas Fairbanks, Rudolf Valentino, Greta Garbo, John Gilbert and John Sullivan

Facing Page:
Prithviraj Kapoor in 'zarra bakhtar' (armour).

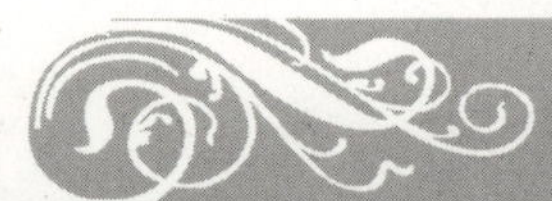

were his idols. His father Lala Basheshirnath wanted him to study law, so he joined a law college but gave up after flunking the first year. His mind and soul was already lost to the movies.

Determined to become an actor, Kapoor bought a ticket one day and boarded a train to Bombay. He got off at Grant Road. As he recounted to *Filmfare* in an interview in 1952, 'I managed to commandeer a coolie, loaded his trolley with my tennis racket, hockey sticks, violin and suitcase, and got out of the station'. Unlike other aspirants, Prithviraj had landed at Bombay in grand style. Besieged by cabbies that were curious about the tall, handsome man, he refused a taxi and instead made for the *ghoda gaadi*. Not sure where to go and eager as any tourist to look around, he told the tonga-driver to give him the reins of the horse. Travelling in this manner for sometime, the driver called for a halt at Kashmir Hotel, Colaba.

On 2 October 1929, a friend fixed up an appointment with Khan Bahadur Ardeshir Irani, the owner of Imperial Film Company. Irani, a top-ranking producer, took to Prithviraj instantly, but had no vacancy at that moment. Prithviraj offered to work as an unpaid extra. A few months later, he was put on the payroll on a fixed salary of Rs 75 per month.

After minor roles in some insignificant films, he was cast as a leading man in *Cinema Girl* opposite the Goan beauty Ermeline. He then acted in seven more silent films. He also had the privilege of acting in the first talkie *Alam Ara*.

Calcutta was then emerging as the new centre for film-making. So, off went Kapoor to join B.N. Sircar's New Theatres. It was during this period that he met the pioneer filmmaker Kidar Sharma, who shared his passion for *sher-o-shairi* (reciting couplets) and Urdu

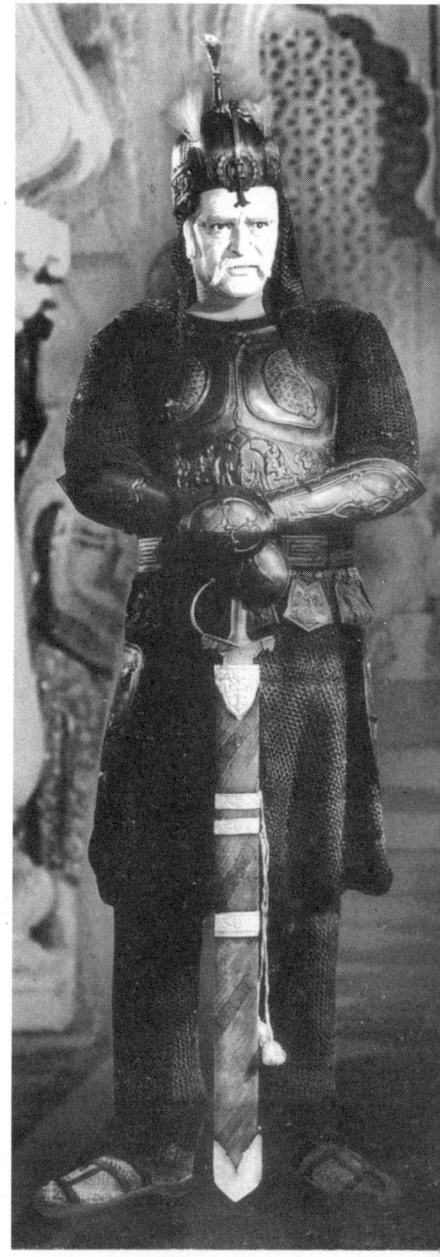

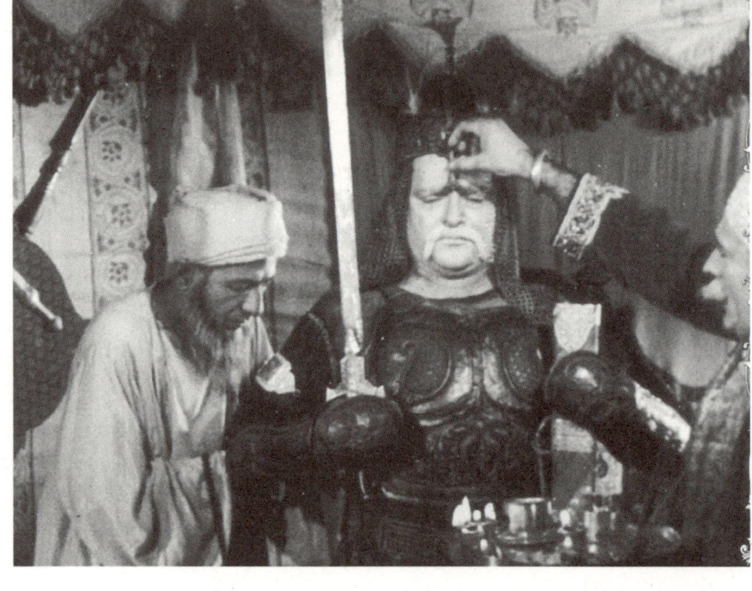

Prithviraj Kapoor as Akbar, the symbol of secularism! 'Religious tolerance, the only right path'

Pandit Jawaharlal Nehru was a patron and a fan of the actor. Prithviraj himself was an ardent admirer of Nehru and used to recount his meetings with Nehru with pride.

literature. Kapoor went on to work in New Theatres' *Vidyapati, Ananth Ashram, Manzil, Abhagin, Milaap, Dahej* and *Awaara*. After six years he returned to Bombay, which then rivalled Calcutta with its own prosperous film industry. He joined Ranjeet Studios and later founded the famous Prithvi Theatre which staged a series of plays including *Pathan, Ghaddar, Shakuntala, Dewaar, Kisan* and *Kalakar.* These became immensely popular, and he often travelled across the country staging them with a group of ninety actors, technicians and musicians. Prithviraj's son Raj, Shammi and Shashi Kapoor learnt the ropes of acting at the Prithvi Theatre. Pandit Jawaharlal Nehru was a patron and a fan of the actor. Prithviraj himself was an ardent admirer of Nehru and used to recount his meetings with Nehru with pride.

By the time Asif cast him in the role of Emperor Akbar he had aged and put on some weight. However,

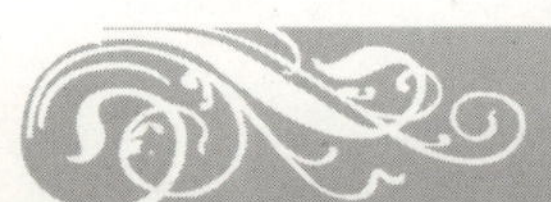

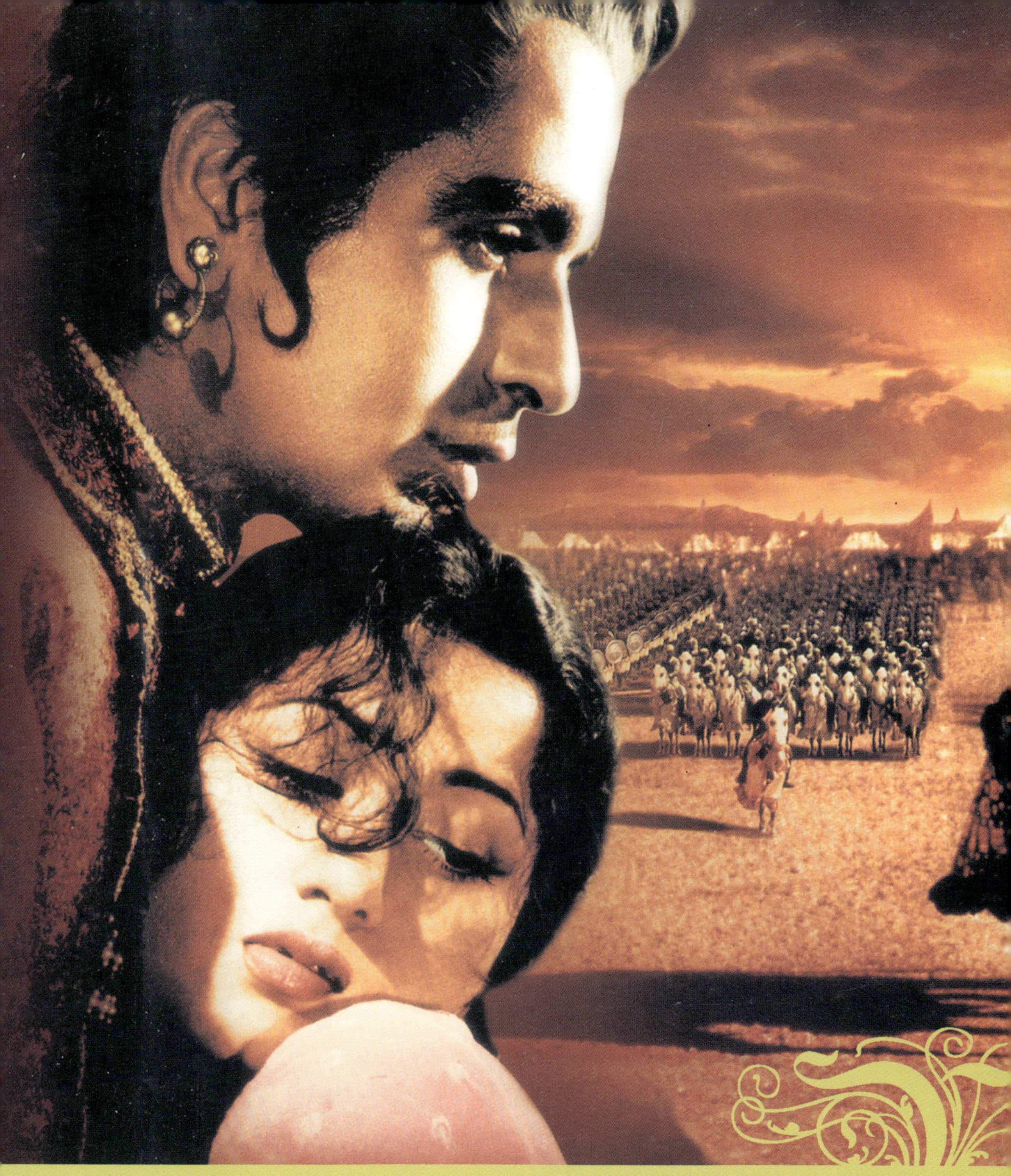

The irresistible beauty...worth fighting a war for. Madhubala and Dilip Kumar in a highly dramatic love scene 'Mohabbat jo darti hai woh mohabbat nahin ...gunah hai ...ayyashi hai'... (Love...that fears...is no love...it is a sin...it is indulgence instead...!)

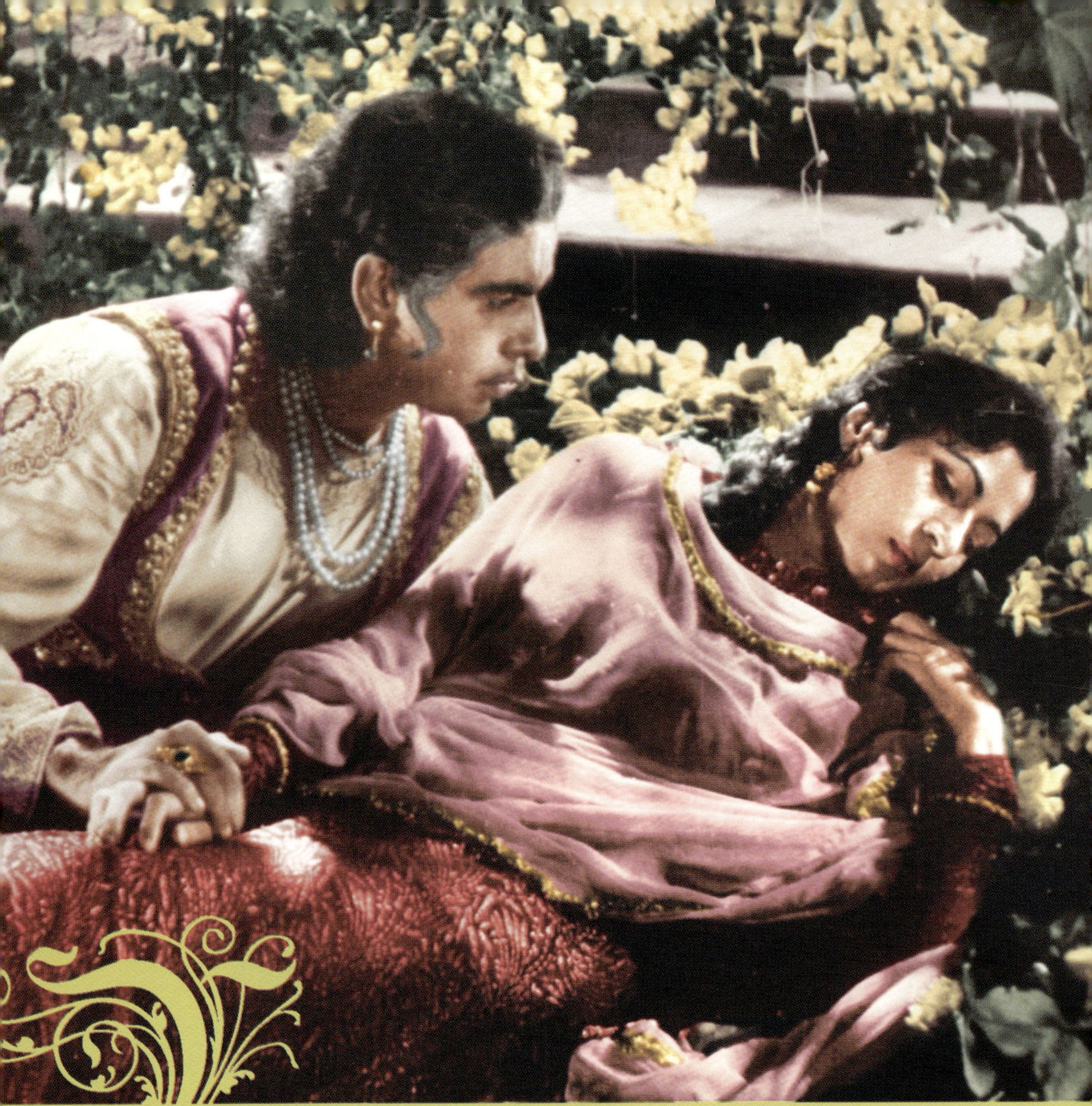

'Aql tamasha dekhti rahi aur ishq apni hud se guzar gaya'
(Love crossed all limits ...and wisdom kept wondering)
Dilip Kumar and Madhubala, the moments of submission and acquiescence.

Facing page:
above: *The pomp and power could not suppress the undying love.*
A tense Akbar (Prithviraj Kapoor) in his palace after declaring the death sentence upon his son
below: *Prithviraj Kapoor on the battlefield.*
The most spectacular war sequence, ever shot in historical films in India.

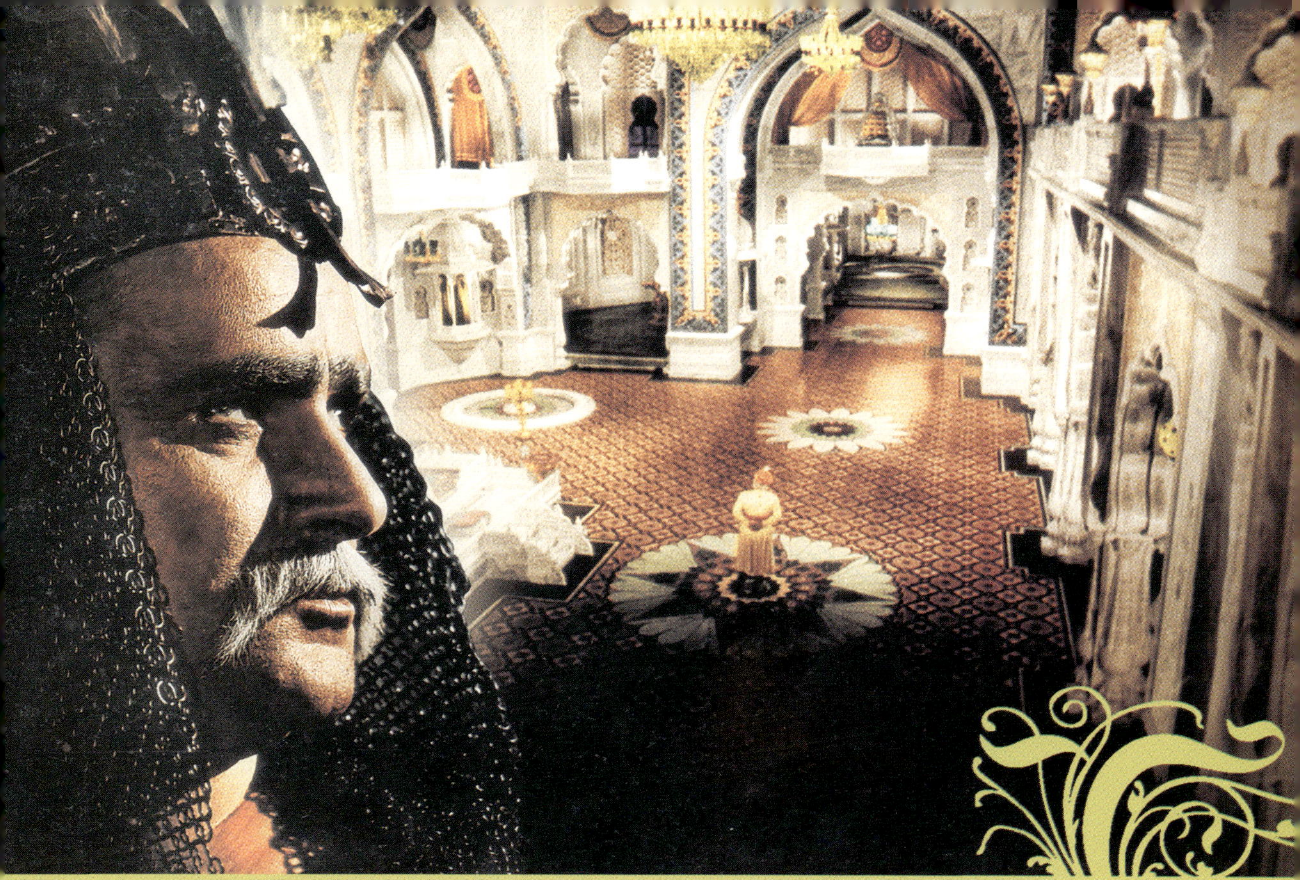

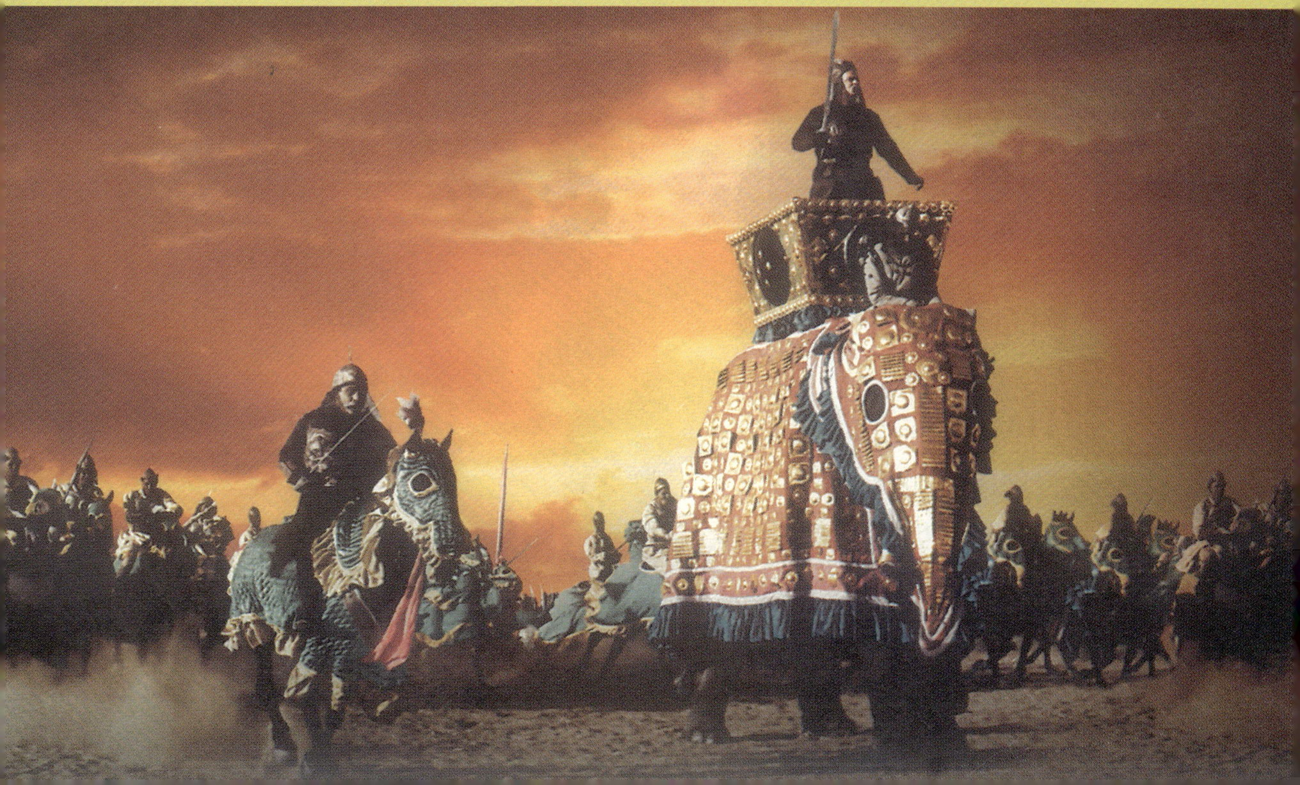

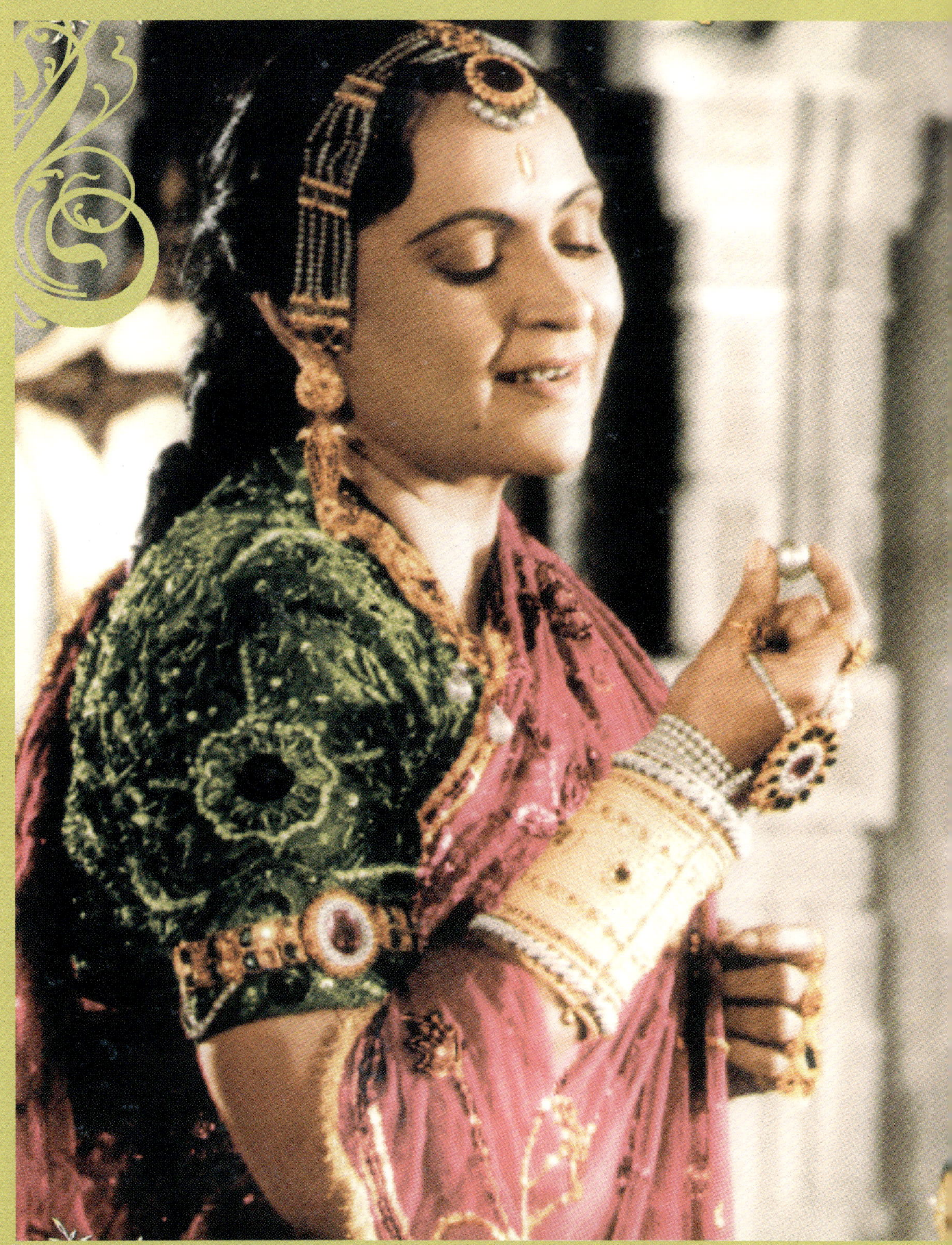

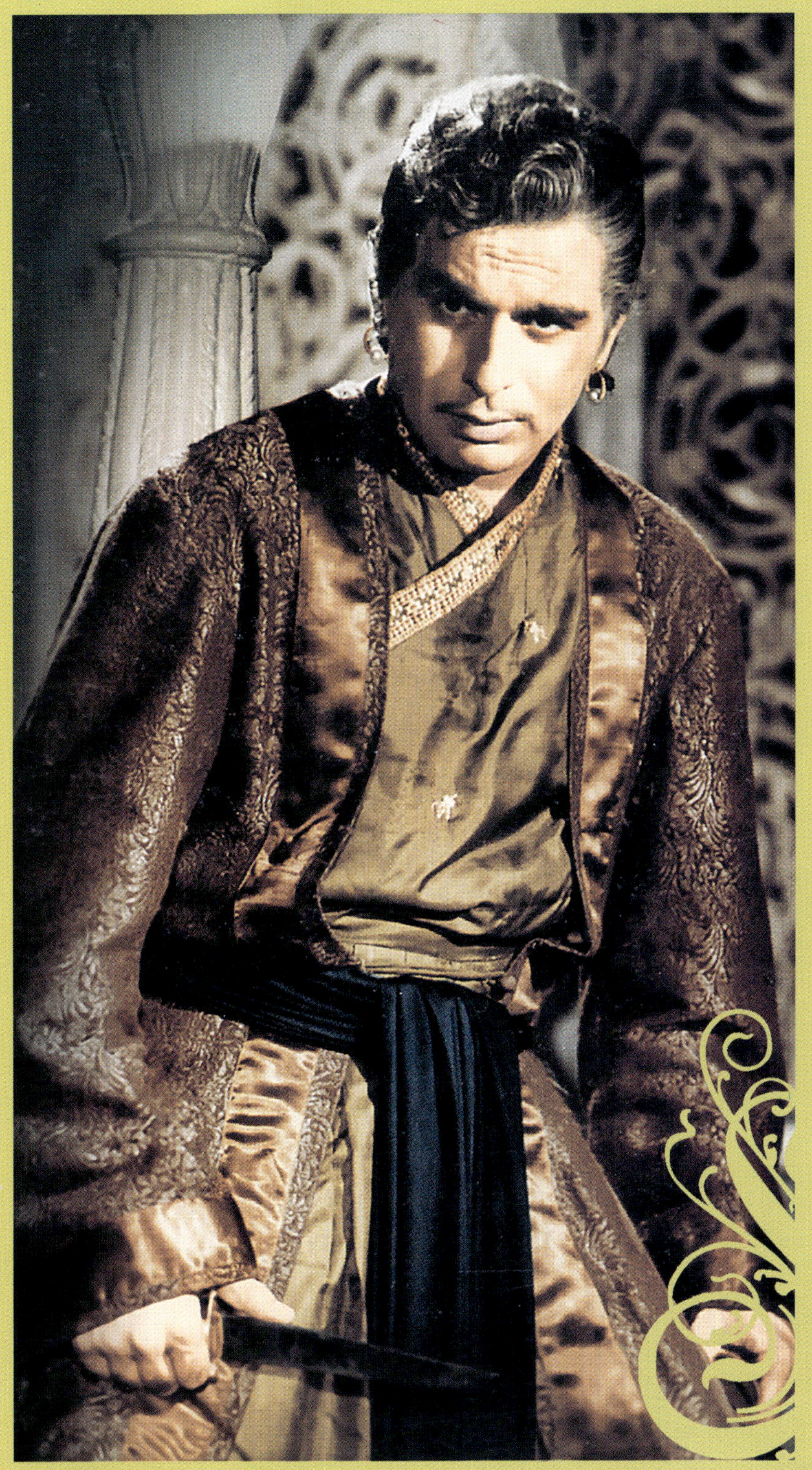

Dilip Kumar..... Prince Saleem with a dagger determined to honour his love.

Facing page: *Durga Khote as Maharani Jodha. 'Raat ghadi ka akhiri moti....' good news for the mother... her son is about to reach the palace after fourteen years of separation.*

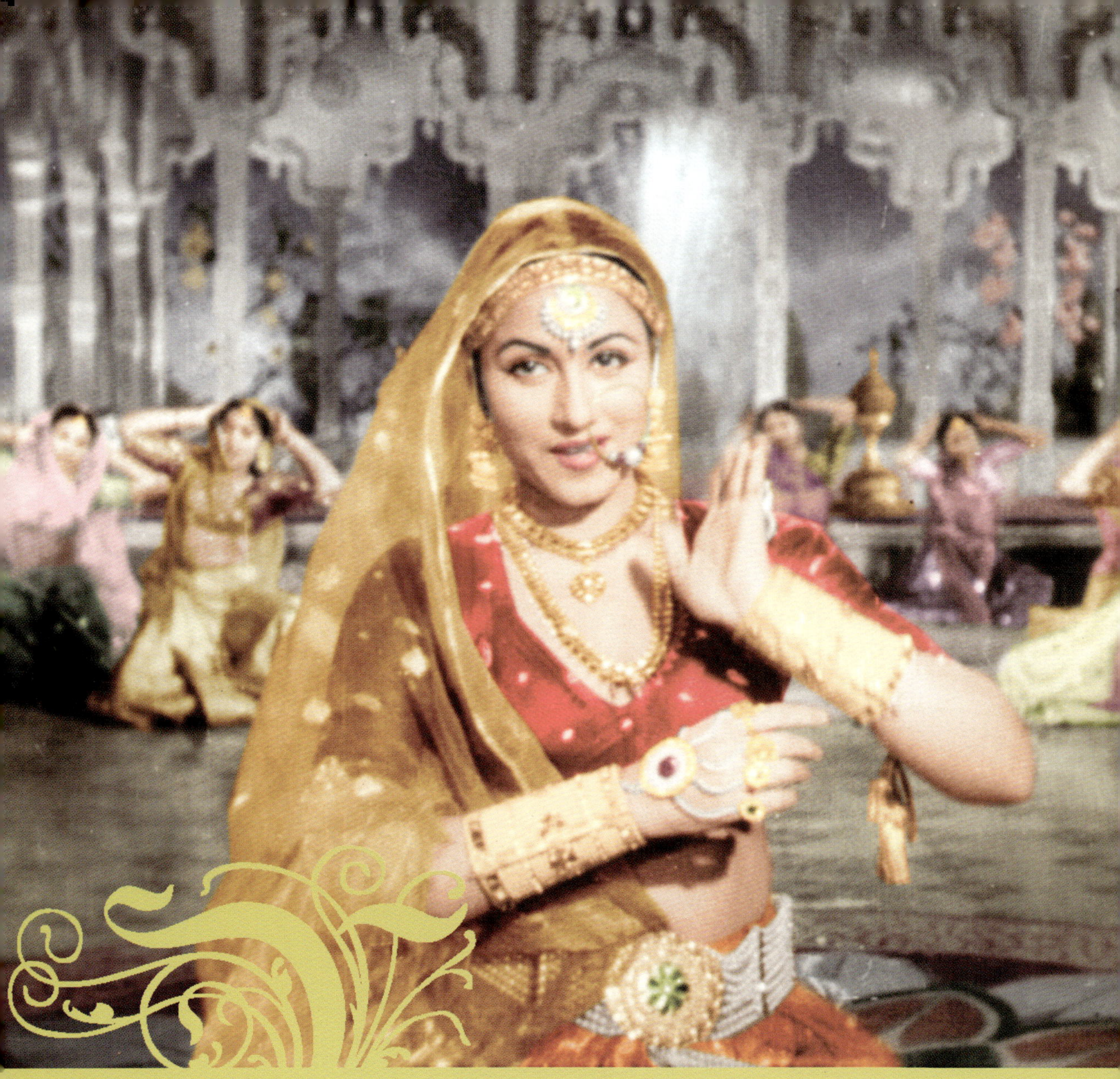

"Mohey panghat pey Nandlal ched gayo rey ..."
Madhubala (Anarkali), dancing on the occasion of Krishna Janm ashtami.
She looked gorgeous as she gazes at her 'Nandlal' Dilip Kumar

Facing page:
above: *Nigar Sultana, the imposing vamp ...*
A dream... a delusion to become the empress of Hindustan
below: *Dilip Kumar and Madhubala in one of the most romantic sequences of Indian cinema... when... silence spoke volumes of poetry*

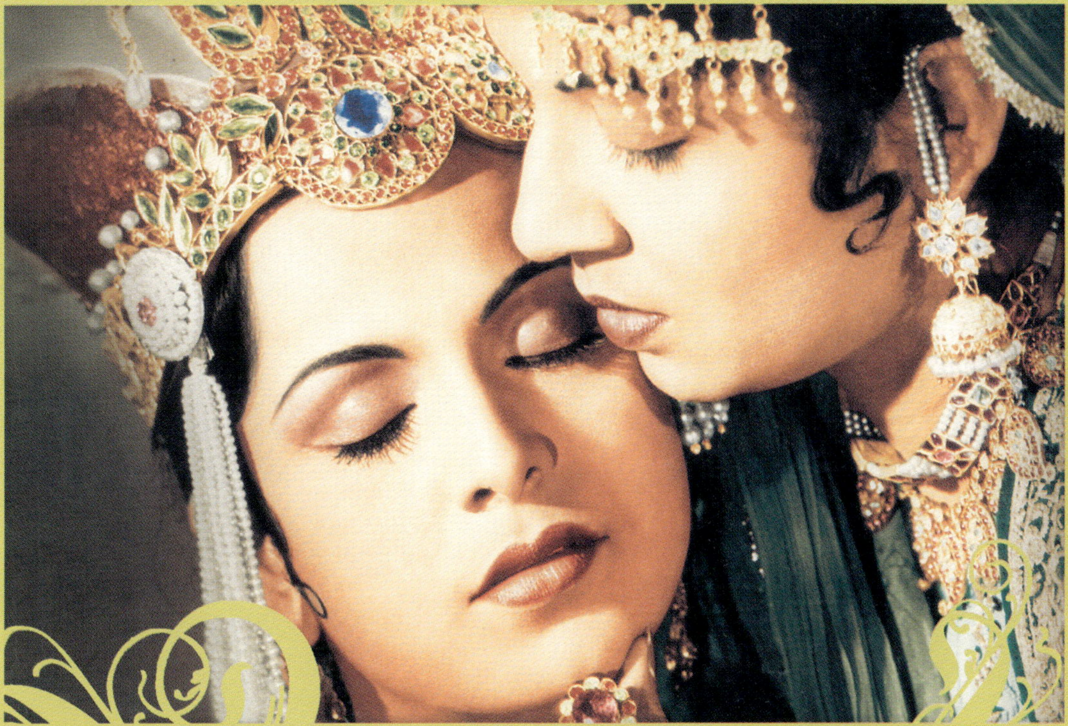

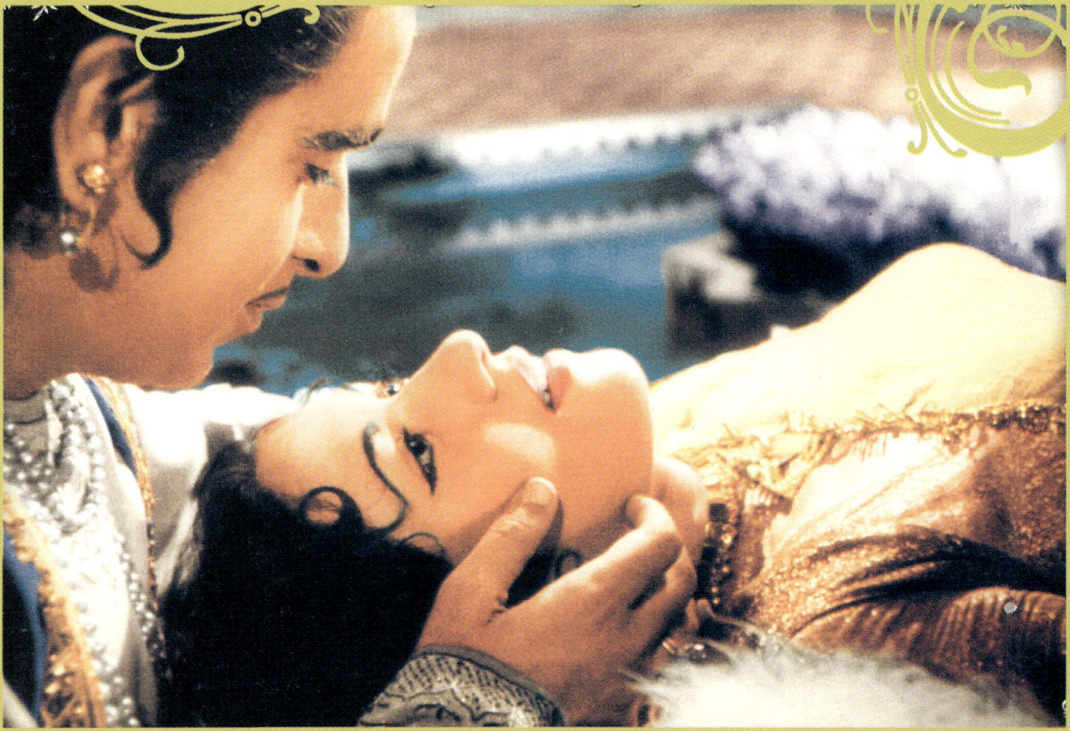

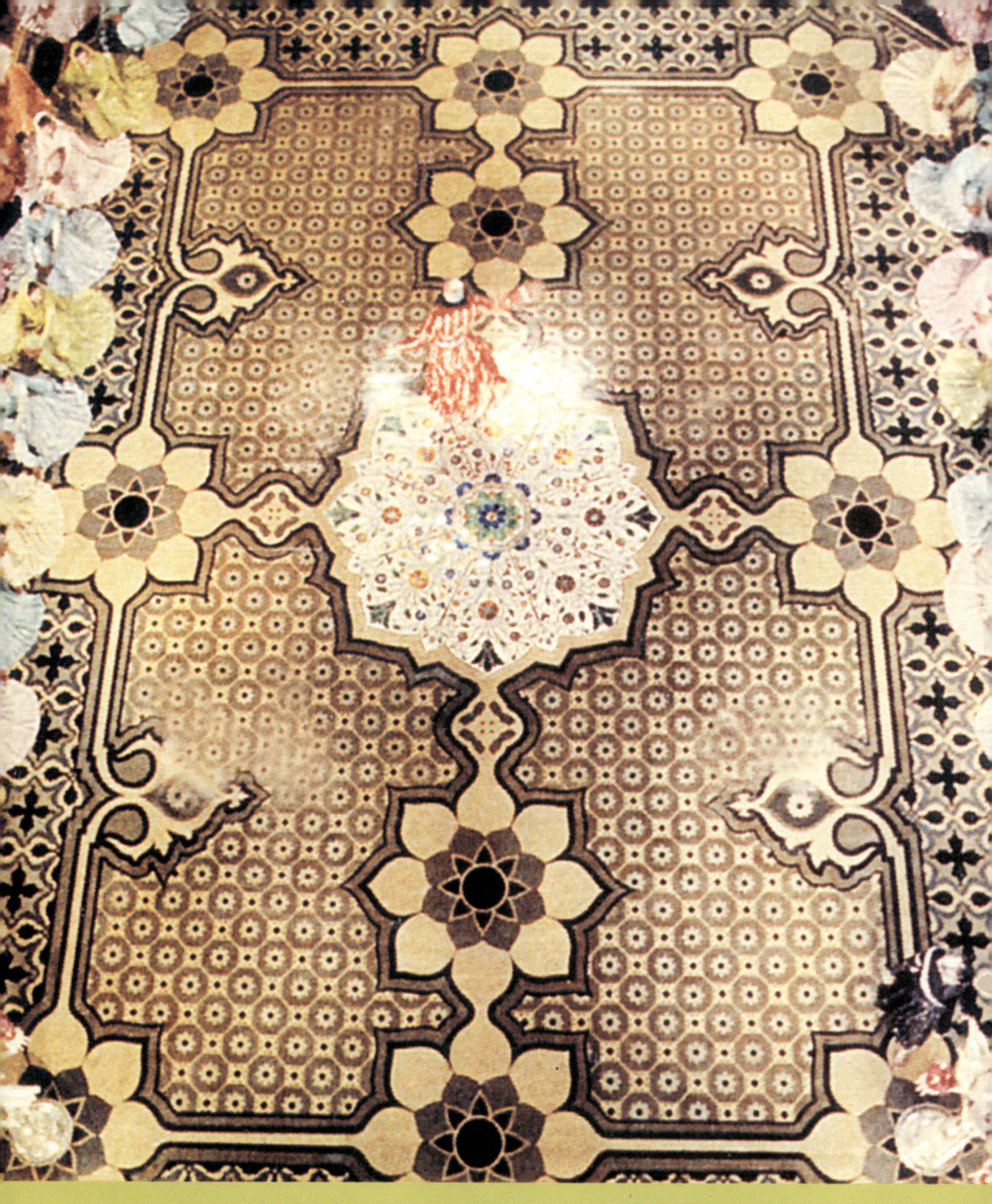

The beautifully designed dance floor.
The opulence of the Mughal era is apparent in every frame.

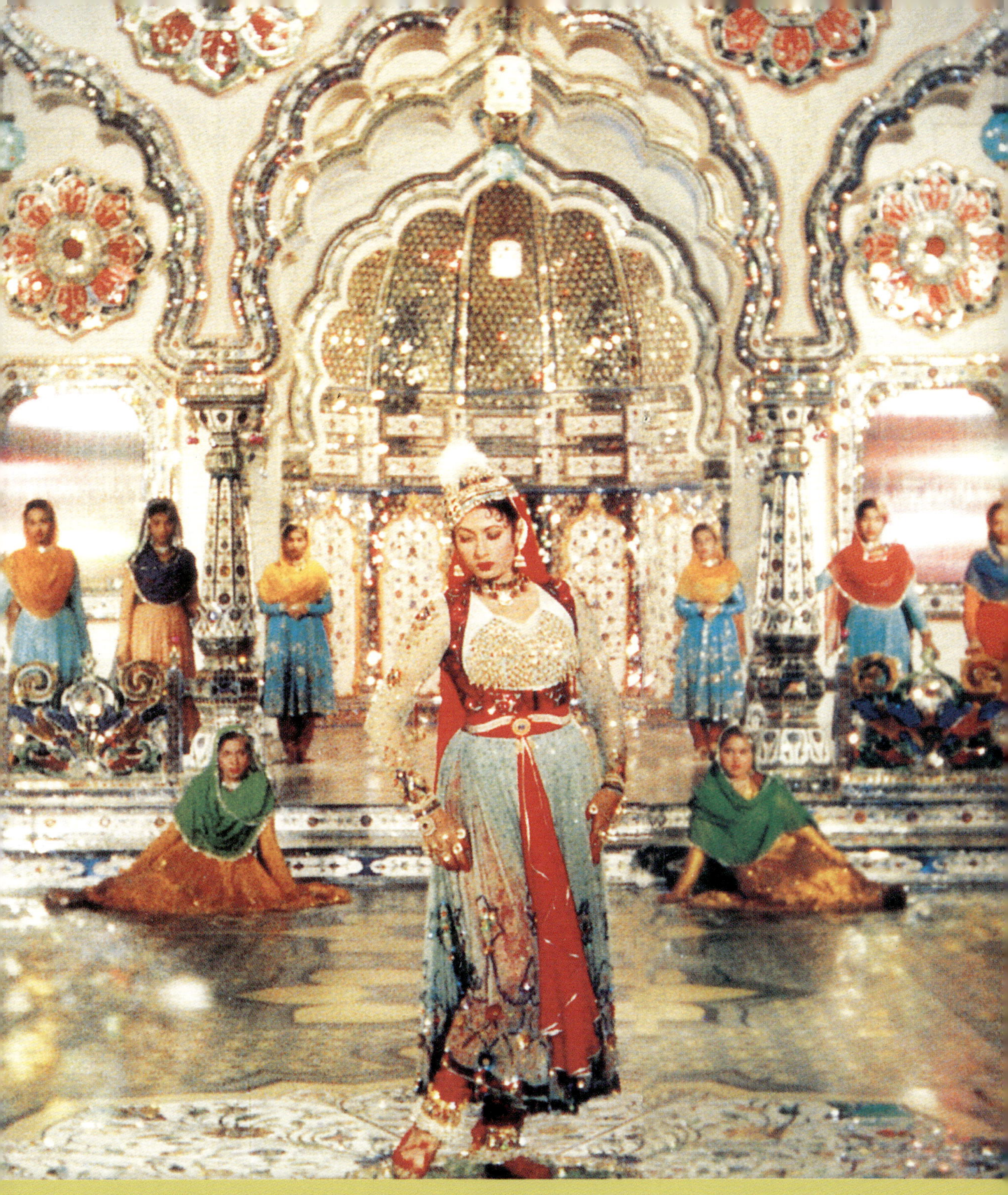

Madhubala, dancing in the fabulous Sheesh Mahal... 'Insaan kisi sey duniya mein ek baar mohabbat karta hai' 'Is dard ko lekar jeeta hai, is dard ko lekar marta hai...' (A person falls in love only once, ... and the agony lives on and endures till he is no more)

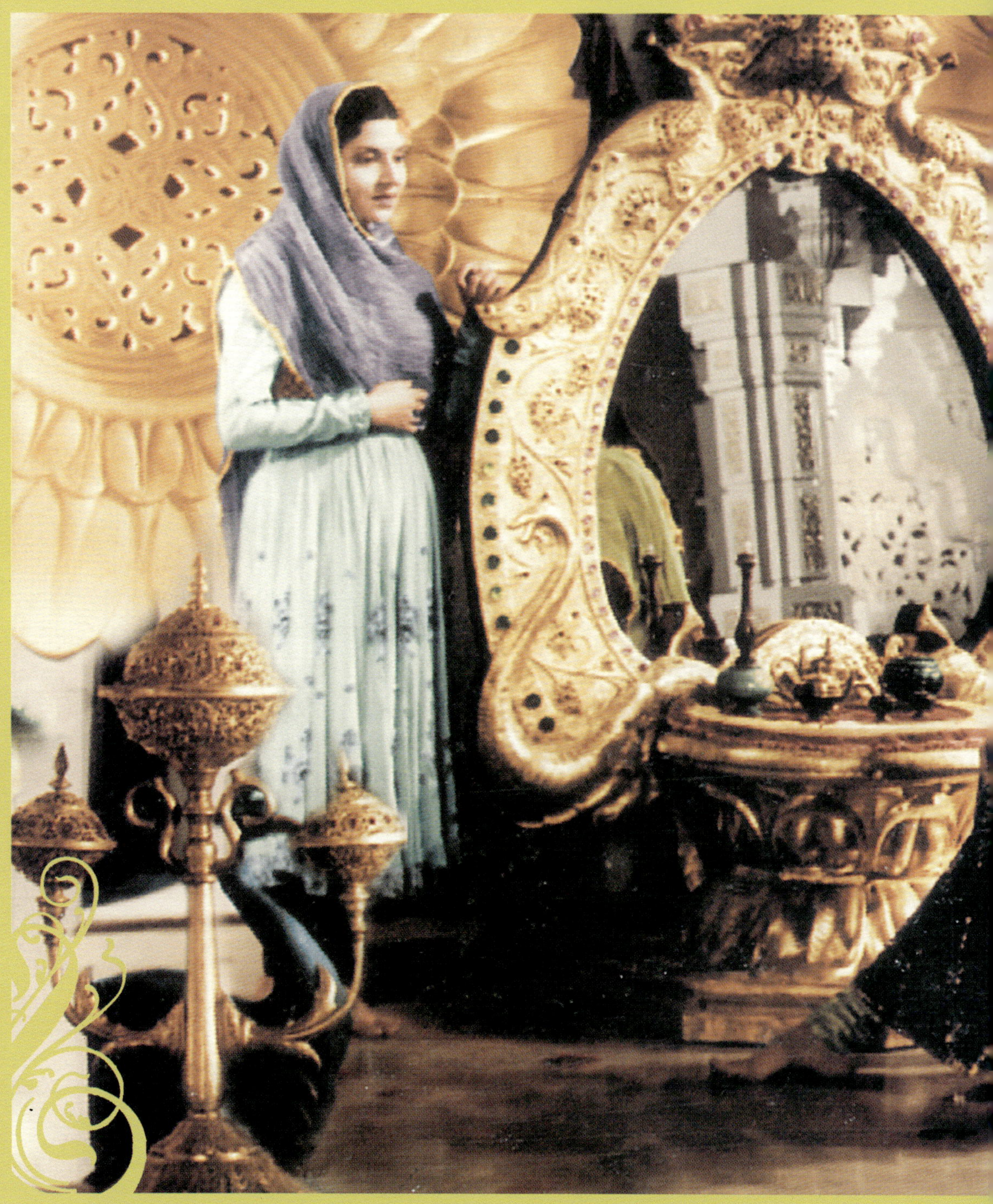

Nigar Sultana (wearing the crown), with her friend... the ruthless 'other girl'

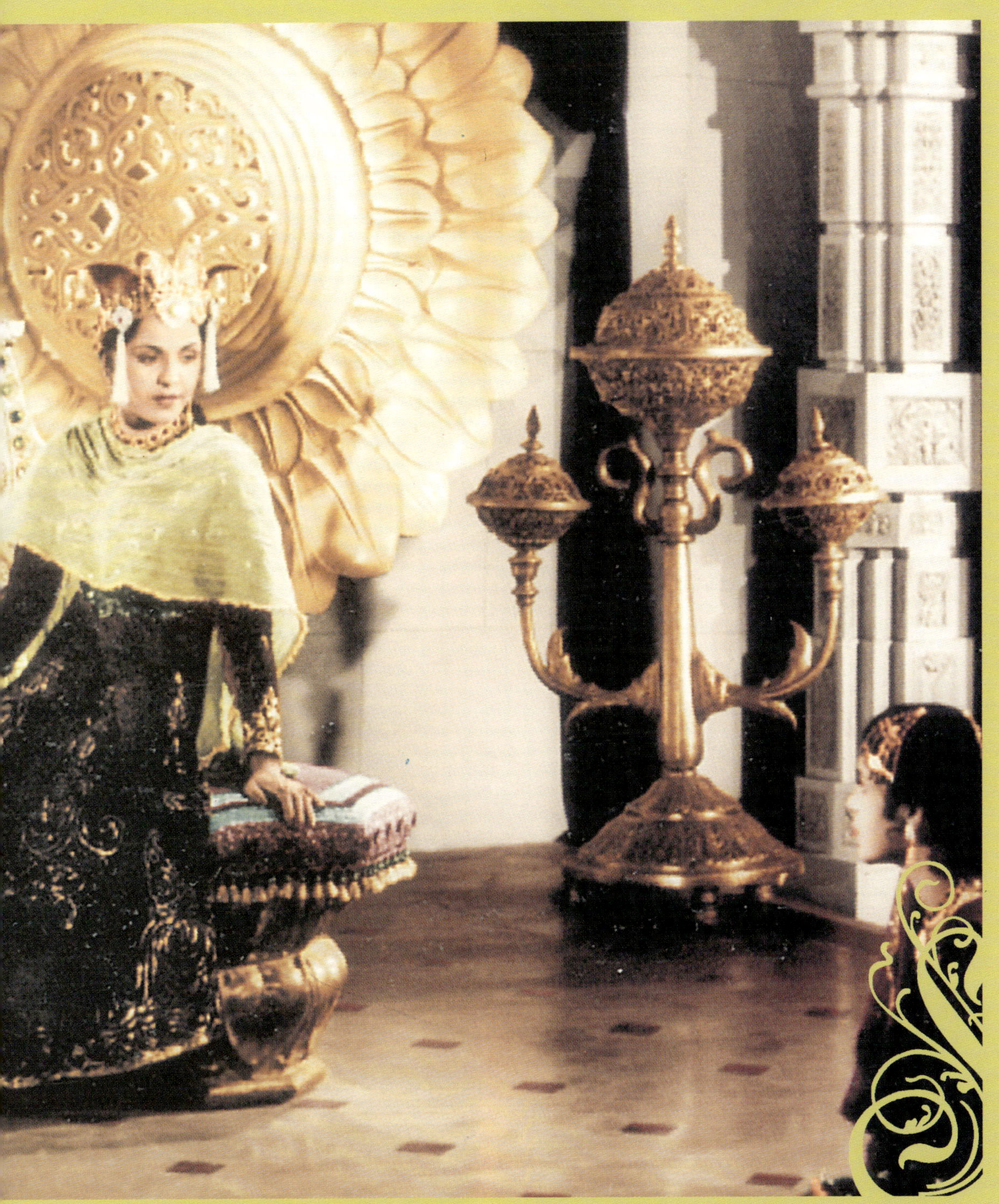

'Kya aasman se tare todne ka irada hai?'
'Kabhie kabhie tare khud toot kar zameen par gir atey hain.'
(Do you want to pluck stars from the sky?)
(Stars do fall on earth some times...)

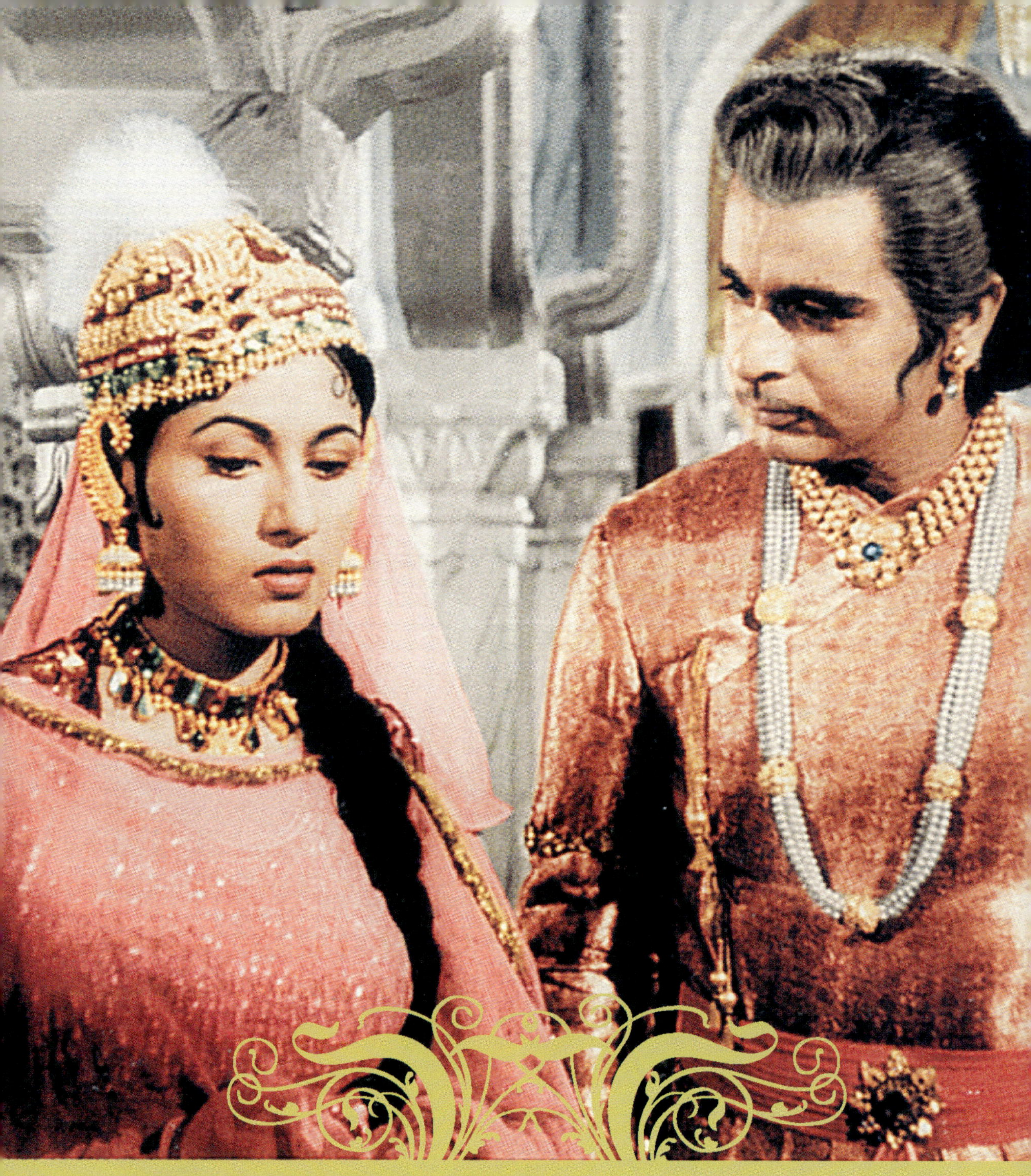

Dilip Kumar and Madhubala in a dramatic scene when, on the provocation of Bahar, he talks of her unfaithfulness. 'Akbar ki buzdil londi.. tu Saleem ki mehbooba nahin.. ek jhooti qasam thi jo mera iman badal gayee..' 'You are Akbar's coward slave girl! You aren't my sweet heart… It is a false oath that ruined my faith.'

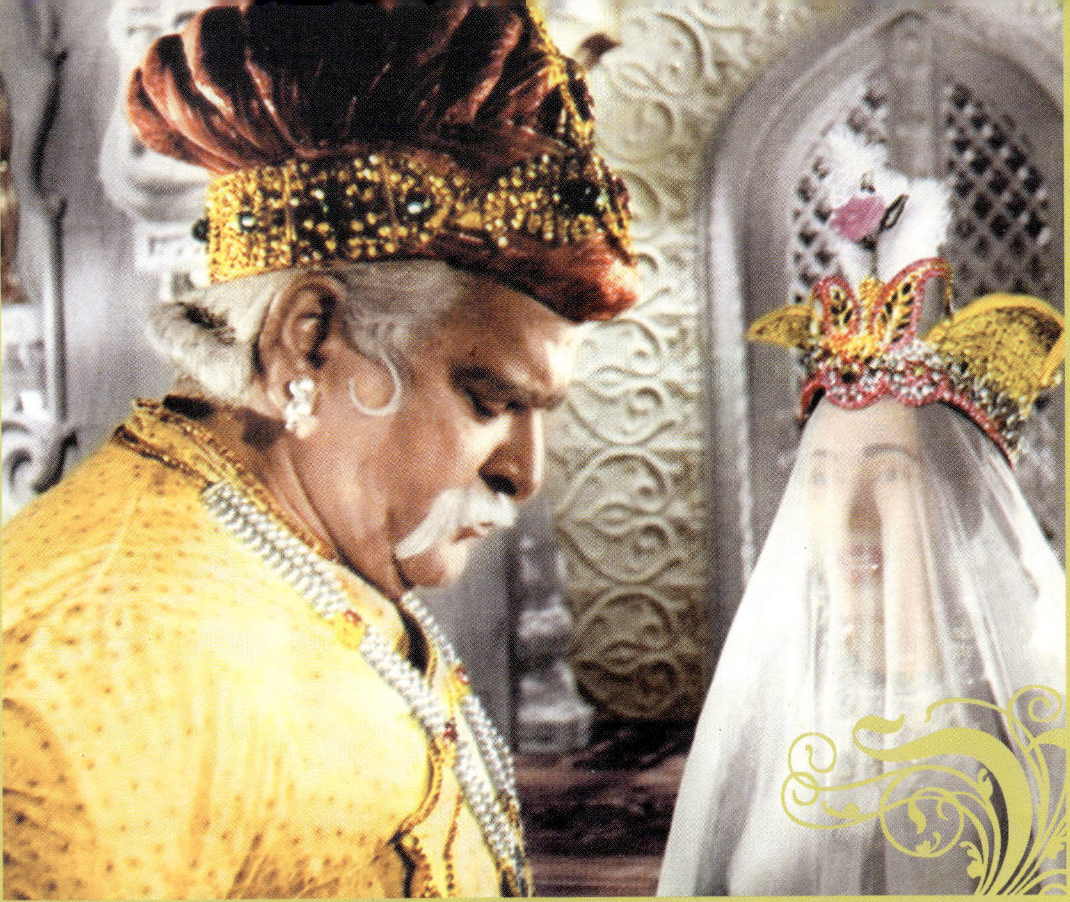

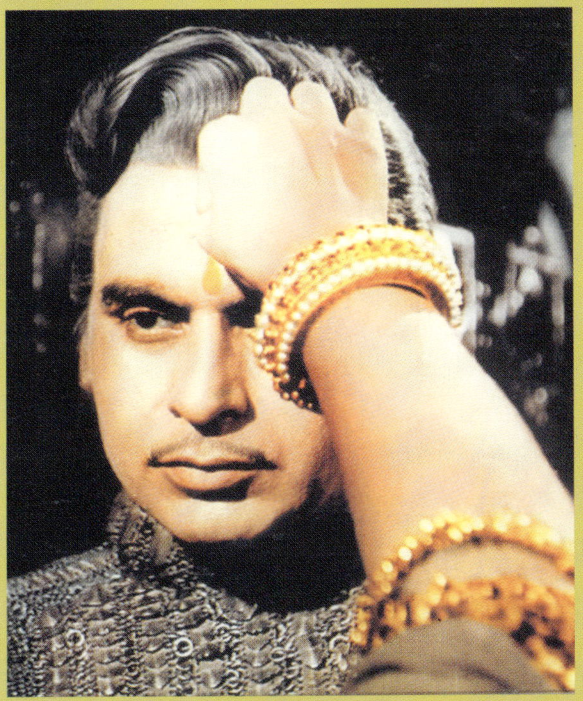

Above:
True love that is destined for devastation and inevitable death, yet it transcends life:
'...Yeh kaneez Jalal-uddin Mohammad Akbar ko apna khoon maaf karti hai!'
(...this courtesan forgives Jalal-uddin Mohammad Akbar for her murder)
Prithviraj Kapoor and Madhubala in a touching scene before she was made empress for one night as her last wish.

Left:
Maharani Jodha applies tilak on her son's forehead when he is about to get the death sentence.
She utters with pride:
'Rajput soormaon ka byah
Mout sey bhi hota hai...'
(Valiant Rajputs, married death as well)

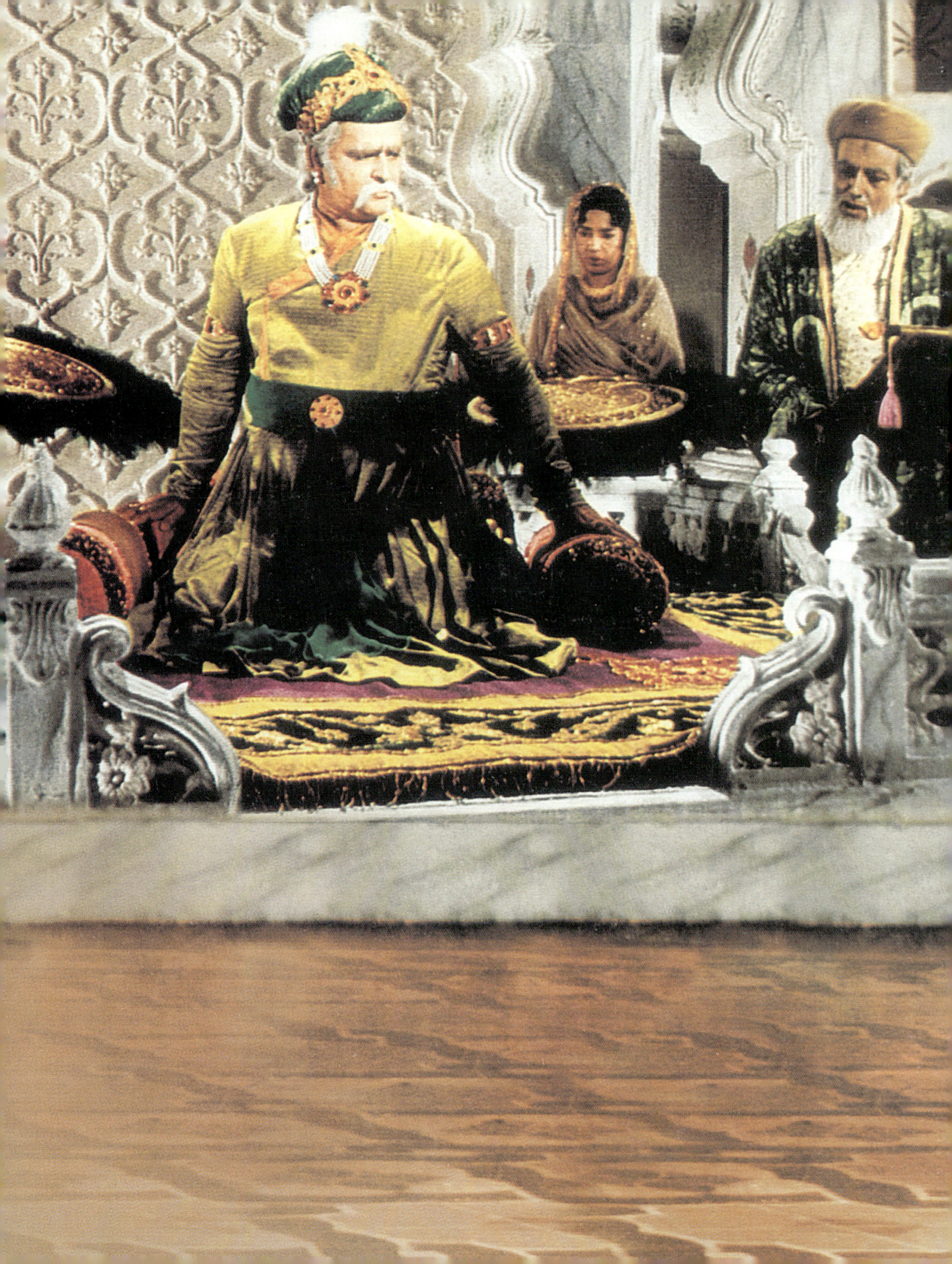

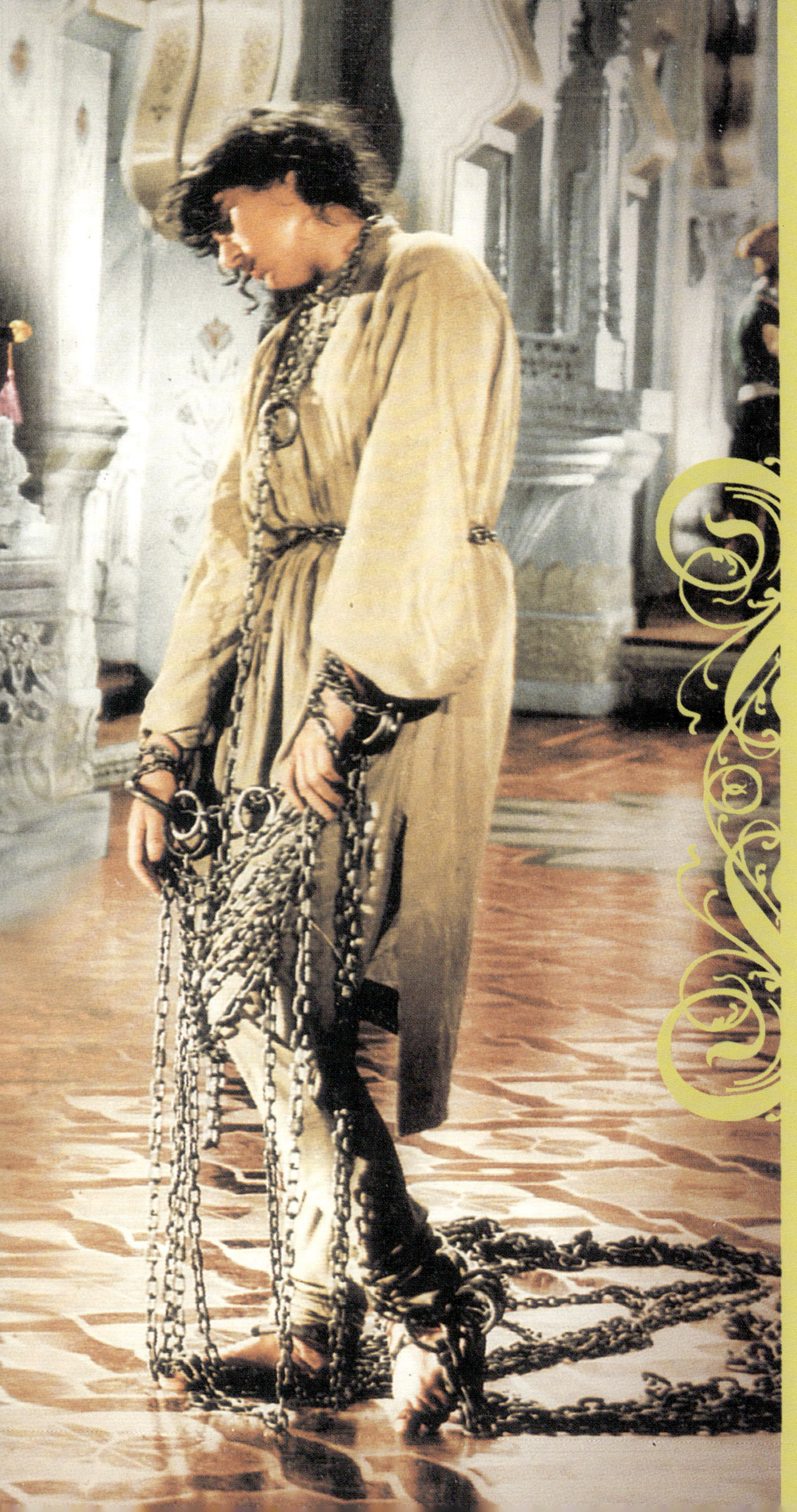

Prithviraj Kapoor as Akbar, enraged by his son's revolt, retorts: 'Yeh baghawat hamein manzoor hai... Man Singh! Muqabila hoga! Maa-Badolat,... Ba Nafas-e-Nafees jung mein shareek hongey' ('I accept this revolt... Man Singh! We'll meet the challenge... I, with all my soul and mind would be present in the battlefield.')

Madhubala, shackled by heavy iron chains. She had to pay a price for such dedication, as she spent many days in bed after each shoot schedule, nursing the abrasions caused by the chains.

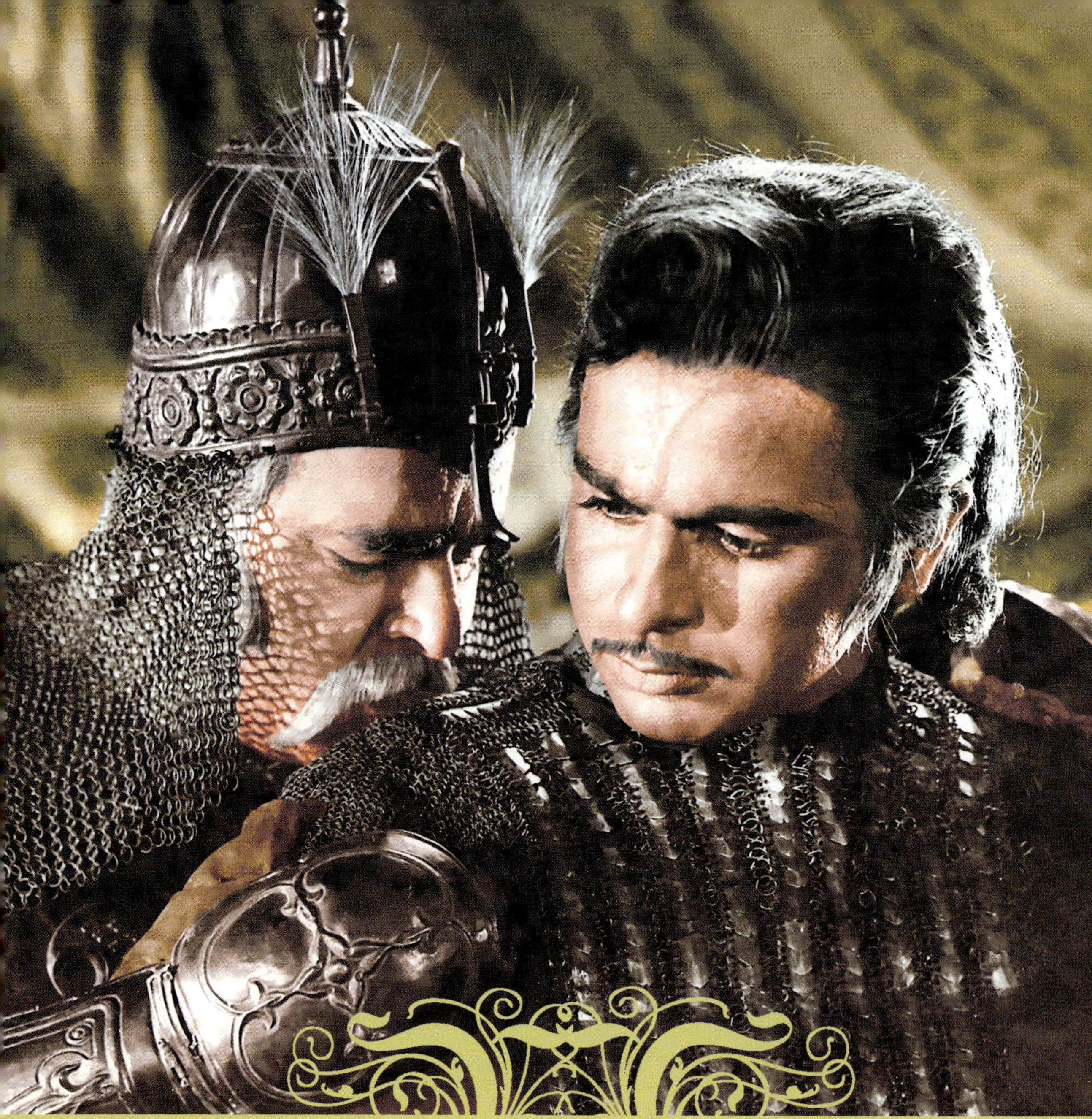

Akbar wants to give peace a chance, but in vain Saleem protests: 'Bete ki mohabbat barbad karkey muhabbat chahtey hain?' ('How can you expect love from your son after ruining his?') Prithviraj Kapoor and Dilip Kumar, wearing real zarra bakhtar (armour) weighing about eighty pounds. According to Dilip Kumar this was the first scene he shot for Mughal-e-Azam, a fine example of emotions blending with drama.

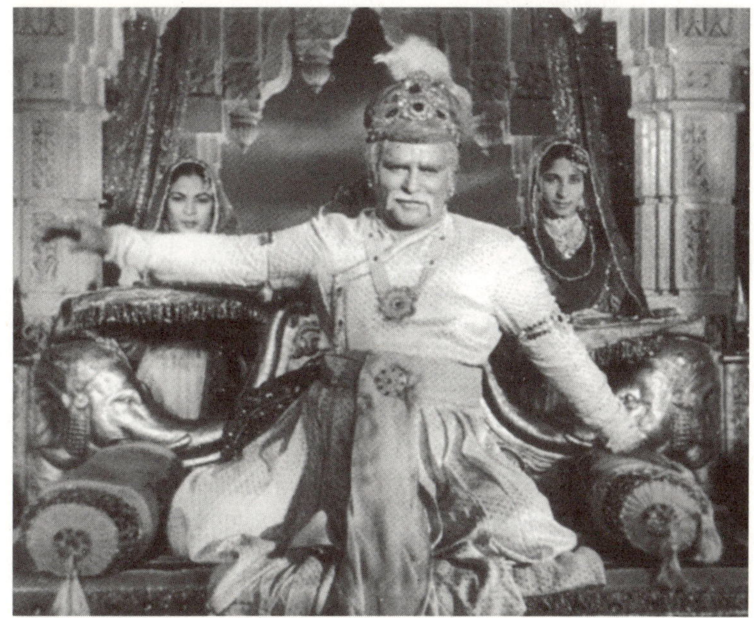

...the devastatingly handsome face remained untouched.

the devastatingly handsome face remained untouched. Kapoor worked hard to develop a particular manner of speech and gait for the role. His royal baritone and declamatory style made the emperor come alive. His portrayal was just what Asif needed to impress Shapoorji.

Prithviraj, who played the sitar, was a fellow of the Sangeet Natak Academy and a nominated member of the Rajya Sabha for eight years. He was honoured with Padma Bhushan in 1969. He won the Czechoslovakian National Acadamy of Arts and Music award for his outstanding performance in K.A. Abbas' *Aasmaan Mahal* in 1966. He also won the Dadasaheb Phalke award in 1972. This was the first time that this prestigious award was given posthumously, and it was received by his eldest son Raj Kapoor.

A deeply religious man, his day began with prayers and a reading of the *Bhagvad Gita*. He believed in and

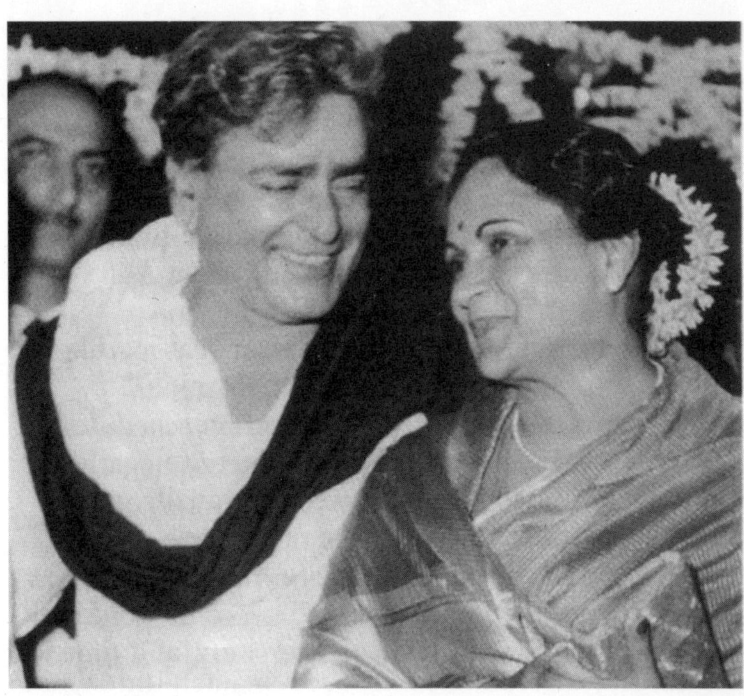

Prithviraj Kapoor and Durga Khote at the premiere (1960).

respected other religions, too. His home had the holy scriptures of all faiths, and he would often quote from them. He was not fond of ostentatious living, though he could have easily afforded it. Nothing made him happier than helping the needy. A chain smoker, Prithviraj Kapoor died of throat cancer on 29 May 1972.

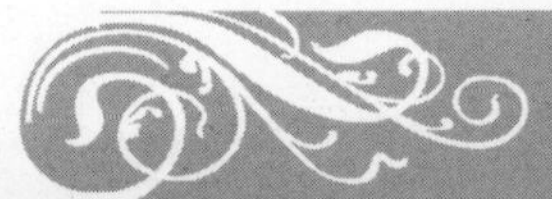

Dilip Kumar

Prince Salim

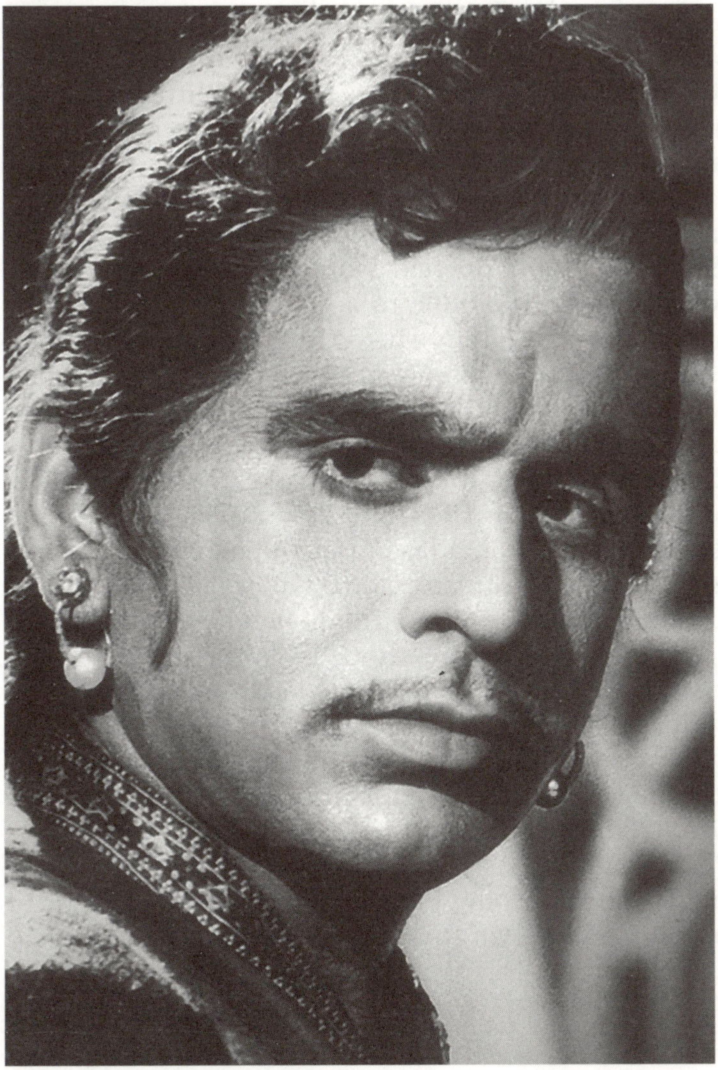

On the first day when Dilip Kumar stood in front of a mirror to be dressed up as Prince Salim, he suddenly complained of feeling uneasy and awkward...

Once Dilip Kumar had, apparently, dreamt of himself as a prince. He says, 'When I was a boy, I dreamt that there was a big pavilion lined up by the Romans and a huge carpet in the middle on which I was walking, flanked by guards in resplendent uniforms. I was wearing a flowing robe and everything glittered around me....And then at the end of the passage an old man garlanded me.'

The boy did not know that a dream merchant called K. Asif would fulfil his childhood fantasy on celluloid. This happened with Chandramohan's exit from *Mughal-e-Azam* due to a fatal heart attack, which made Asif replace him with Prithviraj Kapoor.

Naturally, all the scenes of Sapru and Chandramohan as Salim and Akbar had to be reshot. Asif then decided to replace Sapru too with a classier and more saleable actor, Dilip Kumar. In fact, Asif had earlier rejected him for the same role in 1945. But by now Dilip Kumar had become a huge star, a legend in Indian cinema. When Asif asked him to play Salim, Dilip Kumar, who had never acted in a costume drama before, hesitated.

Asif had earlier rejected him for the same role in 1945. But by now Dilip Kumar had become a huge star, a legend in Indian cinema.

He remained unsure, though. On the first day when he stood in front of the mirror to be dressed up as prince Salim, he suddenly complained of feeling uneasy and awkward in the heavy costume of the prince. Asif reassured him, 'If the real Prince Salim could put up with it, surely so can you.'

After a while Asif realised the problem — it was the wig! It was not doing justice either to Dilip Kumar or to Prince Salim. Asif took a quick decision and whisked

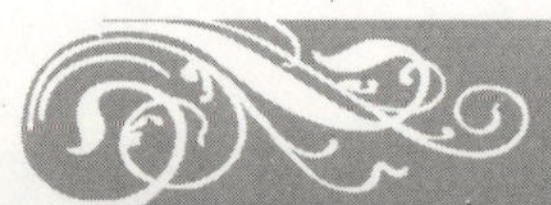

Dilip Kumar off to London. It took six months of patient trials before the perfect wig was ready. Wearing it and watching himself in the mirror, the actor was finally convinced that he was indeed Prince Salim of *Mughal-e-Azam*.

Dilip Kumar was born as Yusuf Khan on 11 December 1922 in a middle-class Pathan family of Peshawar. His father Gulam Sarwar Khan had a large joint family comprising Yusuf's grandparents and thirteen brothers and sisters: seven sisters and six brothers. 'My arrival was accepted in a normal manner, without excitement, firstly because it was a chilly morning, and secondly because I was the third son in the family,' says Dilip Kumar.

(l to r): Murad, Prithviraj Kapoor, Dilip Kumar and Nigar Sultana.

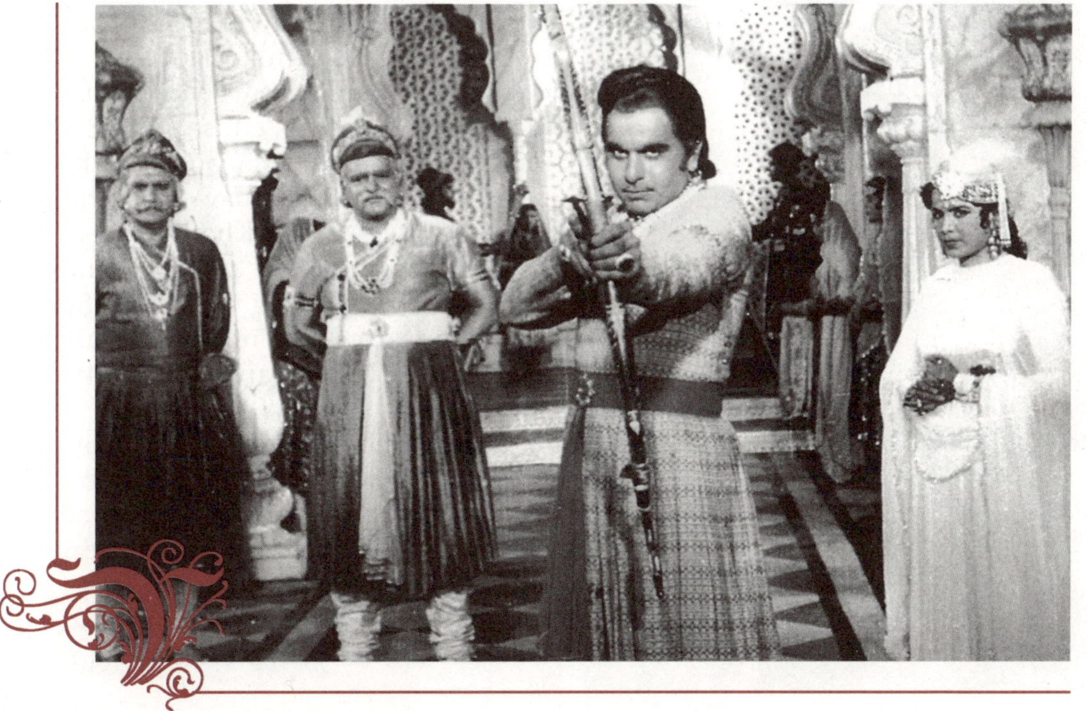

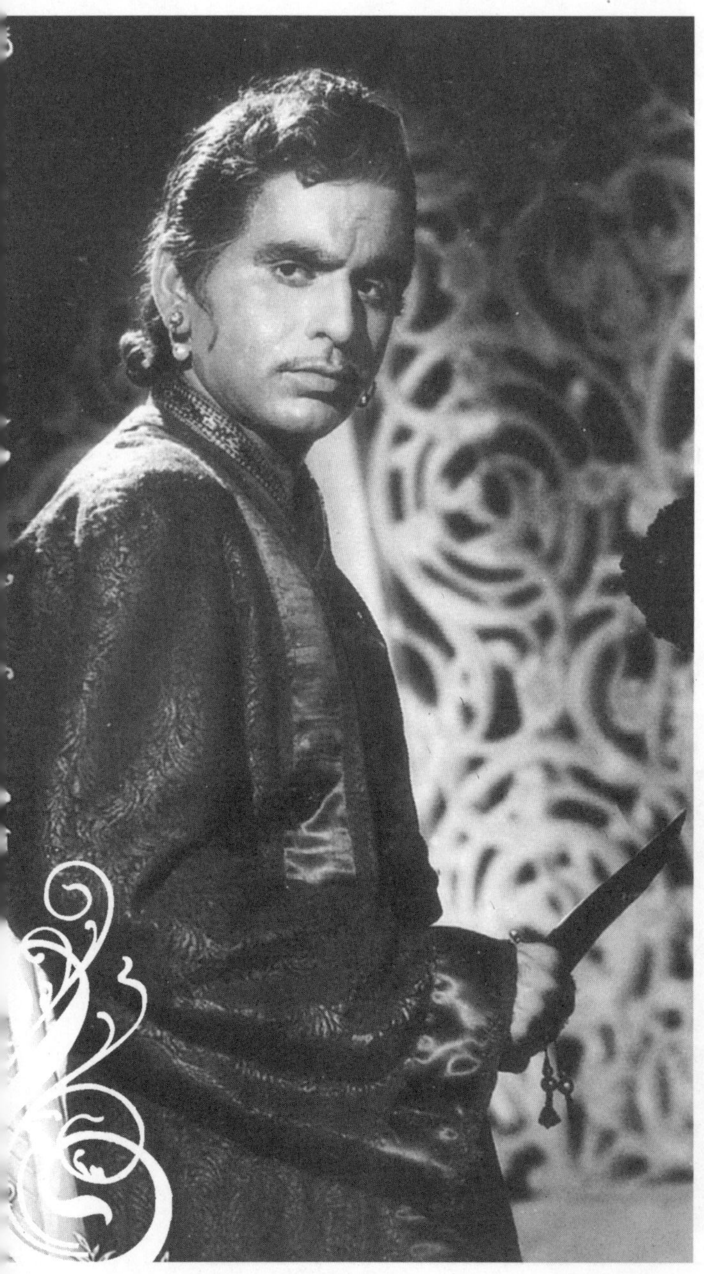

The family was very traditional. They were devout Muslims with cultural values that had no place for fanaticism. Lala Basheshirnath, father of Prithviraj Kapoor, was a close friend of Gulam Sarwar Khan. This laid the foundations of strong bonds of friendship between the Khans and the Kapoors, which continued over the ages.

Gulam Sarwar Khan was a fruit merchant and had extensive business associations in central and southern parts of India. He also had a wholesale establishment at Crawford Market, Bombay. The family business was sufficient to fend for the large family and provide a comfortable and decent living. Little Yusuf got his early education at a local school in Peshawar, but soon the family shifted to Bombay due to his elder brother Ayyub Khan's illness. Ayyub once fell off a horse, and doctors advised a long treatment. So Gulam Sarwar Khan rented a house at Nagdevi Street and his family settled in Bombay.

However, Bombay's humid climate had an adverse effect on Ayyub's recovery and the family soon migrated to Deolali, a cantonment town near Nashik which was much cooler. Yusuf was admitted to a local school at Deolali and stayed there for eight years with his family. Following the start of the Second World War in 1939, Sarwar Khan's bungalow at Deolali was requisitioned, and the family had to move back to Bombay. Yusuf was admitted to the Anjuman-e-Islam School near V.T. (now C.S.T. station) in Bombay. After matriculation, he joined Wilson College and took up science as his main subject. During the entire period at school and college, Yusuf had no taste for movies. He was an average student more interested in sports than studies. The shy and absentminded boy was often teased in class for invariably forgetting his cap or notebook. His professors would find him dribbling the football in the classroom and ask him to leave in order to do justice to the ball on the field. His only ambition then was to become a Test cricketer and score a century one day. But destiny had something else in store.

Dilip's only ambition then was to become a Test cricketer and score a century one day. But destiny had something else in store.

During his student life itself, his family's fortunes dipped and Yusuf's father asked him to lend a hand with the business. Yusuf dropped out of college in his junior B.Sc. and began looking for work in areas other than his family trade. He got an offer to join an army canteen at Poona (now Pune). The job was of an assistant canteen manager for a salary of Rs 35 per month. After sometime, to augment his income, he put up a small fruit counter at the canteen's swimming pool and started selling them to soldiers who came for recreation. His income increased, but the canteen closed down due to the government's field ration scheme. Yusuf returned to Bombay with a respectable bank balance.

He joined his father's business reluctantly because he wanted to do something more exciting. His father started sending him out of Bombay to finalise deals. It was during one such visit to Nainital that he met Devika Rani, the famous actress-producer and owner of Bombay Talkies.

Facing Page:
Sahibe-e-Aalam determined to honour his love.

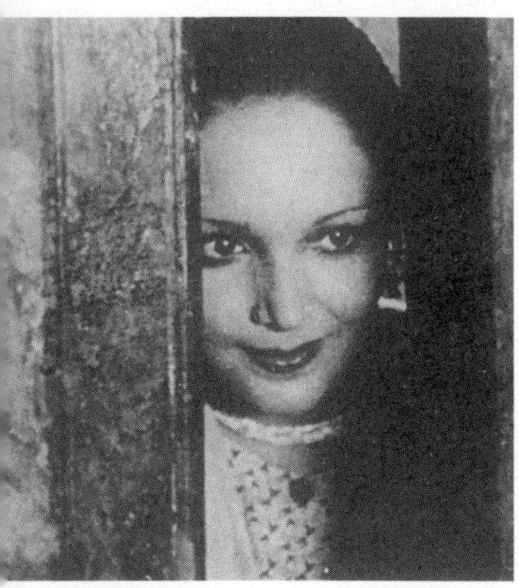

Devika Rani in Achhut Kanya.

Ashok Kumar was, at that point, on the verge of leaving Bombay Talkies to join his brother-in-law S. Mukherji (grandfather of Kajol and Rani Mukherjee) in Filmistan. Devika Rani was on the lookout for a suitable actor. Yusuf's Pathan looks and soft-spoken manner impressed the lady. She asked him to meet her in Bombay. After a formal interview with the lady at Bombay Talkies, Yusuf got his first break in *Jwar Bhata* in 1944. Devika Rani considered 'Yusuf' an unsuitable screen name and hence asked him to choose one of the three names — Dilip Kumar, Vasudev and Jahangir. Yusuf blurted out 'Dilip Kumar', and thus a shy, introvert Yusuf became Dilip Kumar, the superstar of Indian cinema.

A Bengali director Amiya Chakravarty directed his first film *Jwar Bhatta*. Mridula, a newcomer like Dilip, was its heroine. Agha and Shammi played the other lead. The film flopped miserably. The actor's second film *Pratima,* directed by Jai Raj, also sank without a trace. Dilip Kumar's acting abilities were by now being questioned.

The then leading film magazine *Film India* published some unkind reviews and Dilip Kumar was naturally concerned. Devika Rani had, by 1945, already left Bombay Talkies and settled in Bangalore with her husband. After Devika Rani, Hiten Choudhary, the chief production controller, became the virtual boss of the company.

He was a well-wisher of Dilip Kumar and cast him in a new film, *Milan,* based on Rabindranath Tagore's story *Nouka Dubi* (the shipwreck). Dilip Kumar had Meera Mishra and Ranjana as his heroines, and the eminent director Nitin Bose of New Theatres, Calcutta, was called to helm the film. Though *Milan* was not a hit, it proved to be a milestone in Dilip Kumar's career.

Nitin Bose groomed him as an actor and taught him the rudiments of the art of gestures and expressions, which Dilip maintained throughout his film career.

Critics considered *Milan* a film of high standards and artistic values, but it had a mediocre box office run. However, the film announced that its actor Dilip Kumar was here to stay.

After *Milan*, another producer, Shaukat Husain Rizvi, cast Dilip Kumar in *Jugnu* in 1946. He played a young college student against Shaukat's wife Noorjahan in the female lead. *Jugnu* was significant for Dilip Kumar in many ways; he was cast against a big star like Noorjahan for the first time. Noorjahan was a renowned singer and actress of her time, and *Jugnu* was her last film in India, after which she migrated to Pakistan.

"Kanton ko murjhane ka Khouf nahin hota"
Dilip Kumar and Madhubala, after Qawwali Competetion 'Teri Mehfil mein'.

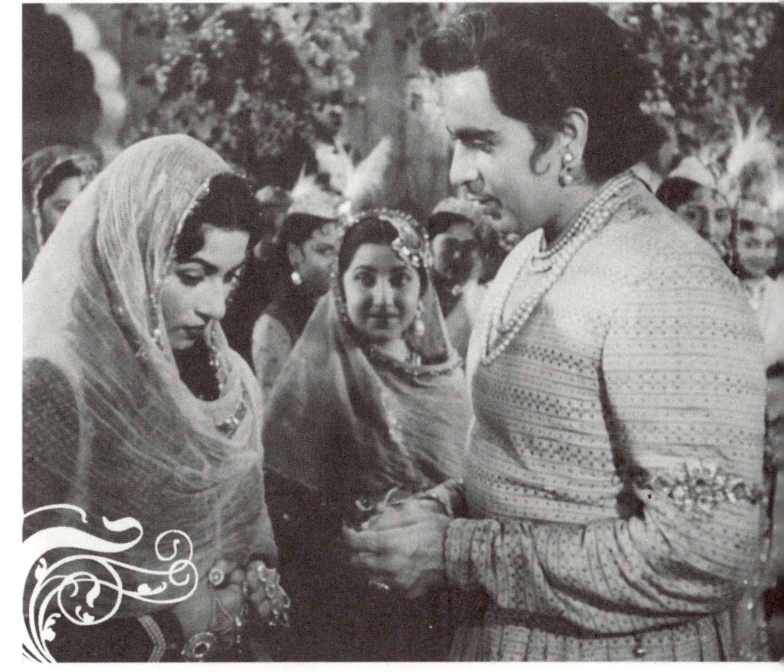

Soulful and melodious music composed by Phiroz Nizami was another highlight of the movie. *'Hamein to sham-e gam me katni hai zindagi apni'*, sung by Noorjahan and *'Yahan badla wafa ka'*, a duet by Noorjahan and Mohammad Rafi, were huge hits.

Jugnu was an important chapter in his career, but Dilip Kumar still longed for a box office smash hit. That was not far ahead. In 1948, music composer Naushad Ali recommended his name to Wadia Movietone for *Mela* opposite Nargis. *Mela* — a simple love story, which suggested that life may be short but love lives long — had some unforgettable numbers. Naushad's music and Shakeel Badayuni's lyrics created a major sensation. *'Ye zindagi ke mele'* by Rafi and *'Dharti ko akash pukare'* by Mukesh and Shamshad Begum became all-time hits. The film proved to be a milestone. It was a roaring commercial success. The nation went crazy for Dilip Kumar. Along with his looks and the innocence on his face, his soft voice, his natural body language — everything was novel and different from the theatrical stiffness of his predecessors. Out of *Mela* thus emerged a phenomenal new screen image.

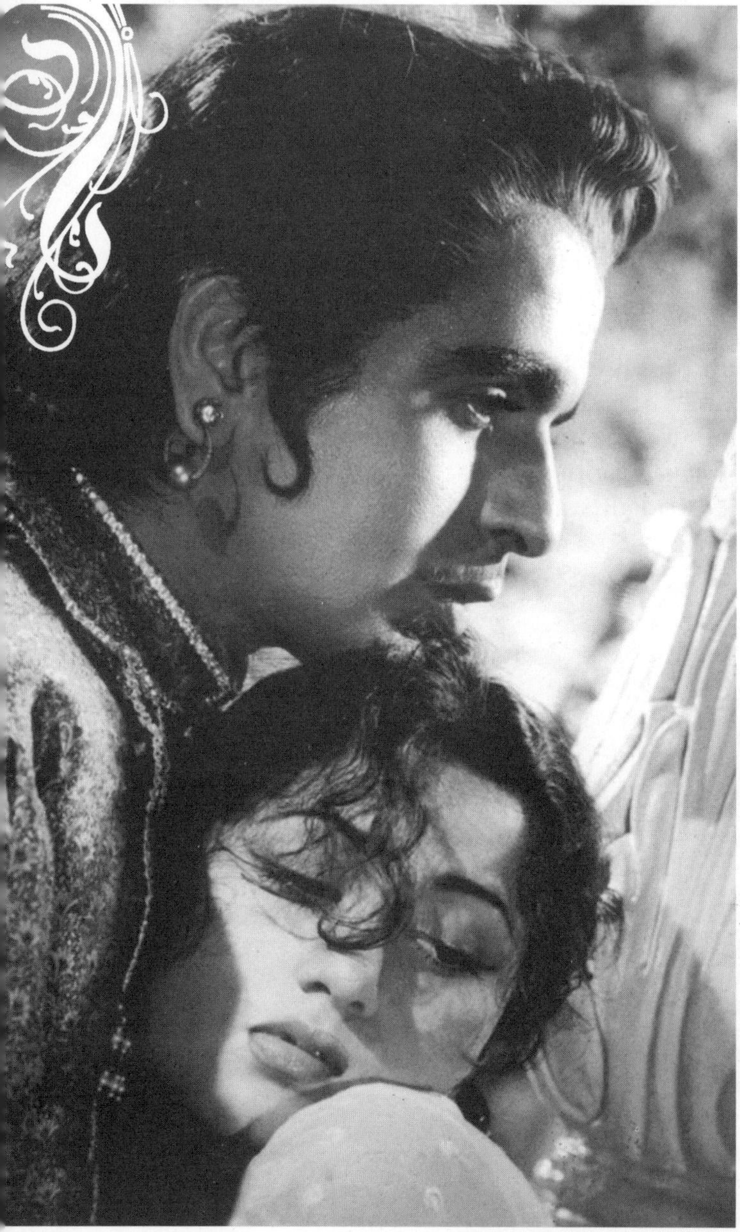

Dilip Kumar, then twenty-five, became a phenomenon — a star was born and a legend began taking shape. After *Mela* there was no looking back. Each successive film served as a histrionic milestone for Indian cinema. *Shaheed, Nadia Ke Paar, Jogan, Hulchul, Sangdil, Andaz, Deedaar, Dagh* and, above all, *Devdas* were all romantic tragedies. Dilip Kumar epitomised a hero who embraced rejection and separation from his love, and this earned him the epithet of 'Tragedy King'. The actor

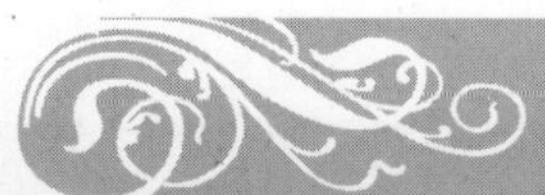

mastered the art of playing the jilted lover on screen; no artiste had as intensely involved the audience in his portrayal of a grief-stricken lover as he did. It was an image that matched director Asif's vision of Prince Salim.

While *Mughal-e-Azam* was on the floors, Dilip Kumar was also acting in *Ganga Jamuna* and *Devdas.* The country bumpkin 'Ganga' of *Ganga Jamuna* and the suffering 'Deva' of Devdas were poles apart from the amorous prince of *Mughal-e-Azam.* Dilip Kumar handled all three roles with ease. '...there was a distance of fifty feet between the sets of *Devdas* and *Mughal-e-Azam*. I switched over from one role to the other . . . I am a difficult man and I take off rather slowly, but once I do, I don't have any difficulty...' (*Filmfare*, 1-15 December 1982) Though Prithviraj Kapoor, with his royal bearing and an author-backed role in *Mughal-e-Azam*, dominated the movie, Dilip Kumar, as a rebellious lover who stakes a kingdom for a courtesan, held his ground. His role as 'Sahib-e-Alam' was truly convincing. His studiedly cinematic language of deliberated gestures, tantalising pauses, his command over his words, his grammar of silence and his body language, everything was simply perfect to portray prince Salim.

Dilip Kumar was nominated to the Rajya Sabha in 1993. Besides numerous *Filmfare* awards for the best actor, he received many BFJA awards, a Lifetime Achievement award, Screen Videocon award, IFFD Samsung award for outstanding achievement in Indian cinema, N.T. Rama Rao award for sterling contribution to Indian Cinema, Ramnath Goenka award for social welfare, Nishan-e-Imtiyaz from the Pakistan government and the Padam Bhushan and prestigious Dadasaheb Phalke award from the Government of India.

Dilip's role as 'Sahib-e-Alam' was truly convincing. His tantalising pauses, his command over his words, his grammar of silence and his body language, everything was simply perfect to portray Prince Salim.

Facing Page:
The ethereal beauty and the insular prince...
The total consumation of love...

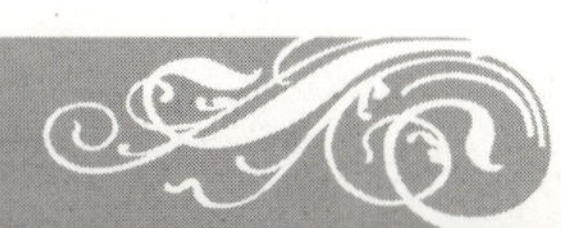

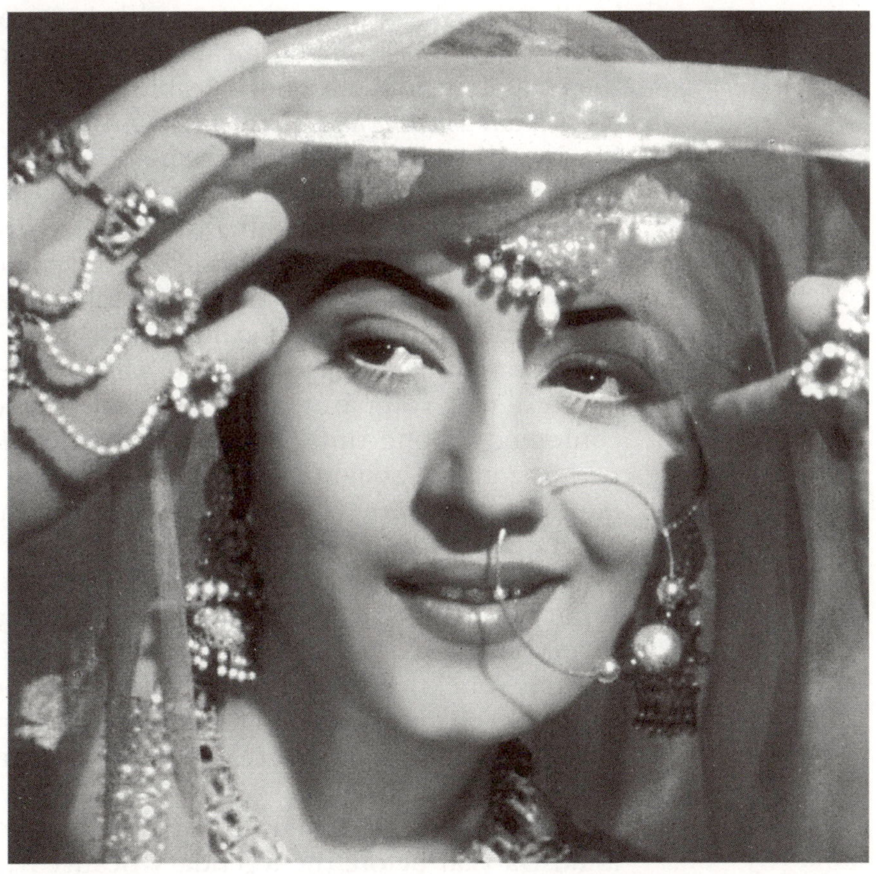

'Mughal-e-Azam' remained without a heroine for almost a year before the legendary beauty Madhubala was finally chosen to play the role.

Dilip Kumar's entry led to the exit of Nargis from *Mughal-e-Azam*. Raj Kapoor's possessiveness did not let his 'lady' make a romantic pair with his professional rival. Nargis was aware of this. 'Raj Kapoor did not like the idea of me making a hot saleable pair with anybody else.' (Ref: *The Life and Times of Nargis* by T.J.S. George) She bowed to the wishes of her 'man' and lost out on a role that every other actress was dying for.

Asif now had a difficult task. He had to find an Anarkali who would be a classical beauty and a great performer as well. All top-ranking heroines were under consideration, but Vijay Laxmi and Begum Para were the front-runners. Naseem Banu was also reportedly offered the role, but she declined. Suraiya was contacted at one time, but her grandmother, whose permission she sought before taking such a decision, quoted an exorbitant fee and consequently the idea of casting her was dropped altogether.

The *Filmfare* issue of 30 May 1952, published a report stating, 'In their search for Anarkali, they interviewed scores of society girls in Hyderabad, Bhopal, Lucknow and Delhi....Many of them were thrilled at the prospect of a film career. History records that Anarkali was more beautiful than queen Noorjahan.'

Mughal-e-Azam remained without a heroine for almost a year before the legendary beauty Madhubala was finally chosen to play the role.

Madhubala was a perfect Anarkali in every respect, but Asif's concern was her notorious father Ataullah

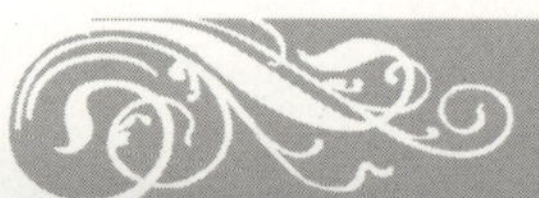

Khan. He was difficult to handle. Apart from other tough conditions, the list of Khan's unreasonable terms usually included not allowing any press reporter or press photographer on the set while Madhubala was shooting. Sometimes, even producers were prohibited on the sets. Night shifts and outdoor locations, too, were difficult to fit in. Leaving the set sharp at 6.30 p.m., irrespective of the work at hand, was a regular practice for her. She was a big star and producers were used to tolerating her father's obstinacy. But Asif was different.

Madhubala was aware of Asif's worries regarding her and did not want to lose the prestigious role. She sent a message through Nazir, a close family associate, informing Asif that she was keen to do the role and none of her father's conditions would be applicable, but Asif was to 'agree' formally to all her father's demands while negotiating the agreement. Asif was satisfied and Madhubala was confirmed to play Anarkali.

Anarkali immortalised Madhubala because not only was she enchantingly beautiful, but she had also

Madhubala was a perfect Anarkali in every sense....

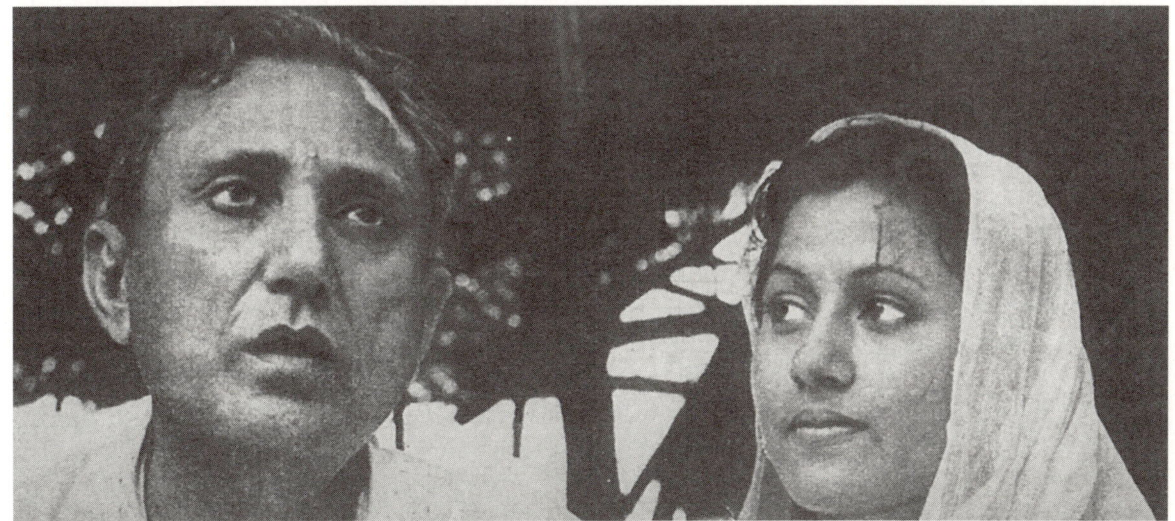

Madhubala and her father Ataullah Khan.

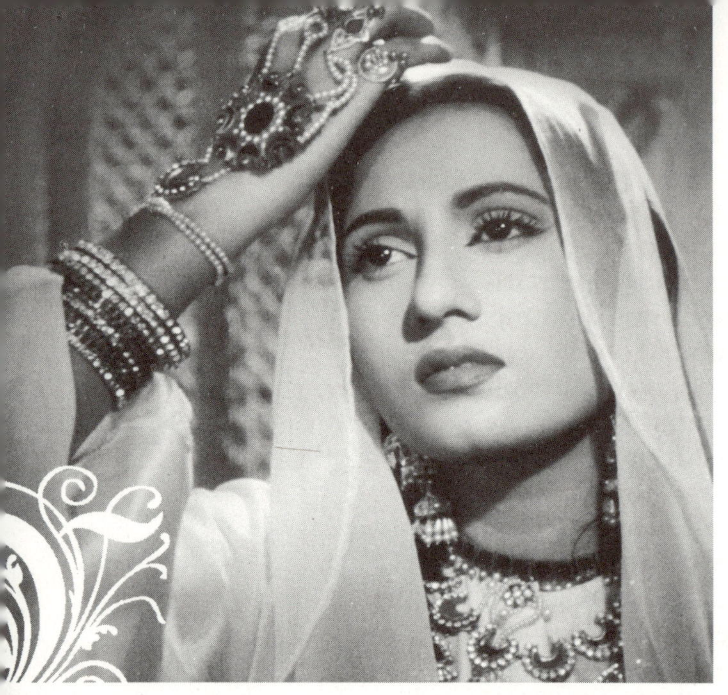

begun identifying with the courtesan. Her own real life love affair had run a similar tragic course as that of the helpless *kaneez.*

There was something unique about Madhubala. Even before she played Anarkali, she had dazzled the nation with her captivating beauty. Her status as an icon lives on, and even today, heroines are flattered if compared to her.

The mystery lies in Madhubala's personality. Most of the women of that era had pensive faces and a theatrical style of acting. But Madhubala was different. She had an angelic face and a bubbly, spirited personality that enthralled audiences with its infectious laughter and the twinkle in the eyes.

There was something unique about Madhubala. Even before she played Anarkali, she had dazzled the nation with her captivating beauty. Her status as an icon lives on...

She was endowed with perfect proportions. Slim, carved legs, shapely curves and long beautiful hands with tapering fingers; all these and more made her the diva of the Indian film world or as she was more popularly called, 'the Venus of Indian Screen'.

Born on 14 February 1933 in Delhi, her real name was Mumtaaz Jahan Begum. She was the third of six sisters, and the prettiest of them. Her father Ataullah Khan had perennial financial difficulties in running the family. When Mumtaaz was eight, some of Khan's friends advised him to allow his daughter to try her luck in the film industry. She was very pretty and had an air of innocence about her. The idea appealed to Khan and he came to Bombay with his family. He planned to reside near Bombay Talkies, Malad, as the studio was the most lucrative dream factory for many film aspirants.

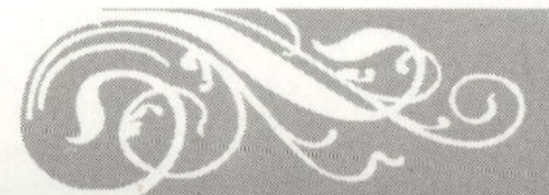

Due to financial constraints, he could manage to get only a small shabby room near the studio. Ataullah Khan took his daughter to the bosses of Bombay Talkies: Himanshu Rai and Devika Rani. They were impressed by Mumtaaz's beauty and innocence. She was cast immediately as a child artist in *Basant* (1942). Mumtaaz sang the popular hit, '*Tum ko mubarak ho unche mahal ye, hum ko pyari hamari ye galiyan*'. After *Basant* she acted as a child artist in Ranjeet Movietone's *Mumtaaz Mahal* (1944). *Dhana Bhagat* (1945) *Pujari* (1946) and *Phulwari* (1946).

Madhubala's journey from a child artist to an acclaimed star involved many disappointments and frustrations. She had to fight hunger and helplessness. Her father roamed from studio to studio for work, and finally in 1947, director Kedar Sharma gave her the first break as the leading lady in *Neelkamal* against Raj Kapoor, who was also debuting as a hero. After *Neelkamal*, she received more offers. By then she had already grown into a vivacious beauty. Producers did not care so much for quality as they banked on Madhubala's beauty to bring in the crowds. Consequently, she worked in some mediocre films namely *Khubsurat Duniya, Paras, Aag* and *Dil ki Raani*. Her most significant one was Kamal Amrohi's *Mahal* in 1949. She was cast against the superstar, Ashok Kumar. A lovely, lonely daughter of a gardener falls in love with the photograph of a man hanging on a wall of the mansion. Her rendering of Lata Mangeshkar's immortal, '*Aayega aanewala....*' on the garden swing, fading away in mist, made for one of the most enduring images of Hindi cinema.

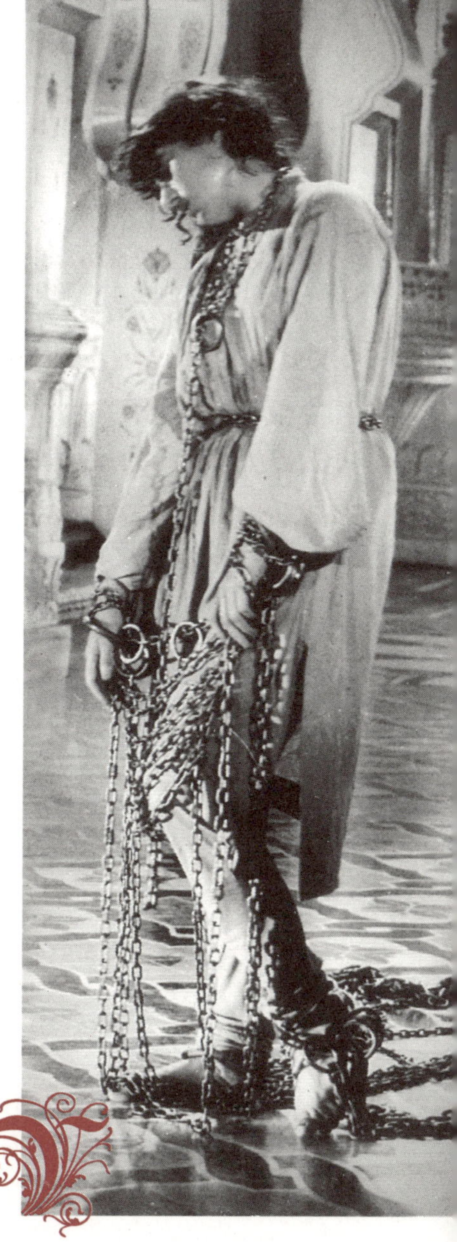

"Tere pyaar ki meherbaani pe roye!", Madhubala shackled in real chains.

She acted in sixty-five films in all and was cast opposite almost every leading hero of her time: Pradeep Kumar in *Raajhut* and *Sherin Farhad*, *Mr & Mrs 55* with Guru Dutt, *Gateway of India* and *Barsaat ki Raat* with Bharat Bhushan, *Ek Saal, Mahal, Howrah Bridge* with Ashok Kumar, *Nirala, Sharabi, Kala Paani, Naadaan* with Dev Anand, *Dhake ki Malamal, Chalti ka Naam Gadi, Jhumru* with Kishore Kumar, and *Badal* and *Saqi* with Premnath, with whom she was linked romantically for a short period.

The cultured and softspoken co-star captivated the sensuous beauty. Dilip and Madhubala worked together in successive films, 'Sangdil' and 'Amar'. Madhubala's father, Ataullah Khan, did not approve of the intimacy, but love found its way.

Madhubala starred with Dilip Kumar in only four films: *Tarana, Sangdil, Amar* and *Mughal-e-Azam*. She was just seventeen when she played a bubbly village belle in *Tarana,* who sings to lure the young doctor played by Dilip Kumar, *'Nain mile nain hue bawre, ab ruke na preet ki ye nav re'*. Their love boat indeed flowed even as the film progressed. The cultured and softspoken co-star captivated the sensuous beauty. They worked together in successive films, *Sangdil* and *Amar*. Madhubala's father, Ataullah Khan, did not approve of their intimacy, but love found its way.

Madhubala used to visit Susheela Rani's house (wife of Babu Rao Patel, the editor of *Film India*) to learn spoken English, making the spot an ideal rendezvous for the lovers. There was mutual care and trust between the two before a rift appeared. It is believed that the famous *Naya Daur* court case in 1957 was the reason for the split. Madhubala was the leading lady in B.R. Chopra's *Naya Daur*. The shooting was in full swing when all of a sudden Ataullah Khan refused to send his daughter to outdoor locations in defiance of a written agreement with B.R. Films. The obvious reason was Dilip Kumar, the hero of the film.

Khan did not want the two to spend free time together in his absence. Chopra then replaced Madhubala with

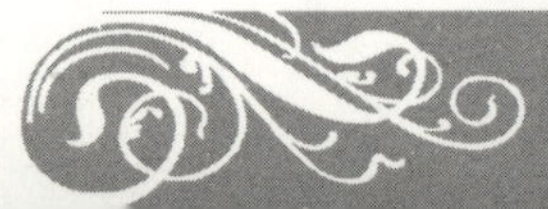

Vyjantimala, crossing out her name and putting the latter's on publicity posters. This infuriated Khan no end; he dragged Chopra to court. Chopra, too, filed a suit against Khan and his daughter for breach of promise and damages. The much-publicised Girgaum court case saw Dilip Kumar being called in as witness and here, standing in the dock, he made a dramatic statement announcing his undying love for Madhubala. Along with this, though, Dilip Kumar testified against Madhubala and her father Ataullah, which led to their defeat and consequently the heartbreak and separation.

Something had gone wrong between the two even before the court case. It might have been Madhubala's extrovert nature that stung Dilip Kumar or her father's obstinacy. In the end, it was too late for her to save the relationship. She was then twenty-four, yearning for matrimonial bliss, and was caught between two hot-headed Pathans.

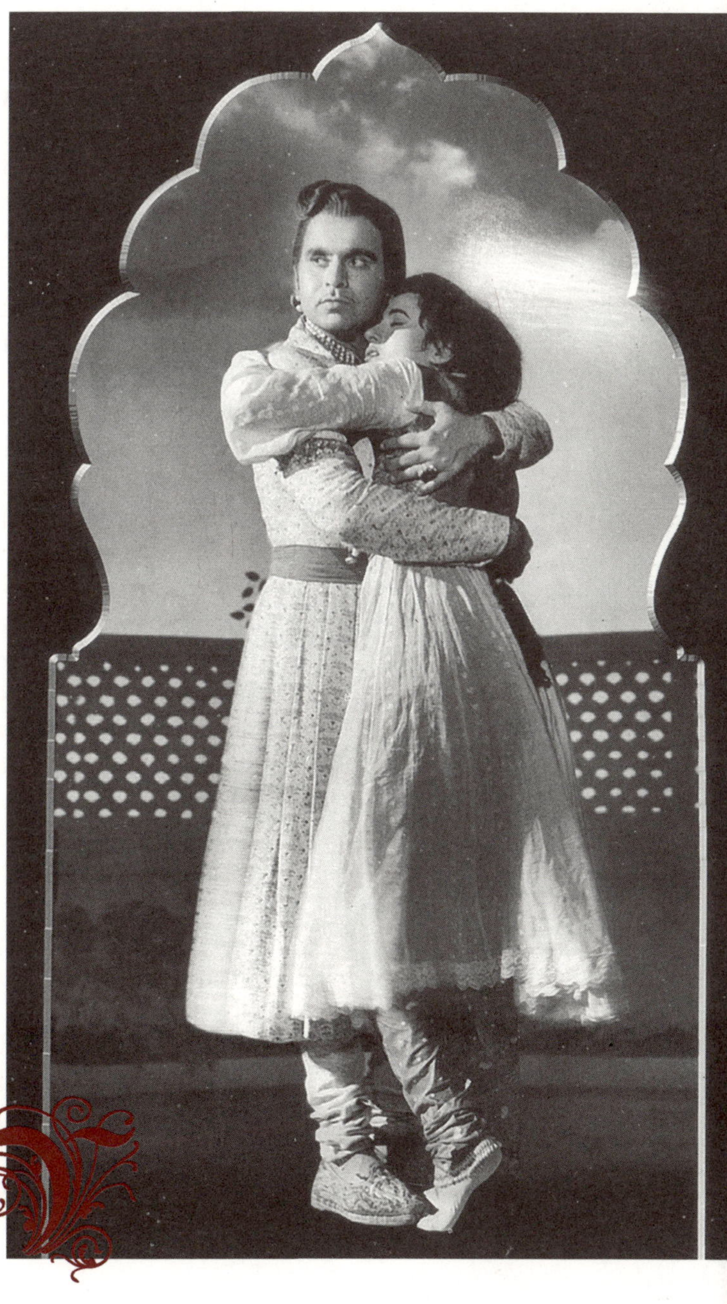

"Pyaar ki aandhi ruk na sakegi,
Nafrat ki deewaaron se,
Khun-e-mohabbat ho na sakega,
Khanjar aur talwaro se!"

'Madhubala captures with her seamless charm the delicate rendering of the character of a tormented kaneez, hopelessly in love with Prince Salim.'

— Saira Bano

In an interview on *Star News* on 11 November 2004, Dilip Kumar when asked about the sour relationship with Madhubala said cryptically, 'It was a matter of principles, which I couldn't let go.'

Madhubala confided once to a friend that she wanted to die a married woman. Heartbroken, she married Kishore Kumar on the rebound. The singer himself was then a disturbed man owing to a failed marriage with Ruma Devi. The marriage between Madhubala and him was solemnised by a civil contract. There were also stories that Kishore Kumar embraced Islam with a new name Abdullah. Whatever the truth be, the loveless marriage soon shattered and she returned to her father's house. People believe that she never stopped loving Dilip Kumar as she wore the ring he had given her even after her marriage to the singer.

On the sets of *Mughal-e-Azam*, the silence between the two star-crossed lovers rang out loud. Her unrequited love and the pain of losing her lover are reflected in every shot. Saira Bano describes her character as follows, 'Madhubala captures with her seamless charm the delicate rendering of the character of a tormented *kaneez*, hopelessly in love with Prince Salim. Dilip Kumar turns in a rare performance almost as if it were in a Shakspearean mould.'

The tormented *kaneez,* once a coquettish belle, was not the same after the *Naya Daur* court case. She was ill and grief-stricken, but determined to bring Anarkali alive on screen. It was during this time that Dr Jaal Vakil detected a hole in her heart when she fainted while shooting for Muhafiz Haider's *Mahlon ka Khwaab* in 1959. She had in fact been suffering from a congential heart disease which had been diagnosed much earlier by her family doctor Dr P.V. Manglik. But her father did not disclose her illness to the world.

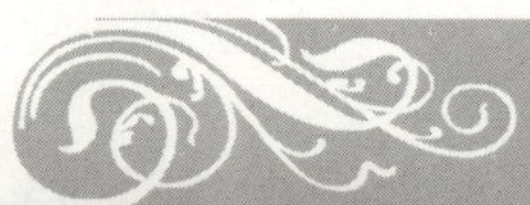

Moreover, K. Asif's quest for perfection forced her to wear heavy iron chains during the shooting of *Mughal-e-Azam*. Ataullah Khan complained that dragging the heavy chains on the dungeon sets of the film caused his daughter's dreaded heart disease. Doctors advised her against any kind of exertion. But she put all that she had into the movie. She insisted on even doing shots that required her to run a distance and ride pillion through the thick dust of the battlefield.

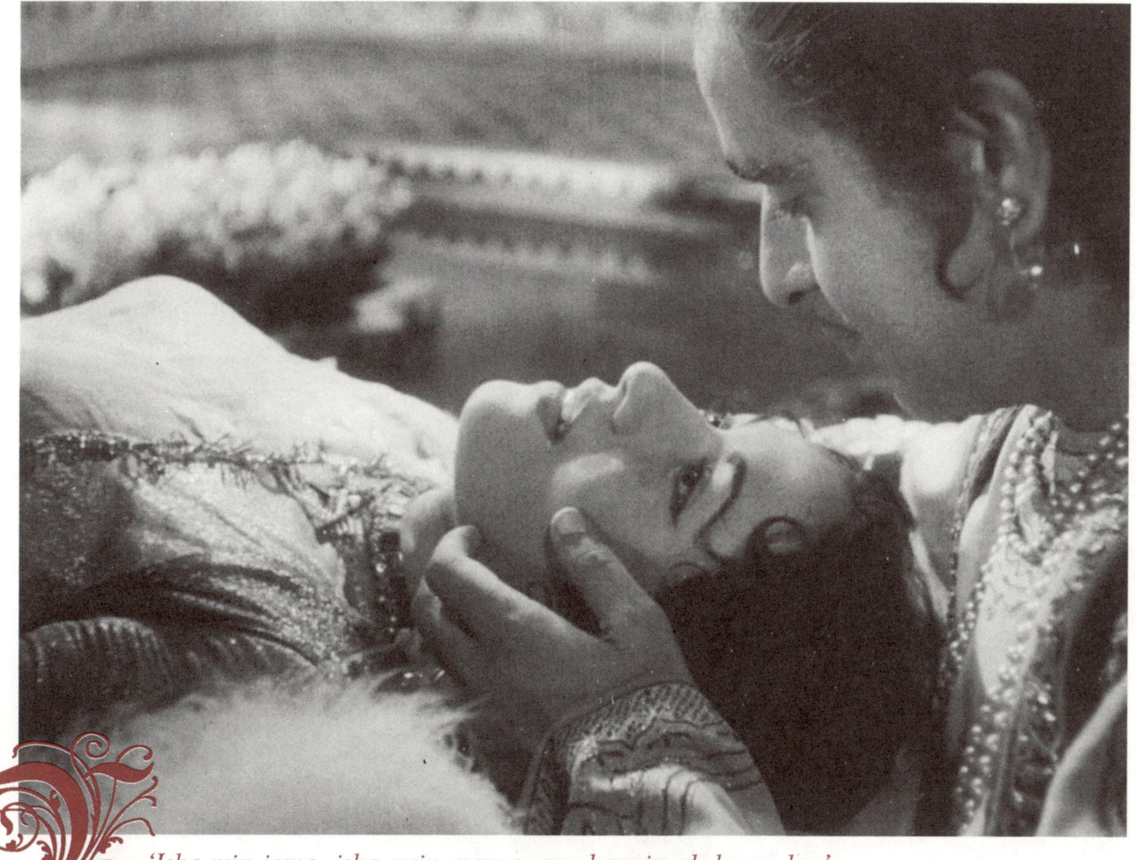

'Ishq min jeena, ishq mein marna, aur hamein ab karna kya'

The late actor Ajit had once said in an interview, 'Madhubala shed many tears during the making of *Mughal-e-Azam*. Every shot with her prince was a trial and caused her trauma.'

In the movie, Dilip Kumar slaps her once accusing her of being unfaithful. He delivers his lines with anguish,

> '... Akbar *ki buzdil laundi...jo* Salim *ki mehbooba nahin...Ek jhooti kasam thi jo mera imaan badal gayaee..Sharmnak badnami ka wo daagh thi jo merey daman par laga aur dhul gaya...'*
>
> (Akbar's coward courtesan! You are certainly not my sweetheart, a false oath instead, that has spoiled my faith, a shameful notoriety that maligned my esteem, but I have got rid of that now.)

The actor reportedly slapped her hard on the sets, perhaps unable to control his anger over the break-up. The slap stung, and Madhubala wept. She complained

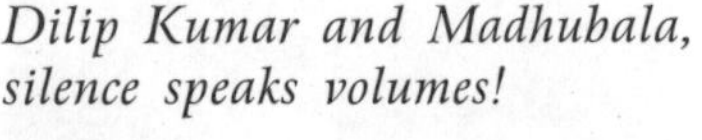

Dilip Kumar and Madhubala, silence speaks volumes!

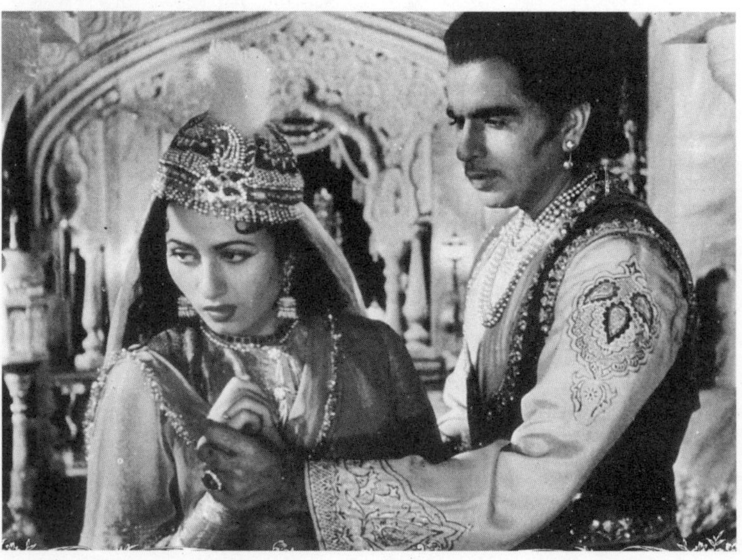

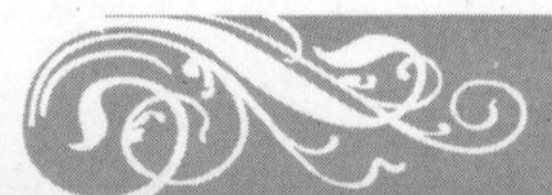

to Asif, who consoled her saying that the incident indicated Dilip Kumar's deep and unresolved emotions for her.

The chemistry between the two lovers was only for the screen though; once the cameras were off, there was a strained silence between the prince and the courtesan. In the privacy of her make-up room, she was often found brooding, haunted by the memories of her lost love.

Though not well-educated, Madhubala had an instinctive understanding of her character as Anarkali. There were long gaps between the shooting schedules, but she managed to maintain the continuity of emotions. She carried the audience with her ethereal beauty.

Madhubala had an instinctive understanding of her character as Anarkali. There were long gaps between the shooting schedules, but she managed to maintain the continuity of emotions.

After the release of *Sharabi* in 1964, she fell seriously ill. It was reported in film magazines that on the floors of *Chalak* (with Raj Kapoor), she became so weak that she would collapse after just half an hour of work. Her dreaded illness and personal traumas took her to her deathbed. She was admitted to the Breach Candy Hospital in 1965 where she lay pale and weak, her beautiful face covered with ugly patches. She returned to her lonely bungalow, Arabian Villa, at Bandra. It is said that during her last days, the most beautiful woman on the Indian screen became such a ghost of her former self that she removed all the mirrors from her home. She faced her illness bravely. The last time she was seen in public was at the Churchgate station with a holy man. Though out of sight for many years, her sudden appearance caused a huge mob to gather. The holy man was believed to be a spiritual healer, but nothing worked. The most sought-after heroine and the first ever dream girl of the Indian screen died young and helpless on 23 February 1969, just nine days after her thirty-sixth birthday. Ataullah Khan, who had sought to protect

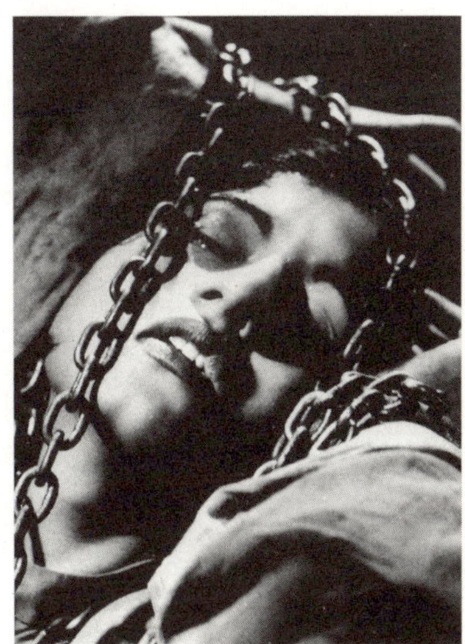

his daughter from the pitfalls of stardom, wept helplessly.

On her last birthday, very few friends and well-wishers visited to wish her good health. Khan recalled her previous birthdays when the house would be deluged with greetings and flowers. Producers sold movies on her name and queued up to lay precious offerings at her feet as if she was a goddess.

It is said that Madhubala yearned for a last look at her real life 'god', but 'he' did not turn up and she met the same fate as that of the helpless *kaneez* of *Mughal-e-Azam* who sang,

'Hamein kaash tumse mohabbat na hoti,
kahani hamari haqueeqat na hoti.'

Significant support

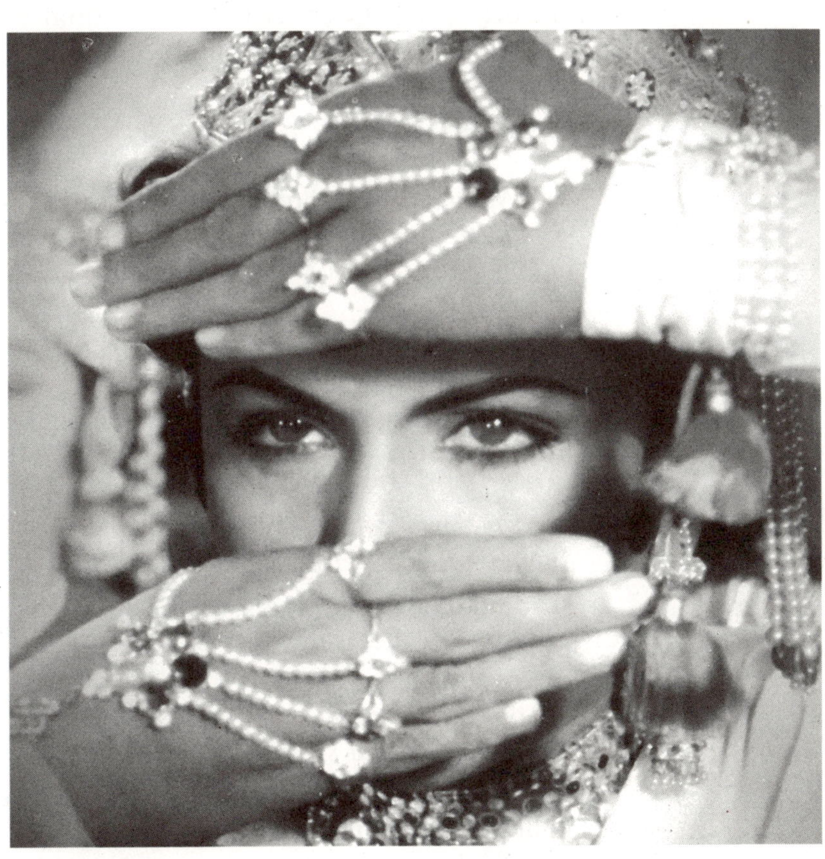

Nigar Sultana... big plans, big aspirations, big dreams
'Na jaane kitni ladkiyan yeh khwab dekh rahi hai
Unhen khwab dekhne do...
...Tum meri aankhen dekho!'

Besides Prithviraj Kapoor, Dilip Kumar, and Madhubala, many other artists contributed in equal measure to make *Mughal-e-Azam* a memorable saga.

Durga Khote

'Uff Mahabali! Yeh Mughlon ki kaisi rajneeti hai jo ek maa ko tadapne bhi nahin deti…? Use rone bhi nahin deti jiske betey ka lahoo is bedardi se lutaya ja raha hai...'

(Your Highness! What politics do the Mughals follow that a mother cannot even wail . . . She can't even cry, though her son's blood is being shed so mercilessly.)…

Meri to donon taraf haar hai, Mahabali! Ek taraf aulaad hai aur ek traf suhaag…'

(I stand to lose both ways, at one end is my son, and on the other is my husband)

Akbar: *Aur is ka faisla apko abhi karna hai…. aulad chahiye yaa suhaag..?*

(Akbar: And you have to choose right now between your son and your husband.)

Durga Khote made a fine Rani Jodhabai with her exquisitely chiselled features, dimpled smile and gracious personality. Khote hailed from an educated

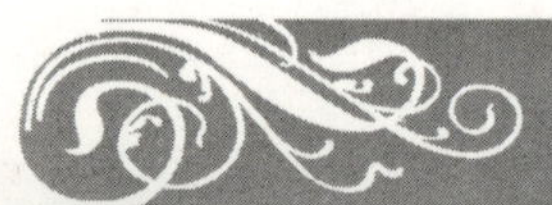

and cultured Maharashtrian family of Bombay (now Mumbai). Her father was a famous lawyer, and her brother a well-known barrister.

The family belonged to the upper strata of society. She graduated from St. Xavier's College and was married off early to the well-educated and broadminded young man Viswas Khote. The couple had two children. Bakul Khote and Harin Khote. Her sister Shalini, who was also married, moved around in distinguished circles.

J.B.H. Wadia, then assistant to Mohan Bhavnani, was a regular visitor and a family friend. Bhavnani had made a silent film starring his wife, and since the talkies had just started, he wanted to toss in a talkie ending. He was looking for a girl to feature with Mrs Bhavnani in the garrulous climax. He asked J.B.H. to approach Shalini, but she refused. She then recommended Durga Khote, who was regarded by the family as a dashing and bold girl. J.B.H. met Durga and offered her the role. She not only accepted it but also travelled to the studio that very day to start work.

The film, *Trapped,* was completed soon and released in 1931. It had a bold theme that put Durga Khote in an awkward position. She hailed from one of the best-known Maharashtrian families in the city and was married into another reputed family. However, this role earned her a certain measure of notoriety. She could not walk around in Girgaum, a Marathi stronghold, without people pointing fingers at her. Her family and her husband's relatives supported her, but the community thought she had let them down. There was one person, however, who appreciated her work and that was none other than the

With zarra bakhtar (armour) of her son.

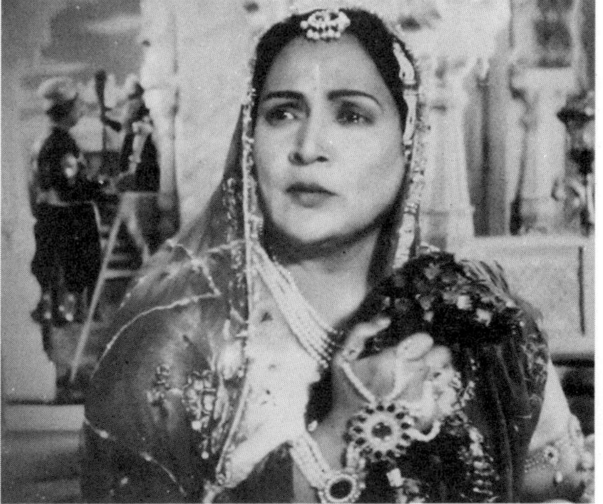

renowned filmmaker V. Shantaram. Shantaram, who was working with Prabhat Studios those days, asked Durga to star in their bilingual film *King of Ayodhya* as Taramati. Determined to vindicate herself and backed by her family, she accepted the offer. The movie clicked in both the Marathi and Hindi versions.

Her next picture *Maya Machindra*, again produced by Prabhat and directed by V. Shantaram, established her as a top star. She went on to play the leading role in many others, including New Theatres' *Raja Rani, Meera*, and *Seeta*. At New Theatres, she was the lady who introduced Kidar Sharma to Debki Bose and guided him through a difficult phase.

Exquisitely chiselled features perfectly matched the grace of a Rajput Rani.

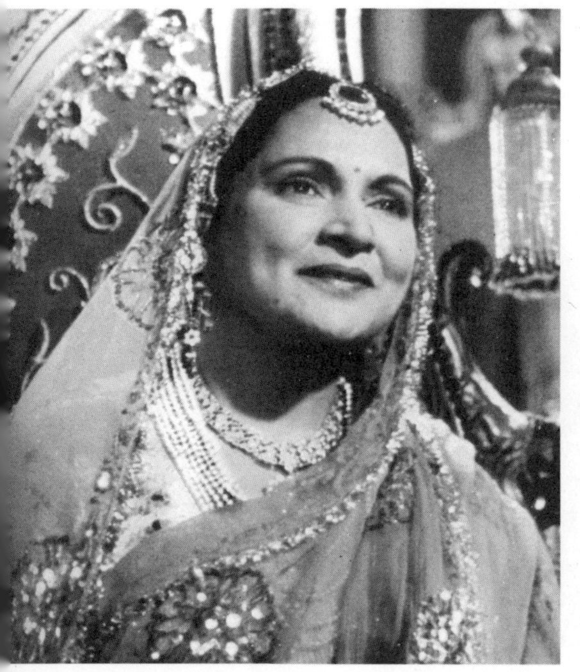

Durga's oeuvre ranged from historicals including Sohrab Modi's *Prithvi Vallabh* and *Chaitanya Mahaprabhu* to social dramas; the roles varied from a termagant mother-in-law to a warrior queen. She even proved a polished comedienne in *Chacha Choudhary,* produced by Kardar Productions in 1953. Her brilliant timing and dialogues made the film a scintillating comedy. In fact, she stole the show from co-star Raja Paranjpye, who was also the director.

In *Chaitanya Mahaprabhu*, her performance as the woman torn between her love for her son and the gratification she felt in his single-minded devotion to god was heartrending. In *Bharat Milap*, Durga played Ram's fiercely resentful stepmother, Kaikeyi. Her jealousy, combined with her verve and beauty, was irresistible.

By the 1940s, she had begun accepting supporting roles. The first one was in *Charno ki Daasi* in 1941. The film was produced and directed by P.K. Atre and met with instant box office success. She won the BFJA award for Best

Performance. In order to imbue the role with reality, she studied a *dhoban*'s (washerwoman's) mannerisms. She continued to play character roles over the next few decades in a series of significant films, including *Anand, Abhimaan, Khushboo, Bobby, Jaaneman, Bawarchi* and *Bidaai*. This film got her the *Filmfare* award for Best Supporting Actress in 1974. Besides, she also received the Padmashree and the prestigious Dadasaheb Phalke award in the year 1984.

... she vindicated his faith by doing full justice to the character of a Rajput queen torn between her husband and her son, '...meri to donon taraf haar hai Mahabali! Ek taraf aulaad hai aur ek taraf suhaag.....'

Durga Khote was also an active and an enthusiastic member of the Marathi Sahitya Sangh, which sponsored and produced Marathi plays. She acted and produced several plays. Added to her many accomplishments and talents was a gift for languages: she could read, write and speak in Marathi, Bengali, Gujarati, Hindi, Urdu, English and French.

She always wore sarees, and her favourite colour was red, which suited her fair Maharashtrian complexion. One of her finest qualities was her punctuality on the sets. Once she had agreed on a date, she would honour her word even if she was unwell. Asif cast her to play Rani Jodhabai, and she vindicated his faith by doing full justice to the character of a Rajput queen torn between her husband and her son, '*...meri to donon taraf haar hai, Mahabali! Ek taraf aulaad hai aur ek taraf suhaag.....*'

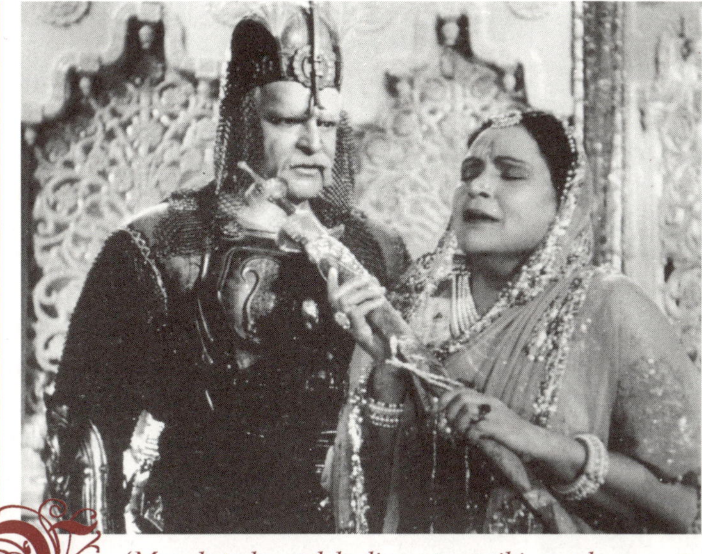

'Mere bete ke qatl ke liye aap mujhi se talwar maang rahe hai!'

Ajit

> 'Rajput *jaan harta hai, Shahzadey! Vachan nahin harta.*'
>
> (A Rajput may give up his life, but not his word).

Ajit had two advantages — one, his rugged looks and physique, and second, a rich baritone.

The line was delivered by Durjan Singh in *Mughal-e-Azam,* and the role was played by Ajit. Born on 22 January 1922 in Shahjahapur, Uttar Pradesh, Ajit's real name was Hamid Ali Khan. He belonged to a conservative Pathan family that frowned on such professions as acting. His father Basheer Ali Khan, who had moved to Hyderabad to join the Nizam's army, did well for himself: he owned properties around Hyderabad including grape and mango orchards.

Basheer Ali Khan wanted his son to follow his footsteps and serve the state army. But Ajit, a student of the Nizam College, Hyderabad, had a poor academic record and could think of nothing else but acting. He was in his element when participating in college plays and extra-curricular activities. To realise his dream, Ajit had to run away from home.

The Rajput friend of Prince Salim, Durjan Singh (Ajit).

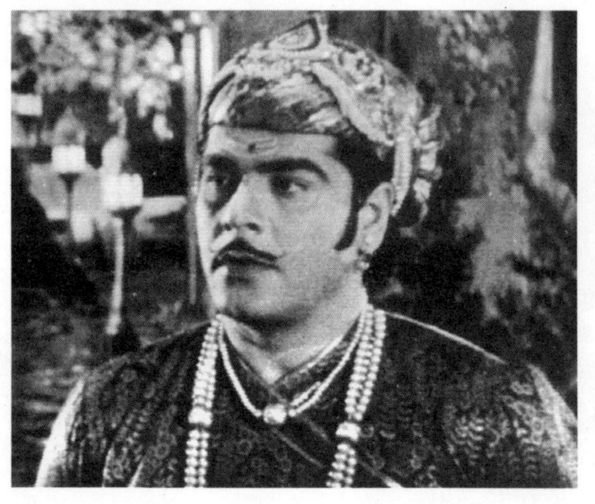

During the period of struggle in Bombay, Ajit did not seek any monetary help from his family, though they could have well afforded it. He would just haunt the film studios, where he luckily got easy entry because he could converse with the Pathan guards in the Pushtu language. After a lot of struggle, he finally landed a job as a junior artist on a daily wage of Rs 4 per day.

Ajit had two advantages — one, his rugged looks and physique, and second, a rich baritone. He soon landed his first break in 1946 as the leading man in *Shah-Misr,* a costume drama. From then on, Ajit did a series of roles as a hero opposite almost every leading lady of his time — Suraiya, Geeta Bali, Madhubala, Bina Rai, Nalini Jayawant, Veena, Nigar Sultan, Begum Para, Kamini Kaushal and Mala Sinha. He almost had fifty films to his credit, from 1946 to 1966. In the first five, he was identified as Hamid. It was only later that one of his mentors K. Amarnath, whom he looked upon as an elder brother, re-christened him as Ajit. Among his best known films were those in which he did parallel roles, namely, *Naya Daur* and *Mughal-e-Azam.* Ajit's career later took a nosedive and he had to work in B-grade films. Eventually, the actor was resurrected when he began to play the role of a villain. Rajendra Kumar cast him in a negative role in *Suraj* and again in Shridhar's *Dharti*. But it was Prakash Mehra's *Zanjeer* in 1972 that proved to be a milestone in his career. The role came to Ajit courtesy writer Salim. He knew Ajit well because he had helped the young writer get his first acting assignment in *Baraat,* produced and directed by K. Amarnath in 1960.

Ajit's role in *Zanjeer* as 'Teja' was that of a suave villain. Dressed in a suit with a cigarette or cigar in his mouth, and a girl on his arm, he looked impressive. Dilip Kumar once described his villainy as that which was aristocratic. Ajit had refused the role of a villain in *Dewaar* because he objected to the scene where Amitabh throws a man out of the balcony clad only in his underwear.

Ajit married his first love, who bore him three sons — Shahid, Abid and Zahid. Shahida, his second wife, is the mother of Arbaaz and Shehzad, who is a well-known TV actor. One of Ajit's pet loves was a football club he formed along with some friends from the industry who shared his passion for the game. Among them were Karan Dewan, Dilip Kumar and Motilal. A heart problem forced the veteran to retirement, and he died on 21 October 1998. His performance as Durjan Singh, who sacrifices his life to save Anarkali in the battlefield, was very convincing and contributed immensely to the success of the film.

His death scene also touched the audiences when he delivers the following lines:

'Jab tak Durjan ke haath mein talwar uthane ki tagat hai, Mout Sahib-e-aalam ke qareeb nahi aasakti.'

(As long as Durjan can hold sword in his hand, death cannot dare come closer to Sahib-e-aalam.)

Kumar (Shaukat Hyder)

'Zindabad ....Zindabad .....Ai Mohabbat Zindabad!'

(Long live…long live, O Love! Long live!)

This song was picturised on the actor who portrays the old and obstinate royal sculptor. His name was Kumar.

Kumar's real name was Shaukat Hyder. He began his career way back in 1932 in *Puran Bhakti* made by Calcutta's New Theatres. He then acted in the famous *Yahudi ki Ladki,* which was the original version of Dilip Kumar's *Yahudi*. Kumar became a top star of his times and acted in dozens of films as the hero. It is said that his popularity started the trend of suffixing Kumar to star names. Eventually, Kumar moved to supporting roles in *Watan, Thokar, Nadi Kinare, Najma, Daayera* and *Tarana,* in which he played the role of Madhubala's blind father. His last film in India was Mehboob Khan's *Son of India*, after which he migrated to Pakistan. Kumar died at Lahore on 30 July 1981. His actress wife Pramila preferred to stay on in India with their three sons —

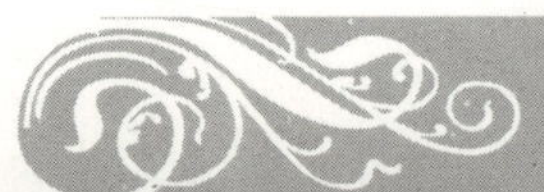

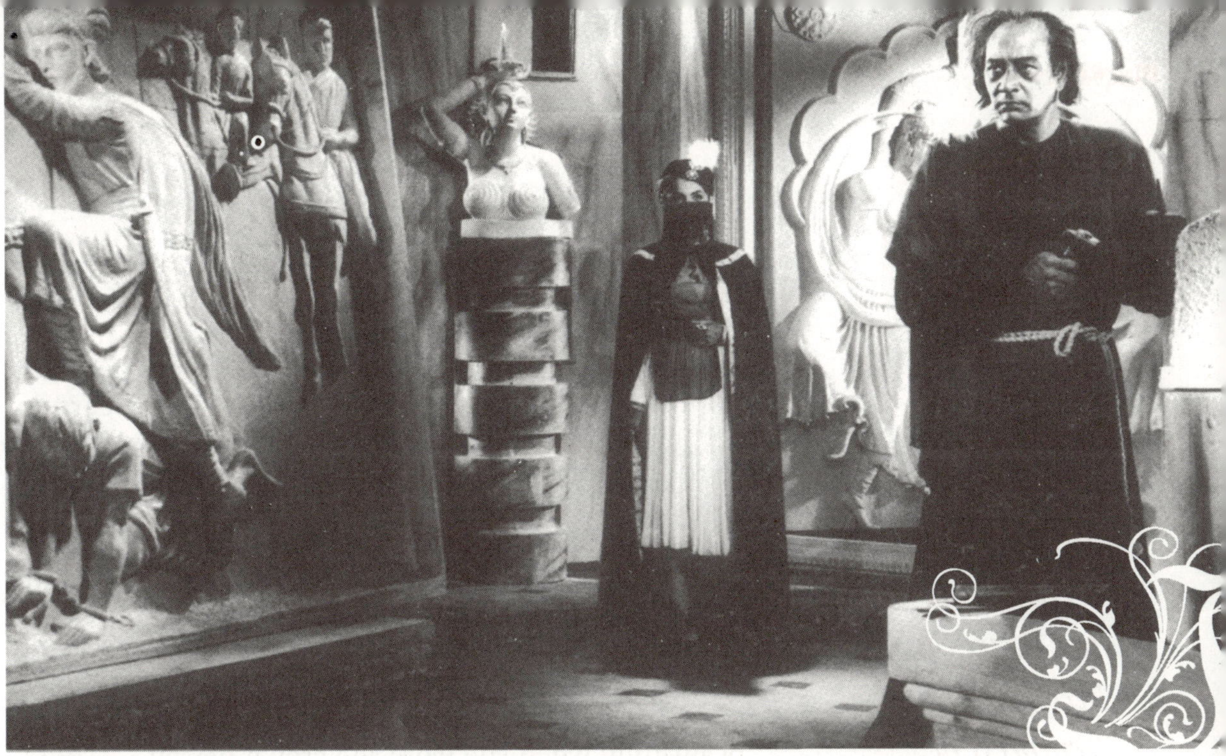

Akbar, Asghar and Hyder and a daughter Naqi Jahan. She acted in a few films but could not achieve much success. Her brother Akbar also played some bit roles but failed.

Kumar's classic looks resembled those of legendary artisans from a golden period. He was perfectly cast as the obdurate and proud sculptor who loved anonymity and was brave enough to turn down Akbar's offer of Anarkali as a reward. His short role as a *sangtarash* (sculptor) was memorable.

In a thought-provoking scene, he tells Bahar, the woman vying for Salim's attention:

> *'....Mere banaye huye Mujassame badshahon aur shahzadon ko pasand nahin aayenge...kyonki yeh such bolte hain...'*
>
> (Royals would not like my sculptures ... because they tell the truth.)

Kumar's classic looks resembled those of legendary artisans from a golden period. He was perfectly cast as the obdurate and proud sculptor.

Her unusual beauty and hypnotic eyes made her an impressive 'other' girl, who had set her heart on becoming the empress of Hindustan.

Nigar Sultana

Nigar Sultana played the vamp Bahar, although Asif initially chose his ex-wife Sitara Devi to do it. After they got divorced, Nigar Sultana jumped in for the role. Her unusual beauty and hypnotic eyes made her an impressive 'other' girl, who had set her heart on becoming the empress of Hindustan and was ready to go to any lengths to fulfil her desire. Born in Hyderabad, she joined the industry in the late 1940s. Her memorable films include *Patanga, Bikhre Moti, Mirza Ghalib, Bazar, Dil ki Basti, Sheesh Mahal, Mastana* and the Dilip Kumar-starrer *Yahudi*.

Sultana as Bahar in *Mughal-e-Azam* looked terrific, especially in the qawwali number *'Teri mehfil me qismat azma kar hum bhi dekhenge....'* She rendered her lines beautifully when she wore the crown herself,

> *'Taj un saron pe nahin rehta jin ke qareeb khouf aa jata hai.... maghroor shahzadon ke liye ek jhuki huyee nazar hi kafi hai.'*

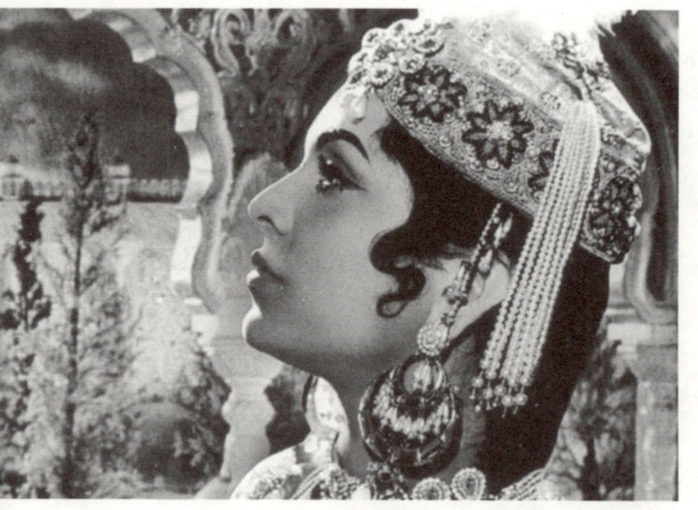

(The crown does not belong to those who fear .... a bashful look is enough for an arrogant prince.)

During the course of the movie, Nigar Sultana married K. Asif.

Their son Akbar Asif, based in the U.K., is a business magnate today. His daughter, Haya Asif (granddaughter of K. Asif) celebrated her eighteenth birthday in London after the release of colour version of *Mughal-e-Azam*. The renowned painter, M.F. Hussain, a *Mughal-e-Azam* buff himself and a fan of late K. Asif,

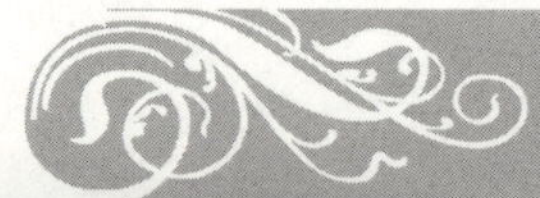

designed Haya's birthday card and painted her portrait in front of the audience, with the beats of '*Teri mehfil me qismat azma kar....*' playing in the background. Haya felt honoured and said on this occasion, 'This song is very special to me as my grandmother (Nigar Sultana) was pregnant with my father when she was shooting the sequence.' Nigar Sultana did full justice to her role in *Mughal-e-Azam*. She passed away on 15 May 2000.

Murad

Murad played Raja Man Singh in the film. Historically he was the brother of Rani Jodhabai. He is the father of present-day actor Raza Murad. Murad, was a familiar face in the 1950s and 1960s. He was highly acclaimed for his rich baritone and dialogue delivery. In the later years, Murad played a judge in various films. In *Mughal-e-Azam*, he steals the show when he

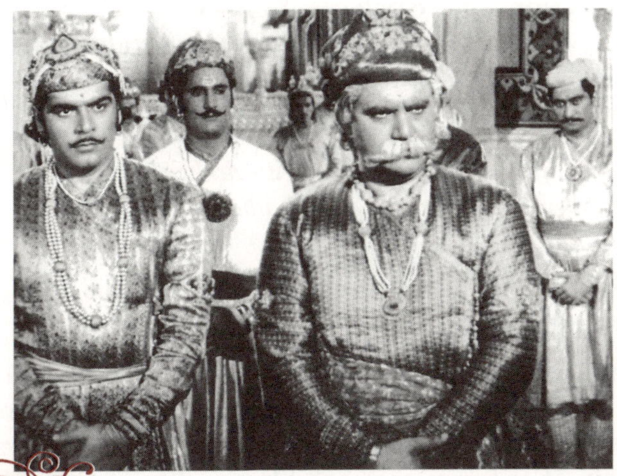

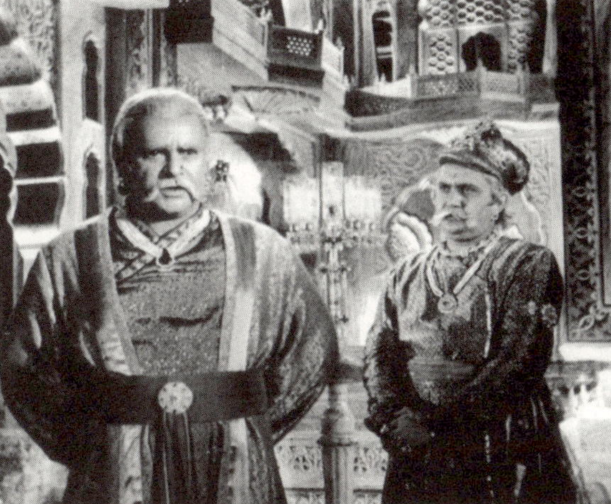

'Maidan-e-jung mein talwar sipahi ke haath mein dijaati hai, mayus ashiq ke haath mein nahi. Shahzaade ki jaan khatre mein na daliye, Mahabali.'

diverts the cannon away from Prince Salim while the death sentence is being executed.

Sheela Deloy

Sheela Deloy played 'Suraiya', the mischievious younger sister of Anarkali, who provides the lighter touches. The lines with Ajit are hilarious, particularly when she tells him, *`Mohabbat kijiyega, dil se dar nikal jayega'*. (Fall in love, you shall become bold.)

She even sings the melodious song, *'Ai ishq ye sab duniya waley bekar ki batein kartei hain'*. This song was cancelled later, perhaps due to the increased length of the film.

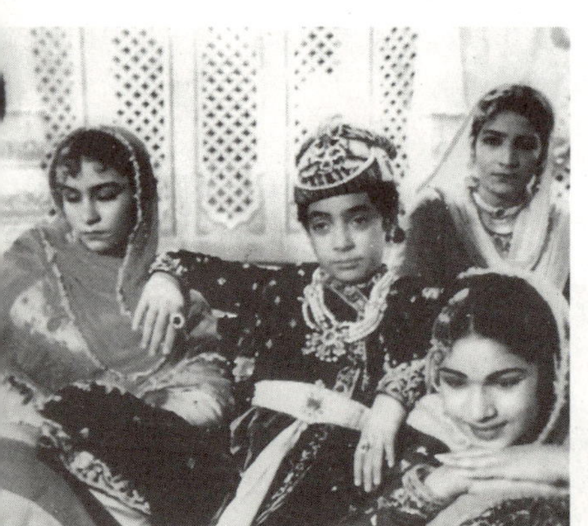

Young Jalal Agha as 'Shaikhu', Prince Salim in childhood.

Besides these talented actors, there were many others who did their roles well. Among them, Johnny Walker was good enough in a small role of Khwaja Sara (eunuchs, who were employed in Mughal darbaars and allowed to roam freely in *mardana* (male) and *zanana* (female) sections of the palace). Young Jalal Agha played 'Shaikhu', the young Prince Salim, very convincingly. This young prince indulges in drinks and female company. Akbar furiously slaps him and says:

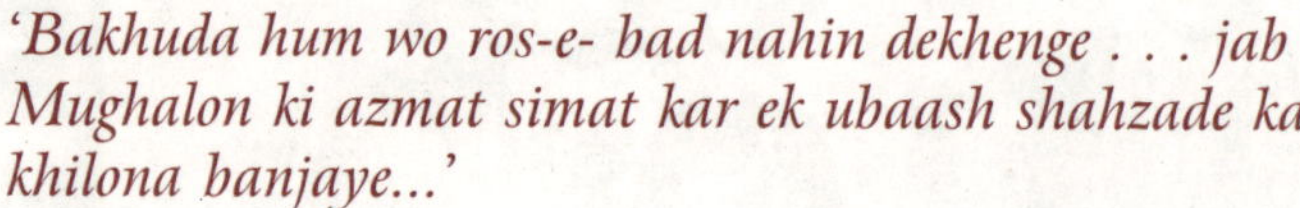

'Bakhuda hum wo ros-e- bad nahin dekhenge . . . jab Mughalon ki azmat simat kar ek ubaash shahzade ka khilona banjaye...'

(By God! I shall hate the day when the Mughal honour would become a toy of a dissolute prince.)

A unique feature of the film was that many leading females of yesteryears, namely Shanta, Kaushalya and Tazi, appeared in bit roles and crowd scenes. Tazi was the widow of the famous hero Shyam. She was signed for rupees one thousand, for her standing role in the film.

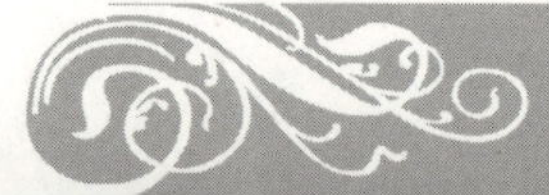

A high note

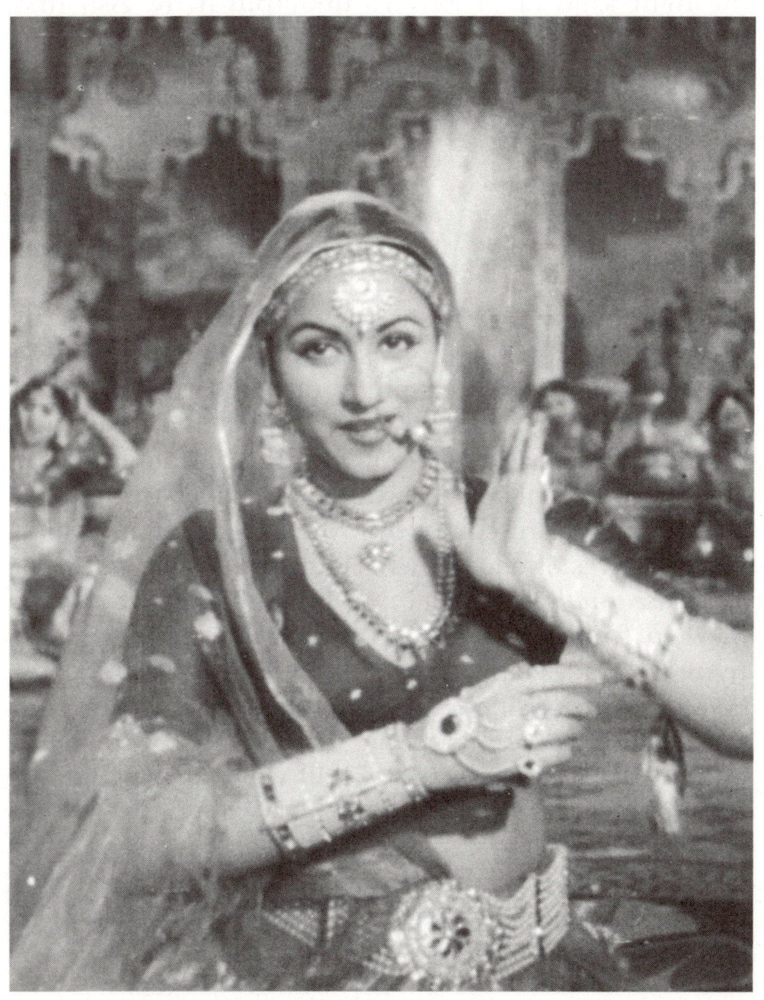

'Naino se jaadu kiya... ... Jiya-ra moh diya!'

'Kaam dil se hota hai, paise se nahi,' Naushad exclaimed. (Passion motivates work, money doesn't.)

Suddenly, a gust of wind blew in from the sea and the currency notes started flying around the music room.

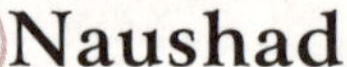

Naushad

Music has always been the lifeline of Hindi cinema. *Mughal-e-Azam,* with its theme of tragic love, needed the right kind of melody to underpin it. K. Asif first engaged Pandit Govindram for the music. He then changed his mind and assigned the work to Ghulam Hyder and later Anil Biswas. Eventually, Asif settled on Naushad Ali when he restarted the project in the early 1950s.

It came about in a very dramatic fashion. One evening, Asif barged into Naushad's music room at his bungalow on Carter Road, Bandra. The composer — an old acquaintance — was at work. After paying his respects, Asif requested Naushad to compose the music for his film. Naushad politely declined the offer and said he was busy with other engagements. Asif then placed a wad of currency notes on the harmonium that Naushad was playing and said, 'I have brought an advance; you are composing the music for my film.' Naushad was offended by his audacity. '*Kaam dil se hota hai, paise se nahi,*' he exclaimed. Suddenly, a gust of wind blew in from the sea and the currency notes started flying around. Naushad reminded Asif of the old days. 'We have been friends from the time we used to drink tea together. Give this money to somebody who needs an advance.' Asif retorted, 'I will work only with you, and you are composing the music for my film.'

A servant, who came in with tea, was stunned to see money flying around. He ran down the stairs to inform Naushad's wife. The sceptical Begum replied

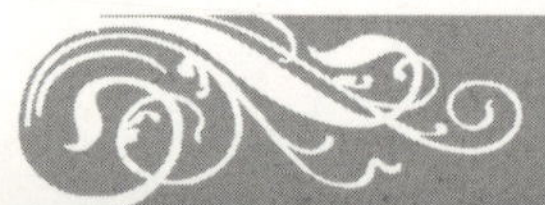

they might be fake notes used during the shoots. When she came up to have a look, she was shocked. After being informed of the altercation, she wryly suggested, *'Rakh lo....,'* and the servant began collecting the notes. A couple of days later, Asif brought along his financier, Shapoorji, to finalise the deal. That was how Naushad became one of the key members of the team.

Naushad's music is rooted in the Hindustani tradition. Born on 25 December 1919 in a middle class conservative Muslim family of Lucknow, Naushad showed a musical inclination at an early age. At the age of six, he was enrolled at the Aminabad High School near his house. It was at the age of ten that his interest in music grew. Those were the days of silent movies when an orchestra would sit below the screen to provide live background music and create an appropriate ambience.

Naushad, music director of Mughal-e-Azam.

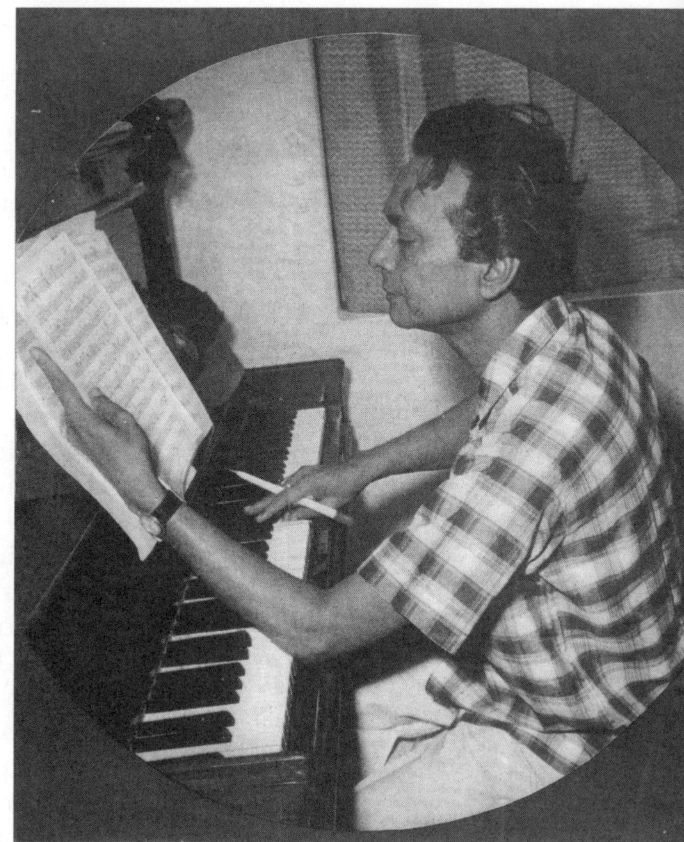

With a fifty per cent discount for children, a visit to the theatre would cost four annas. Naushad would see as many as three shows a day. Sometimes, when he returned home late, his grandmother would quietly open the door to let him in. He would go to bed without dinner for fear of waking his father.

There was a music shop close to his house. Naushad would often stand outside and admire the instruments. The owner, Ustad Ghurbat Ali Saab, used to notice the young boy. Sensing his keen interest in music, the Ustad employed him to keep the instruments and the shop clean. Naushad was overjoyed at the prospect. He was later given the additional responsibility of coming in early to open the shop and tidy up the place. Young Naushad began using this opportunity to play the harmonium. This became a routine till the Ustad stumbled upon him once in the midst of a practice session. Naushad was so engrossed in music that he did not even notice the arrival of the Ustad. When it dawned on him, Naushad sprung to his feet, terrified that he would be fired and driven out of the shop. To his astonishment, the Ustad gifted him a new harmonium to practise at home.

Music was a disrespectful profession in devout Muslim families. Naushad's parents naturally disliked his passion. His father threw his harmonium out and warned him against indulging in a *mirasi*'s profession (a derogatory term for musicians). But Naushad would not give up. He began formal training under Ustad Nawab Yusuf, the younger brother of Ghurbat Ali, and Laddan Miyan, who used to conduct the orchestras at cinema halls. He then went on to learn under Ustad Babban Khan.

These activities enraged his father, who asked young Naushad to choose between home and music. The teenager opted for the latter. He recollects, 'When I was just a boy in my teens, I left my father's protection and formed a touring theatrical company with a group of thirty to forty friends. We toured U.P., Delhi, Marwar and Kathiawad. That tour gave me an opportunity to study the folk music of our land ... I was deeply impressed by the music which sprang from the soil; it was pure and uninhibited. It was then that I realised that anyone wanting to create popular music and pleasing melodies for the masses must seek

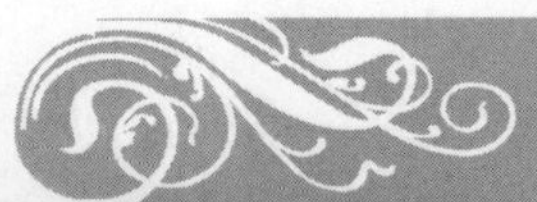

inspiration in this treasure house of folk music.' (*Filmfare*, 27 June 1952).

Working for a local drama company, Naushad provided valuable suggestions and improvised the background scores of many plays. But soon, the company closed down and Naushad was jobless. Some friends then advised him to try his luck in Bombay; so Naushad landed in the city of dreams in 1937. He had big aspirations, but was penniless. Finally, one day, in response to an advertisement, he reached the production office of a company at Khetwadi where music director Ustad Jhande Ali Khan was conducting an audition.

Naushad, being a great fan of the Ustad, was naturally in awe of him. After the audition, to Naushad's disbelief, he was selected as a harmonium player for a salary of forty rupees per month. The film, for which he was hired, was being produced by the Russian producer Henry Darqavitace. Finally, Naushad had a job; but still no place to stay.

Soon, he fortunately ran into an old friend from Lucknow, who worked as a salesman at a shop near Dadar. He was invited to share a little space inside the shop. However, the interiors were very suffocating, and the two friends would take their bedding out and sleep on the pavement. Those were the days of perseverance and hardships. Naushad would often admire the shining lights of Broadway Cinema from his sleeping place on the footpath and dream that one day his luck, too, would shine.

It was around this time (1938) that he befriended a young lad, who was a great film buff and worked at a tailoring shop near Dadar. The boy would boast that one day he would make a big film. Naushad would laugh it off; but he was fond of the young boy and often shared

tea with him at wayside stalls. The boy was none other than K. Asif.

Naushad soon journeyed from pavement to palace, scaling musical heights with films such as *Station Master, Ratan, Dulari, Deedar, Anmol Ghadi, Andaz, Aan, Babul* and *Baiju Bawra*. He had learnt his lessons well under Ustad Jhande Ali Khan: 'The secret of a good and popular film song is that it should have an appeal independent of the music score. It should be capable of being sung and enjoyed even without the aid of an orchestra.'

The lesson inspired Naushad to render his compositions in various ragas. The song would sound like a piece of contemporary music, but he would masterfully underpin it with a raga. Here are a few examples from his vast body of work:

Mohe panghat pe nandlal .... Raga Gaara *(Mughal-e-Azam)*; *Mohabbat ki jhooti kahaani* .... Raga Darbari *(Mughal-e-Azam)*; *Madhuban me Radhika* .... Raga Wamir *(Kohinoor); Uthaye jaa unke sitham* .... Raga Keda *(Andaz)*; *Prem jogan banke* ... .Raga Sohni and Lalit *(Mughal-e-Azam); Mohe bhool gaye sawarya* .... Raga Bhairavi *(Baiju Bawara)*.

Madhubala in the qawaali competition in the film.

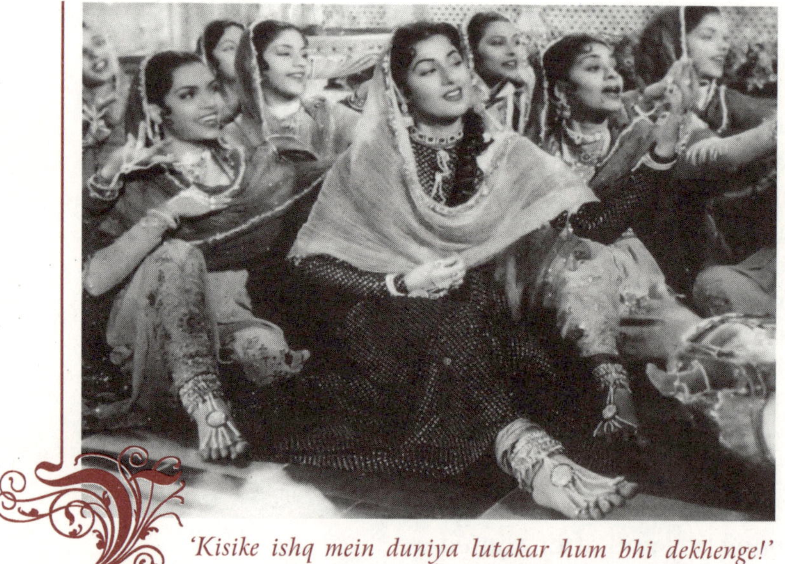

'Kisike ishq mein duniya lutakar hum bhi dekhenge!'

Naushad won the *Filmfare* award in 1952 for *Baiju Bawra*. He also won the BFJA (Bengal Film Journalists' Association) award for *Gunga Jamna* in 1961, the

'Lata Mangeshkar Award' in 1984, the Padama Bhushan in 1992, and the prestigious 'Dadasaheb Phalke Award' in 1982.

Shakeel Badayuni

K. Asif had four writers for the dialogues, but only one lyricist, Shakeel Badayuni.

Shakeel was born on 3 August 1916 in the remote town of Badayun in U.P. His father Moulana Jameel Ahmed Sokhta was a religious scholar, who taught his son Arabic and Persian. The boy inherited his father's poetic sensibility and graduated from the Aligarh Muslim University.

A great admirer of the famous Jigar Moradabadi, his *shairi* often reflected the latter's style. After completing his education, Shakeel found a government job as a clerk in Delhi. Here, he came into contact with the famous poet Neeraj. Shakeel had by now attained recognition and was invited regularly to all the *mushairas*. It was during one such *mushaira* in Bombay, in the year 1946, that Naushad heard him and came away impressed. The poem was,

Wohi karavan wohi raste

(The same caravan, the same routes)

Wohi zindagi wohi marhale

(The same life and the same sufferings)

Magar apne apne maqam par

(Yet at our respective places)

Kabhi hum nahin kabhi tum nahi

(Sometimes you aren't there, sometimes I'm not there)

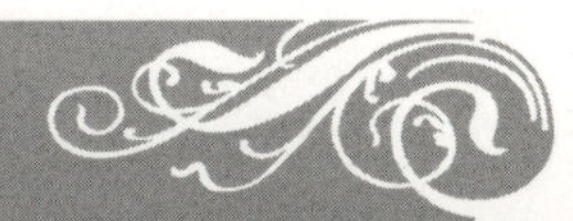

Naushad introduced Shakeel to Abdul Rasheed Kardar, the proprietor of Kardar Studios. Kardar also took to this talented poet, who made an impression despite his shabby appearance. He offered him double the salary and asked him to write the songs for *Dard*. Shakil accepted the offer without a second thought and wrote '*Afsana likh rahi hoon dile beqarar ka.*' This was sung by a newcomer named Uma Devi, who was introduced by Naushad. She later went on to become Tun Tun, the famous comedian. The song was an instant hit and Shakeel became a household name.

After *Dard,* his partnership with Naushad took him to great heights. Both worked together in a series of movies such as *Deedar, Babul, Mela, Mother India, Baiju Bawra, Mughal-e-Azam* and *Mere Mehboob*. The Shakeel–Naushad pair worked together for nearly twenty years. It was a personal bond that extended to their families.

Apart from Naushad, Shakeel also worked with other music directors such as Ravi (*Chaudhvi ka Chand, Do Badan*), Hemant Kumar (*Bees Saal Baad*), C. Ramchandra *(Zindagi Aur Maut*), Ghulam Mohammad *(Kundan*), Sajjad Hussain *(Rukhsana*) and Shanker Jaikishan *(Pyar ka Rishta*). He won the *Filmfare* awards consecutively in 1961, 1962 and 1963 for the best lyrics. Shakeel's lyrics translated passion into sorrow. He brought a strong literary flavour to his creations and was among the few Urdu poets whose work attracted high acclaim in its lamentation over lost love. *'Na milta ghum to barbadi ke afsane' (Amar); 'Huye hum jinke liye barbad' (Deedar);* and *'Nagri-Nagri, dware-dware dhundo re sanvariya' (Mother India*) are a few of his gems. Shakeel earned fame and respect but never enough wealth. He lived in a rented apartment all his life. The great poet and lyricist passed away on 20 April 1970.

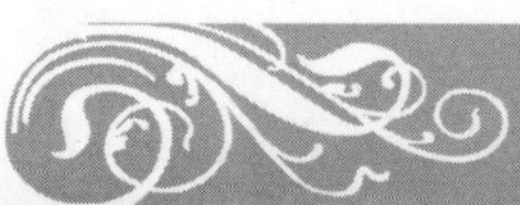

His writings in *Mughal-e-Azam* presented passion with tenderness. The '*bait-baazi*', picturised on Nigar Sultana and Madhubala and sung by Shamshad Begum and Lata Mangeshkar is a poignant example:

'Mohabbat hamne maana zindagi barbad karti hai...'

(I do agree, love ruins one's life)

'Yeh kya kum hai ke mar jaane pe duniya yaad karti hai.'

(Yet, is it not enough that people remember you even after death?)

The lines foretell the fate awaiting Madhubala. Shakeel had written a stanza for Madhubala to depict her inner helplessness:

'Mohabbat ki jhooti kahani pe roye, Badi chot khayee jawani pe roye.'

(Alas! I lament for the love that doesn't reciprocate, it hurts as my youthfulness fades in vain.)

'Na socha na samjha na dekha na bhala, Teri arzoo ne humein maar dala.'

(Alas! I didn't use any wisdom and desired you blindly; this longing is killing)

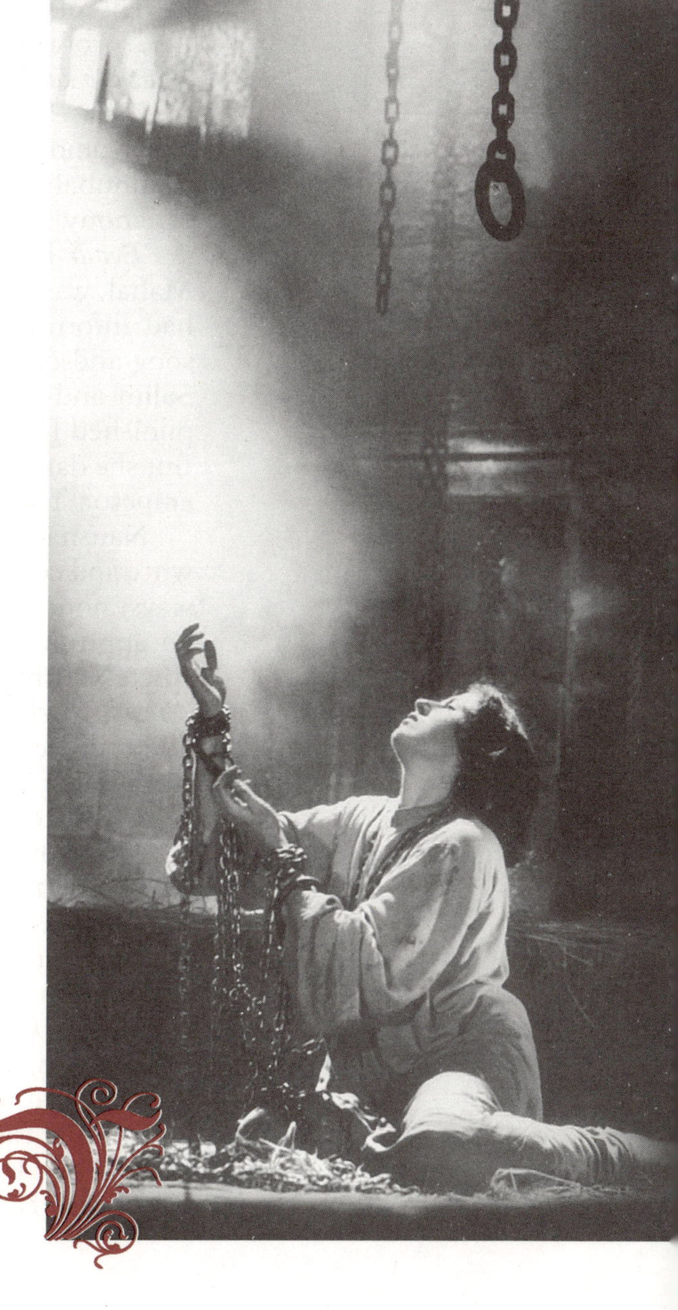

'Bekas pe karam kijiye Sarkar-e-Madina!'

The other song *'Khuda negahban ho tumhara'* (May God protect you) had a more befitting verse: *'Uthe janaza jo kal hamara, qasam hai tumko na dena kandha....'*

(Please do not give shoulder to my dead body when I die tomorrow.) This was almost prophetic in case of Madhubala. Dilip Kumar did not attend her funeral ceremony.

'Pyaar kiya to darna kya,' picturised in the Sheesh Mahal, was an anthem for young rebellious lovers. Asif had informed Naushad about the significance of the song-and-dance sequence, featuring Akbar, Jodhabai, Salim and other courtiers. Anarkali had already been punished for her love and warned of a death sentence. But she dares to challenge and enrage an already furious emperor. The lyrics were the key.

Naushad and Shakeel sat together one evening to write and compose it. But even though they tried several ways, none was satisfying. Shakeel was trying to write an appropriate *geet* or *ghazal*. It was almost midnight when Naushad recalled a folk song which he had heard, *'Prem kari chori kari naye.'* The line appealed to both, and they began working on it. It finally emerged as the memorable *'Pyaar kiya to darna kya.'* It was almost dawn when Shakeel Badayuni finished writing the song.

The words *'parda nahin jab koi khuda se bandon se parda karna kiya'* incensed the emperor as the lowly *kaneez* reminded him of the existence of the Almighty — the true harbinger of love. And the fearless declaration, *'Maut wahi jo duniya dekhe, ghut-ghut kar yun marna kya,'* turned out to be a line that inspired many young couples to elope.

Naushad used eight sitars, eight sarangis, pakhawaj and tabla for the score. He selected three noted maestros — Ustad Niyaz Ahmed Khan, Hafeez Ahmed Khan and Faiyyaz Ahmed Khan. Pandit Ram Doshi,

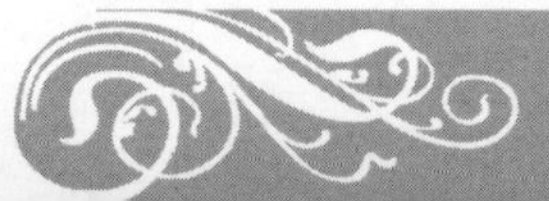

the noted pakhawaj player from Benaras, was especially invited to play the pakhawaj. Sarangi and sitar sections were led by Pt. Rama Narayan and Ustaad Haleem Jaffar Khan, respectively. The basic raga was Darbari Kanada.

Asif insisted that the song still needed to evoke the image of Anarkali as reflected in the thousand mirrors of the Sheesh Mahal. This was difficult because the composition was ready. But an idea suddenly struck Naushad. He asked Lata Mangeshkar to sing the verse without music. Her voice was then recorded on four different soundtracks with different effects, like hollowness, at a distance from the microphone, and then far away from the microphone. The four voices were then transferred to the original track of the song. The effect was splendid! It seemed as if the images were echoing the original voice. This was done very neatly and ingeniously at a time when advanced technology was absent.

Lachchu Maharaj

To choreograph the dance sequence *'Mohe panghat pe nandlal ched gayo re'* at the Mughal court on Krishna Janmashtami, Asif wanted the best. Naushad suggested the name of the great Kathak exponent, Lachhu Maharaj.

'Kankari aisi maari, gagariya phod daari!' Madhubala in 'Mohe-pangat pe'.

Lachhu Maharaj, whose real name was Pandit Basanth Prasad, was born in 1901. Lachchu, Achchan and Shambu were the last three of the Lucknow gharana of Kathak. Their great-grandfather, Pandit Iswari Prasad Handia, is said to have perfected the dance form under the patronage of the Nawabs of Avadh, and is the founder of this gharana. The three brothers were the disciples of their uncle Bindadin Maharaj. Lachhu Maharaj's father, Kalka Prasad, and grandfather, Thakur Prasad, were also consummate exponents of this art form.

In a strange coincidence, the opening lines of *'Mohe panghat pe'* were composed by Thakur Prasad, Lachhu Maharaj's grandfather. Music director Naushad said in an interview that Lachhu Maharaj wept when he first heard the song on the sets. He informed the director that it was his grandfather's favourite composition, which he used to play in Nawab Wajid Ali Shah's darbar. Naushad also wrote in an article that 'the *mukhda* (beginning line) was written by Kalka Bindadin. Based on this, lyricist Shakeel Badayuni wrote a song...' (Ref: *Notes of Naushad*, compiled and edited by Shashikant Kinikar; p. 81).

After the release of the colour version of the film in November 2004, one Raj Brahmbhatt, a sexologist by profession, had announced that the song was wrongly credited to Shakeel Badayuni and that it had been written by his grandfather, Raghunath Brahmbhatt for a Gujarati play, *Chatravijay,* in 1920. There is a strange confusion as Nawab Wajid Ali Shah ruled over Awadh around 1840, which is in fact much before 1920, as claimed by Mr Brahmbhatt. Besides, there have been many songwriters who got inspired by lyrics, mukhdas and compositions of other poets. For example, Gulzar used the universally known couplet by Mirza Ghalib,

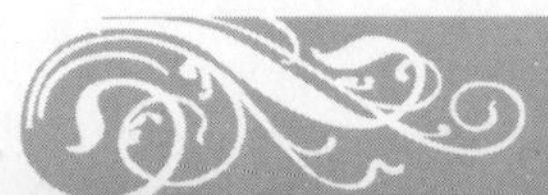

'*Dil dhoondta hain phir wohi fursat ke raat din...*' in *Mausam*. Similarly, Majrooh Sultanpuri used '*Patta patta, boota boota haal hamara jane hai*' in *Ek Nazar*, originally written by renowned Urdu poet Mir Taqi Mir.

Asif liked '*Mohe panghat pe....*' but disapproved of the solo voice. He wanted a chorus to picturise it on Madhubala along with some girls. So, Naushad had to re-record it with a chorus at appropriate places. The scene depicts Lord Krishna teasing Radha and the other *gopis* when they go to the river to fetch water. It was reported that Madhubala took three years to learn the dance; she was a beauty, but no dancer, and Lachchu Maharaj would not give up the challenge. (Ref: *Cine Advance,* September 1978)

The three inheritors of the Bindadin legacy — Achhan, Lachhu and Shambhu — took their art to great heights. The entire history of their tradition is said to have burnt down in a fire, but the disciples had learnt their skills well (Ref: *Cine Advance,* September 1978). Lachhu Maharaj further studied music under Ustad Fayyaz Khan and went on to work in films for thirty-two years. *Teesri Kasam* and *Guide* are examples from a memorable body of work. He also imparted training to a number of leading female stars. Madhubala learnt Kathak in *Mughal-e-Azam* and Waheeda Rehman learnt the famous *nagin* (snake) dance in *Guide.* Lachhu Maharaj was later appointed director of the Kathak Kendra of Uttar Pradesh Sangeet Natak Akademi.

He died on 18 July 1978, freeing the dance form of kathak from mathematical cliché and infusing it with a liveliness which is manifest in '*Mohe panaghat pe.*' Incidentally, during the picturisation of this song, a young handsome lad was often seen on the sets. He was Zulfiqar Ali Bhutto, the late prime minister of Pakistan, who once aspired to become an actor.

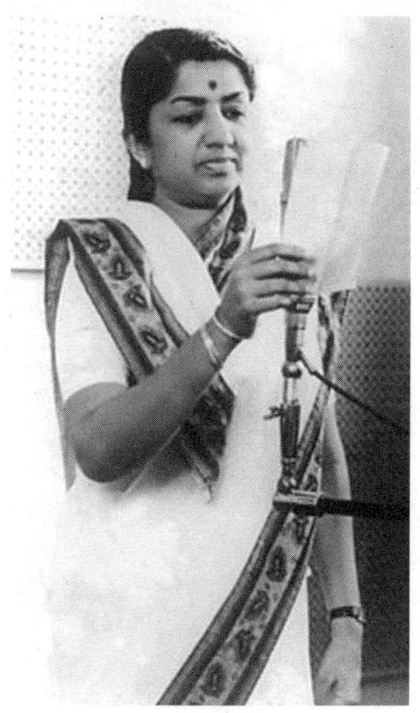

The nightingale of India: Lata Mangeshkar. Mughal-e-Azam has some of the most glittered jems of her entire career.

Each song in the film was a gem. Naushad says, 'Actually, some of the most detailed work in my life was done in *Mughal-e-Azam*. I remember some songs I composed and rejected, recomposed and again rejected many many times before I came up with the perfect version.' He believed that unless you feel the pain and ecstasy of music within your heart, you cannot communicate these feelings to the listeners of your music. Originally, twenty songs were recorded for *Mughal-e-Azam,* but only ten were retained. Several songs, including one by Shamshad Begum, Mubarak Begum and Lata Mangeshkar — *'Husn ki barat chali'* — were left out on the editing table along with a beach house scene of Salim presenting trophies to the court dancers. Another Shamshad Begum number *'Chala jaa re name chalakte hue'* was also scissored out of the final print. So was '*Akele mujhe chod ke kahan chale*'. Lata Mangeshkar's melodious '*Ai ishk ye sab duniya waley bekar ki batein*' and '*Hamein kaash tumse mohabbat na hoti*' were first excised but later added. Unfortunately, in the new colour version, these two songs have been chopped out. Though *Mughal-e-Azam* buffs missed seeing such beautiful songs in colour, it seemed a wise decision to have the film pace as the songs were likely to hamper the tempo of the scenes where they were inserted. Probably, K. Asif too might have eliminated the said songs intially for the same reason. The music of *Mughal-e-Azam* was an unqualified success and touched everybody — the common man, eclectic music lovers, critics and journalists. Yet, to everybody's great surprise, it lost the *Filmfare* award for Best Music to *Dil Apna aur Preet Parai* for the year 1960. When J.C. Jain, the then editor-in-chief of *Filmfare* was asked about this, he replied, 'The music of *Mughal-e-Azam* was *ilmi* (intellectual) and that of *Dil Apna aur Preet Parai*, *filmi*.' What a strange reply!!

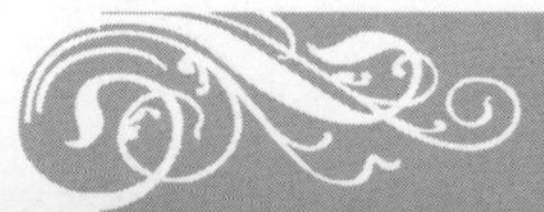

Unforgettable moments

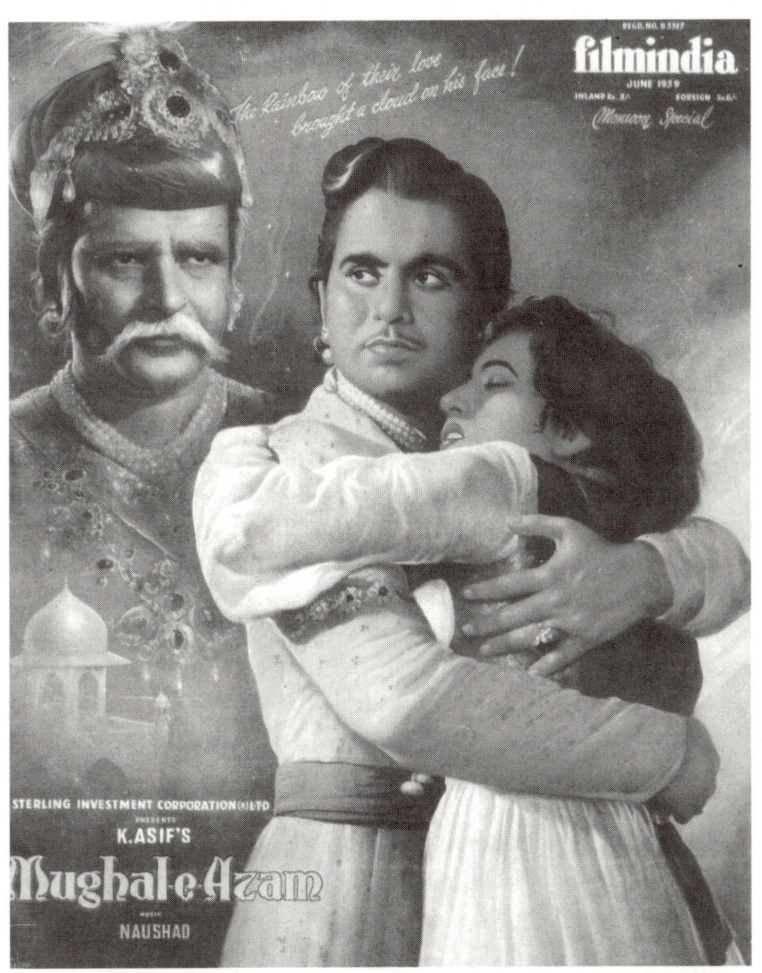

The cover of the June 1959 issue of Film India.

The erotic undercurrent, the silence and the song contribute to make it a transcendental moment in cinema.'

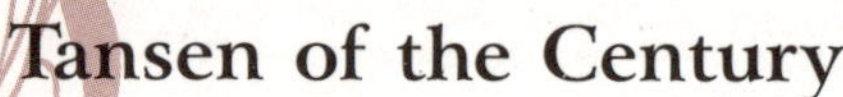

Tansen of the Century

What is it that makes a scene memorable? It could be the pleasure of watching a real life romance on screen or the imaginative manner in which a scene is enacted or written. Emperor Akbar had nine distinguished personalities in his court. They were known as the *Navratans,* each renowned for a particular skill — Raja Todar Mal for revenue and administration; Raja Birbal for his wit; Abul Fazl for literary talent; and so on. For music, it was Tansen. Asif wanted a unique voice to render Tansen's ragas in Akbar's darbar.

The most sensuous situation in *Mughal-e-Azam,* most critics and cinema lovers agree, is when the lovers meet secretly for the first time. Salim conveys the message to Anarkali through her sister Suraiya, '*Jab Tansen raga chedenge, tum mujh se milne chali aana,*' Naushad composed a classical number, '*Prem Jogan ban ke*' in raga Lalit and Sohni for the scene. The lovers would spend an entire night on the terrace of the palace, the notes signifying the transition to dawn, drawing out an erotic nuance. K. Asif, on Naushad's suggestion, wanted Ustad Bade Ghulam Ali Khan Saab to sing for this sequence as he was regarded as the 'Tansen of the century'. The problem was that the Ustad, a doyen of the Patiala gharana, never sang for movies. But Asif was adamant. 'He will sing for my film,' he swore.

Ustad Bade Ghulam Ali Khan, doing his Riyaz (practice).

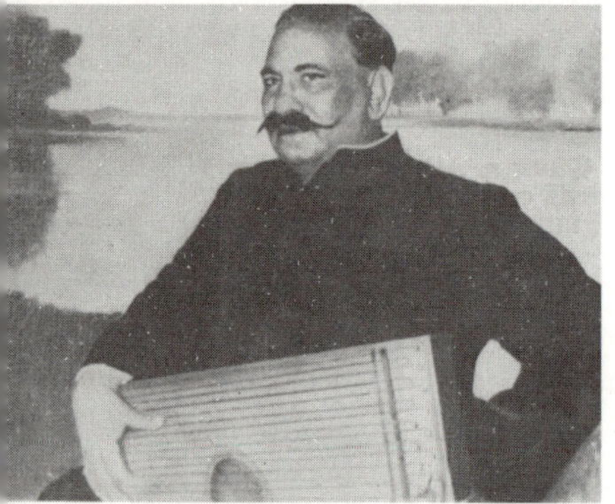

Bade Ghulam Ali Khan Saheb, born in 1902 at Kasur in the western part of Punjab (now Lahore), was known as the Tansen of modern India. He came to Bombay in 1924 and presented his rare art in

Vikramadittya Sangeet Parishad, held at Bombay University's convocation hall. The audience that evening included eminent artists of the era, namely, Ustad Fayyaz Hussain Khan, Ustad Alauddin Khan (guru of Pandit Ravi Shankar), and sarod player Ustad Hafiz Ali Khan (father of Ustad Amjad Ali Khan). It is on records that all these stalwarts were completely enthralled by Bade Ghulam Ali Khan Saheb's melodious rendition, and his voice and unique style unfolded the most attractive and elaborate picture of raga Marwa. The ustad later composed some of the best khayals and thumris. His thumris, *'Yaad piya ki aayi', 'Terchi nazar ke baan,'* and *'Kaati hai birah ki raat'*, are still popular with enthusiasts though recorded half a century ago. Music was not a profession for him; it was his way of life.

Dr Susheela Mishra, an authority on the subject, describes his ability to create emotions through music and communicate the same to the listeners. She writes, 'When he would sing "*Kali Ghata Ghir Aayee Re Sajni*", the audience could almost hear the rumbling of thunder, see the flashes of lightning, and share the agony of the separated one.' In the ustad's vision, ragas seemed to have a strong bond with nature. Prof B.R. Deodhar, in his book *Pillars of Hindustani Music,* reminisces an evening

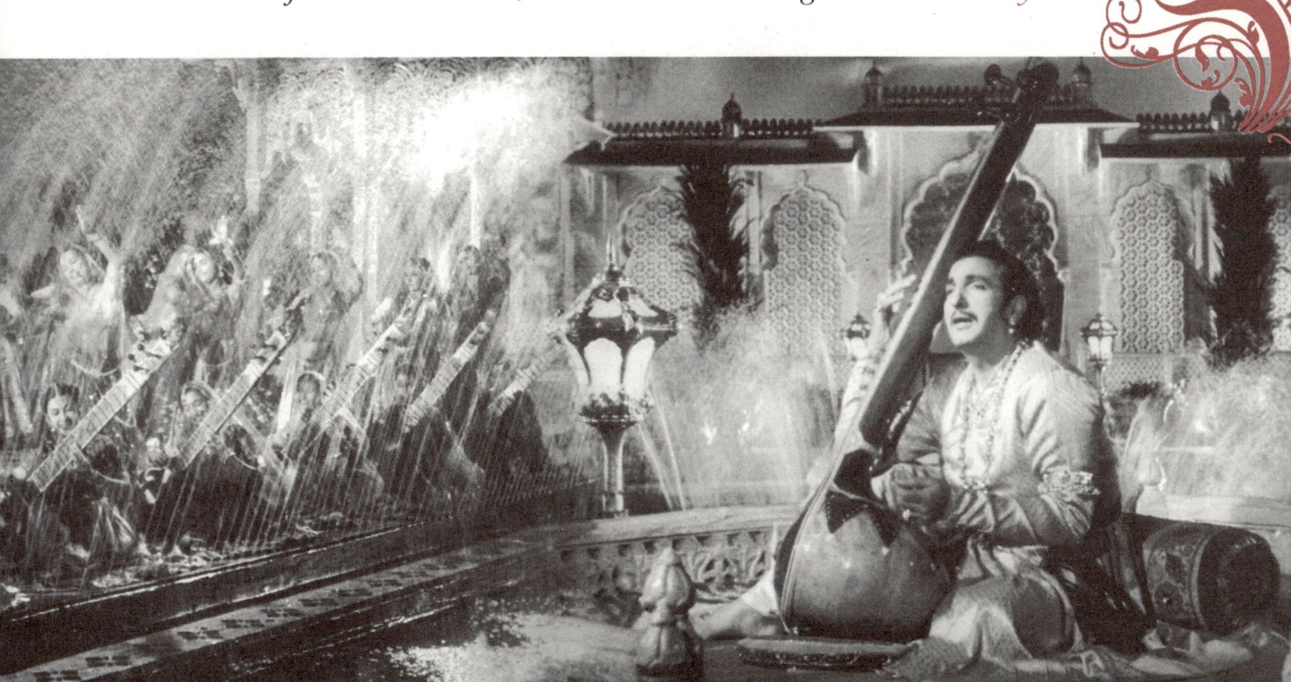

'Shubh din aayo re'.

in 1945 when the ustad would walk along Chowpatty beach to watch the sun set over the vast Arabian sea. One such evening, the ustad, accompanied by the professor, watched the last red rays of the sun setting over the western skies, and the sea reflecting this in the vast spread of water. Transfixed by the scene, he told the professor: 'This is the precise hour to sing raga Marwa, because the hour of sunset is the most fascinating time when lovers, who have been separated, begin to wonder how they are to spend the night in loneliness. The same happens to people who do not have a roof over their heads. The day passes by itself, but at night they start worrying about finding a shelter..... I am of the opinion that the chief aim of Marwa is to portray this anxiety or uncertainty.'

G.N. Joshi also observed the same relationship between nature and the ustad's mood. He writes in his book *Down Melody Lane:* 'The exhibition of nature's strength always inspired Khan Saab. One evening, during the monsoon, I had the good fortune to find Bade Ghulam Ali in a very exuberant mood. From the balcony of his flat on Malabar Hill one could see the turbulent sea with its rising waves, and he gave vocal expression to his feelings in a number of variations of raga Malhar; his *gumak taan* on every clap of thunder seemed as if a *jugalbandi* show was in progress between nature and this great man.'

He is credited with the introduction of the magnificent sur mandal, an instrument which has become popular today with leading vocalists. Though a staunch Shia Muslim, he had no problem singing the Vishnu *mantra* 'Hari om Tatsat' or 'Deva Deveshwara Mahadev', his famous drut khayal in raga Bhupali. In this way he exemplified the practical secularity of Hindustani classical music. He was bestowed with many

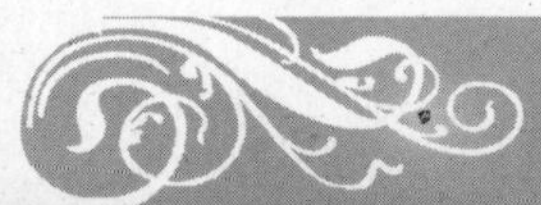

honorary awards, including the Padma Bhushan. He was also elected as a fellow of the Sangeet Natak Academy. The Vishwa Bharati University conferred on him a Doctor of Literature (Ph.D.) degree. Music lovers feted him with titles like Aftab-e-Mausiqui, Sangeet Samrat, Sur Devta and of course, the Tansen of Modern India.

The ustad was fond of good food and was a good cook. Bhuna chicken, mutton paya and karela mutton with scotch were some of his favourite combinations, with lots of sweets to top it all. His gastronomic indulgences were perhaps responsible for a weight problem in later years. It was difficult to believe that this huge man, with a walrus moustache, was capable of producing soul-stirring notes that would enchant generations of music lovers. The mellifluous voice was finally silenced in 1968 by a fatal heart attack at the age of sixty-six.

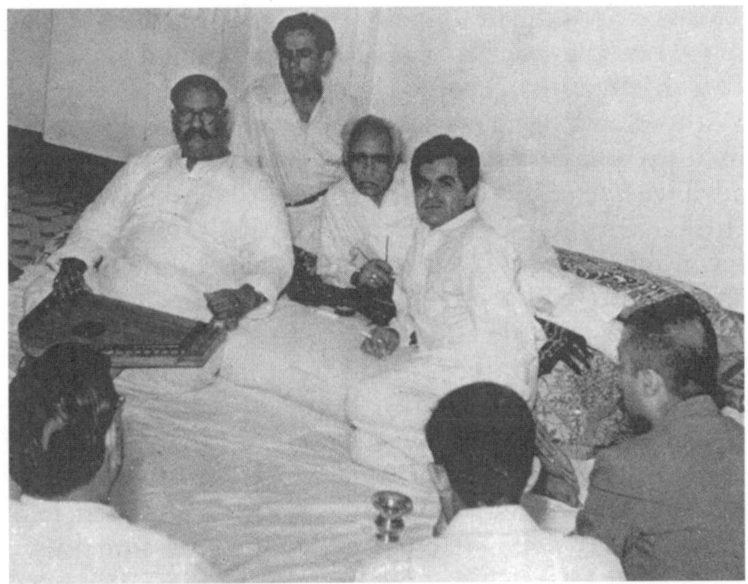

Ustad Bade Ghulam Ali Khan, Dilip Kumar and friends.

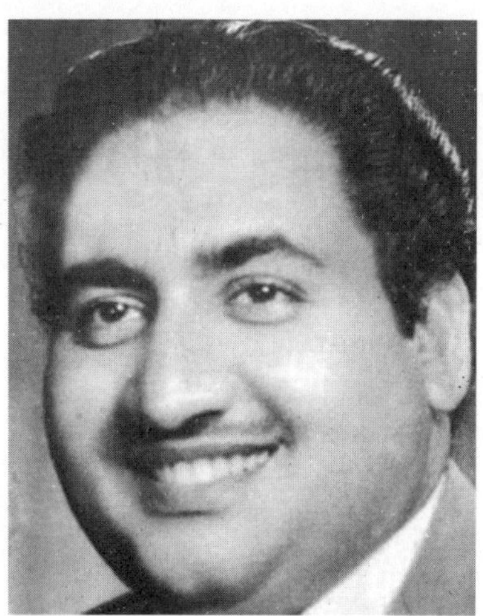

Zinada baad Ai Mohabbat Zinda Baad...,
Mohammad Rafithe velvet voice of India.

Asif wanted this great singer to perform in his film and asked Naushad to fix up a meeting. The two then drove down to Walkeshwar where the ustad resided. With due respect, Naushad informed him about the purpose of their visit. Khan Saheb replied that he was not interested in films. 'Even an *alaap* can't be done justice to in three minutes,' he commented. 'But this song cannot be sung by anyone else,' Asif reacted. This annoyed the ustad. '*Ye kaun badtameez hain?*' (Who is this rude man?), he chided. Asif was unrepentant. 'Khan Saheb, only you can sing...name your price.'

Asif's talk about money further infuriated the maestro. But Naushad managed to pacify him and introduced Asif as the director of *Mughal-e-Azam*. Bade Ghulam Ali Khan took Naushad aside and said, 'I will quote a price that he won't be able to afford; he will go back disappointed.'

Khan Saheb then told Asif, 'So, you want to know my price? I will charge twenty-five thousand rupees.' This was an unheard of sum for singers that time. Even renowned playback artistes like Mohammad Rafi and Lata Mangeshkar charged only four hundred rupees. Without batting an eyelid, Asif put ten thousand rupees in front of the artiste, saying *'Aap to anmol hain, ye* advance *hai, baki* recording *ke baad (*You are invaluable, this is the advance. I will pay the rest after the recording*).*' So, it was that the ustad was burdened with an unwanted film assignment with a director he did not know anything about.

On the stipulated date, Khan Saheb reported to Mehboob Studios on the dot. Immediately a rug, sheets, pillows and cushions were arranged and the recording studio was transformed into a *baithak*. Mollified, the ustad assumed his position and launched into a *gumak taan*. 'It's too heavy. I'd like something

softer,' Asif suggested. The maestro flared up in anger. He would sing only after viewing the scene, he proclaimed.

But the scene had already been shot. So, Asif had to hastily edit it overnight to arrange a special preview. After watching Madhubala and Dilip Kumar enact the love play, a pleased ustad responded, 'Anarkali *kafi khoobsurat hai, Shahzada bhi khoobsurat hai (*Anarkali is quite beautiful, so is the prince*)*.' He then returned to the studio's *baithak* and cheerfully rendered the song four times over with unflagging interest.

Thus, one of the finest sequences of the film was created: Lovelorn Madhubala gets ready at a dressing table to meet her lover. Adorned and ebullient with desire, shy and hesitant, she moves; the rhythmic sound of her *payal* (ornament for the feet), coupled with the soulful classical song '*Prem jogan ban ke sundari, pee ki oar chalee...*' playing in the background, captivated the viewers. The romantic interlude between her and Dilip Kumar, as he strokes her face using a feather, is simply enthralling. Madhubala smiles sensuously at every touch of the feather. Dilip Kumar's intense eyes convey the yearning. The erotic undercurrent, the silence, and the song contribute to make this a transcendental moment. This sequence, about 200-feet long, which does not contain a single dialogue or physical contact, makes for the most romantic visual in Indian cinema.

After the sensual *Prem Jogan..*, the ustad was cajoled to render yet another song '*Shubh din ayo'*, which Tansen sings at the request of Jodhabai to drive away the battlefield dust and cannon blasts from the mind of Prince Salim, who is returning from war after fourteen years. This segment cost Asif yet another Rs 25,000! Bade Ghulam Ali Khan Saab's voice contributed immensely to immortalise these sequences in *Mughal-e-Azam*.

There is a scene in the film between Maharani Jodhabai and Salim where he is willing to give up everything, including throne of Hindustan for her. He says,

'Mujhe apne kimti Hindustan mein se ek zarra tak na dein. Main Maharani Jodha ke jaan-o-maal ka sadqa aur saltanat-e- Akbari ki khairaat mangta hoon, mujhe Anarkali *bheek mein de dein...'*

(Please do not give me a penny from your precious Hindustan! But I beg of you . . . just give me Anarkali as charity of the great Akbar's kingdom and alms of Queen Jodha's life.)

His eyes full of tears, desperation in his voice, an expression of longing and helplessness, together with the lilting Urdu words, make the scene memorable.

Much like *Devdas,* Salim is a romantic at heart, who is sent far from home, away from the comforts of the palace, at the age of ten. After years of hardships on the battlefield, his melancholic temperament does not change. He defines his sword as 'Shakh-e-gul' (shoot of the flower) that amuses his friend Durjan Singh. He expresses his astonishment in the following words:

'Jo mizaj choudah baras tak jung ki varsha mein nahata raha, woh aaj bhi kavita mei racha hua hai...'

(Your nature is still embellished by poetic thoughts despite being nurtured for fourteen years by war and violence . . .)

To this, Dilip Kumar gives a fitting reply:
'Omar Khayyam *ki rubaiyee ko sunehri warq ke bajaye agar pathreeli zameen par likh diya jaye to kya uske maani jaaenge badal?*

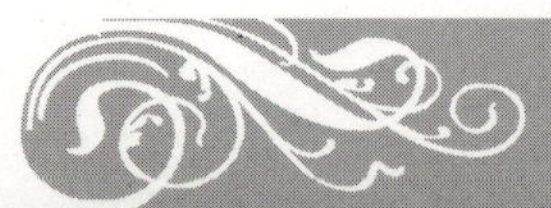

(Would Omar Khayyam's verse change its meaning if written on a rough stone instead of a golden leaf?)'

Dilip Kumar had no role model for Prince Salim. He once said:

'When I was playing Prince Salim, my style was totally different. I had done roles which had an air of informality around them. I could not think of anything, nor was there any film running, from where I could go pick up some mannerisms. So, I put on the costume and requested Asif to make a set. He pitched a tent, and the first scene he did was when Akbar comes in to try and make peace with his son. And I still feel it was one of its best scenes. I put on the costume – eighty pounds of steel amour — and was moving around in that for three or four days to get the royal feel.' This scene, undoubtedly, is a great example where emotions and drama reach new heights, making the imperial Akbar emerge as a caring father. He tries to conciliate Salim, '*Shahanshah roya nahin kartey Shaikhu...Ghareeb baap ki aankho mein ansoo hain*.... (Kings don't wail.... there are tears in the poor father's eyes...)

Although the first half of the film is slow drama, the lavishness mesmerises the viewer. Moreover, the powerful dialogue delivery of the actors adds to the imagination of the already dazzled audience. For instance, the scene between Prithviraj Kapoor and Dilip Kumar, after Anarkali openly declares her love in '*Pyar kiya to darna kya*', is a fine example of the subtle histrionic capabilities of the two legends.

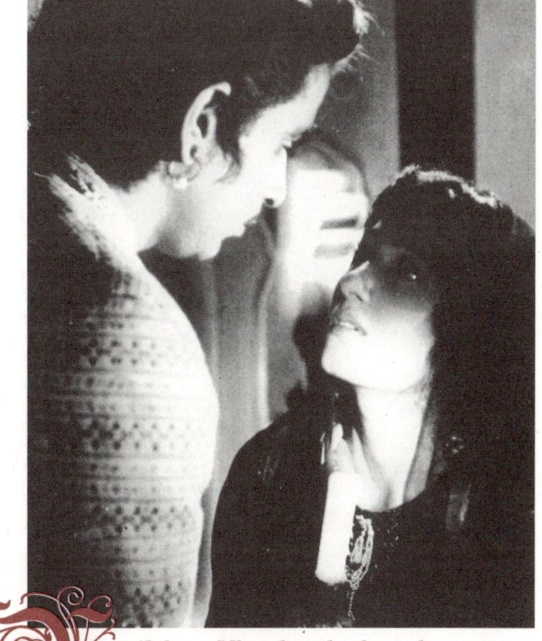

'Main Khwabon ko haqeekat mein badal doonga.'

Akbar declares '*Takhliya*' (A royal way of saying 'leave me alone'). Everybody leaves except Salim, and this is followed by the famous confrontational scene between the father and son. Akbar is anguished and tells Salim:

'Tumhari moujoodgi nafarmani ki daleel hai'

(Your presence proves your disobedience)
Salim ignores his father's displeasure and asks:

'....Aaj Zill-e-Ilahi ko apne zulm aur merey zabt ki ek hadd muqarrar karni hogi'

(Today, Zill-e-Ilahi must set a dividing line between my tolerance and his tyranny.)

Akbar roars:
'Agar tumhari aarzooyen ek kaneez hain, ek bandi hain, to sari zindagi isi tarah zabt karna hoga'.

(If your desire is just an ordinary courtesan, a slave girl, you will have to suffer like this for the rest of your life.)

The scene where Madhubala snuffs the candle with the palm of her hand is also a rare example of cinematic beauty, where romance speaks volumes. Dilip Kumar utters his lines with his usual mastery: *'Main tumhari aankhon me apnee mohabbat ka iqrar dekhna chahta hun'.* (I want to see the approval of my love in your eyes).

She replies in a choked voice that reflected her real life dilemma: *'Inhen na dekhiye, Shahzadey! In mein ek kaneez ki sehmi huyei hasraton ke siwa kuch nahin...'* (Please don't see them, O Prince! There is nothing but a fearful hopelessness in my eyes).

Dilip Kumar interrupts: *'Bhool jao ke tum ek kaneez ho....'* (Forget that you are just a courtesan).

Madhubala pleads in a manner that expresses her eternal love for her 'shahzada': *'Meri ankhon se mere*

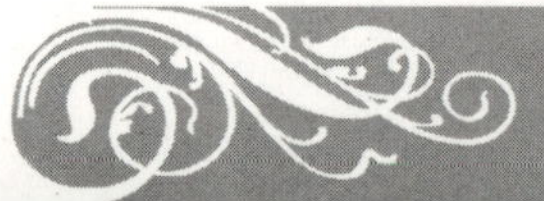

khwab na chiniye shahzaday... main mar jaongi'. (Please do not take away the dreams from my eyes! I'll die!)

She is not just performing in this scene but in fact seeking to unravel the deeper mysteries of life and a total consummation of love. The beauty of the scene lies in her helplessness as she appeals to an insular prince, who seems to belong to an ethereal world.

Then there is a court room scene where the accused Salim is asked to present Anarkali before the court. This highly dramatic sequence between an imperial father and a rebellious son was never seen before. Salim flatly refuses to meet Akbar's demands:

> Akbar: *Tumne ek adna kaneez ki khatir Vali-Ehdi ke aizaz ko badnam kiya, shahi ehkaam ki toheen kee, mahakma-e-fouj ke motamid aur wafadar Rajput Durjan Singh ko ghaddari par uksaya..aur Anarkali ko farar karaya, Shahanshah-e-waqt ki foujon ko vargalya..aur baghavat kee.*
>
> (You disgraced the status of Vali-Ehed (legal heir), for the love of an ordinary slave girl, abused royal mandates, incited the trustworthy and faithful soldier Rajput Durjan Singh to rebel, made Anarkali's escape possible, instigated the royal armies to revolt.. and . . . committed the crime of waging war against the state.)
>
> *. . . Yeh tamam ilzamat wapas liye jasakte hain, tumhari tamam nadaniyan aur nafarmaniyan maaf keejasakti hain, aur hum ek bar phir tum par meherbaan hosaktey hain..Agar tum anar kali wapas kardo.*
>
> (All these charges may be withdrawn, all your disobedience and foolishness may be forgiven, and I may bestow upon you my kindness once again.... if you just return Anarkali)

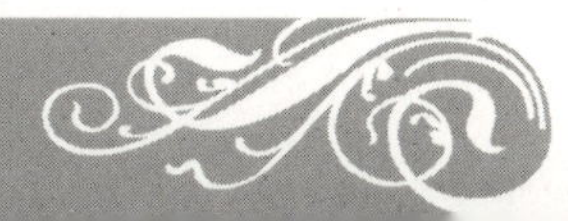

Salim: *Taki aap use saza-e-Mout desaken?*

(So that you execute her with death sentence?)

Akbar: *Yaqeenan* (Certainly)

Salim: *To phir aadil Shahnshah ko, apni hukumat mein un narfarman parvanon ko bhi saza dena chahiye jo shama par nisar hojate hain, phulon par mandrate huei us bhanvre ko bhi qaid karlena chahiye jo mohabbat key meethey raag gata hai and nadi key machalte huye us paani ko bhi rok dena chahiye jo samandar ki aghosh me apna namo-nishan khot deta hai...*

(Then the 'honest' king must also punish the obstinate and fluttering moths, living within his territory who sacrifice their lives for shama (candle), he must arrest the buzzing bee too, who hangs around flowers, humming love songs, and he must also check the flowing water of the river, yearning to vanish into the ocean.)

Akbar: *Yeh adalat deewane jazbat me ubalti, mohabbat ki daleelein sunna nahi chahti...Anarkali chahti hai.*

(This court is not interested in insignificant arguments of love tales ... it demands Anarkali instead!)

Salim:...*Wo main dena nahin chahta*

(That I cannot give)

Akbar: *To phir Nasle-Taimur ke jah-o-jalal ki qasam! Tum is azimusshan takht-o-taj se hamesha ke liye mehroom kardiye jaoge.*

(I swear upon the glory and dominance of Taimur's blood-line, you shall be deprived of this majestic

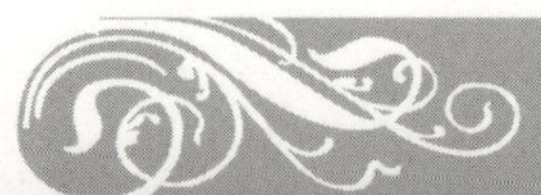

crown and throne forever … [Taimur was the great warrior and forefather of Mughals]

Salim: *Mujhe manzoor hai, lekin wo takht manzoor nahin jis ke payey Anarkali ke janaze par rakhe hon…who taj jis ki kalghi mei khud mera hi dil pevast ho mujhe manzoor nahin.*

(That is acceptable to me … but I don't accept a throne whose foundation is laid on the funeral of Anarkali; the crown whose crest is adorned by my own wounded heart is not acceptable to me)

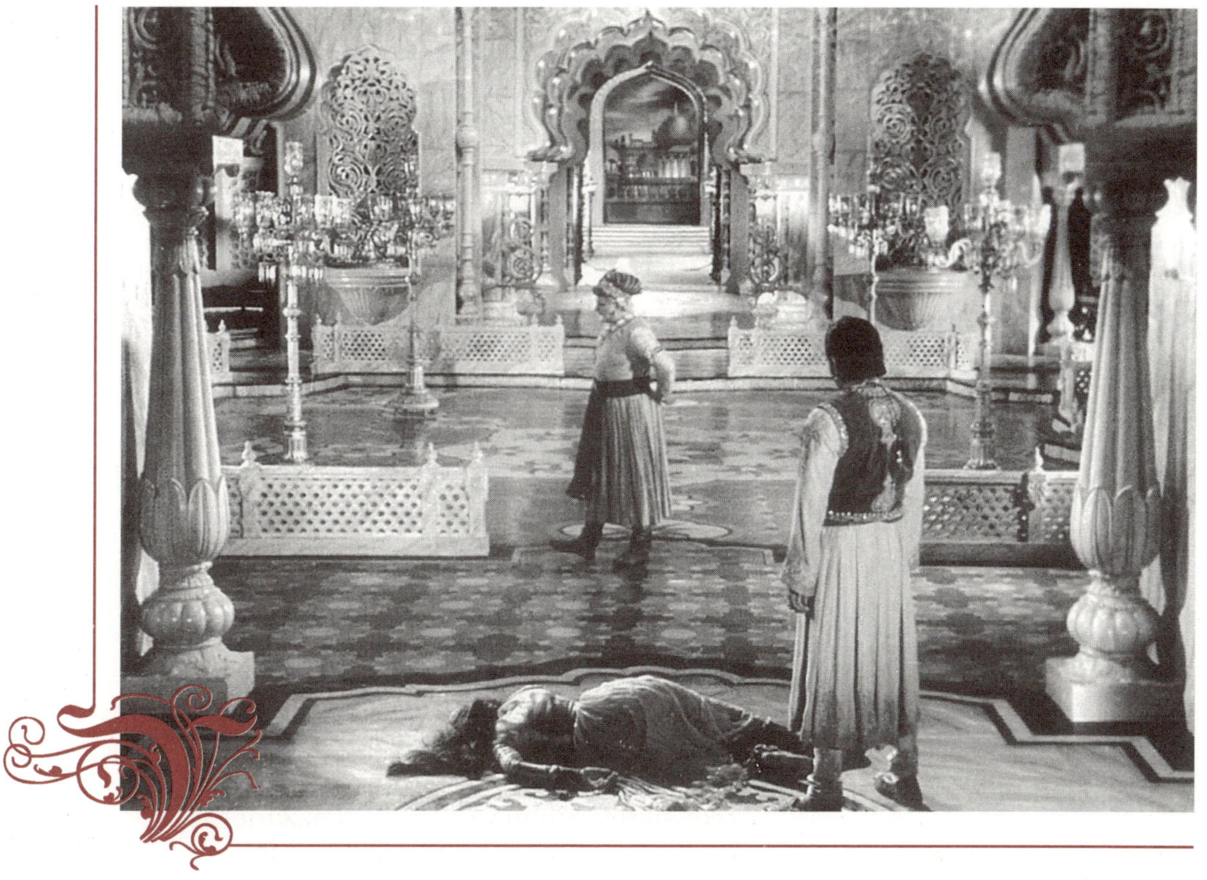

Akbar: *Maloom huaa.. tum Mughlon ka taj pighlakar ek raqqasa ke pairon ki pazeb banana chahte ho, tum Hindostan ke muqaddas takht par ek haseen londi ko nachana chahte ho…*

(Obviously you intend to prepare a *pazeb* [ornament of feet] for a nautch-girl, by melting the crown of the great Mughals; you want to desecrate the throne of India by making a slave girl dance on it . . .)

Salim: *Aur aap…is bharey darbar mei apni honei wali bahu ko zaleel karna chahtey hain . . .*

(And you are abusing your 'would be' daughter-in-law in this packed court room.)

Akbar: *Khamosh!* (shut up!)

Salim: *Agar shahnshah insaaf ke parde mein apni shikast ka intiqam hi lena chahta hai to usey Anarkali nahin mileygi.....Use apne betey ki jaan lena hogi...'*

(If the king seeks revenge for his defeat on the pretext of 'justice', Anarkali will not be given to him....He will have to kill his son.)

And, Akbar proclaims the death sentence for his son.

Anarkali's famous last words are perhaps indelibly etched in everyone's memories: '

Ab janaze ko rukhsat ki ijazat dejiye...'

(Please allow the funeral to leave now).

She pauses for a while and says:
'Zill-e-Ilahi ki in beyshumar bakhshishon ke badley yeh kaneez Jalaluddin Mohammad Akbar ko apna khoon maaf karti hai.'

(For all the 'kindness' that the emperor has bestowed, I forgive him for my murder).

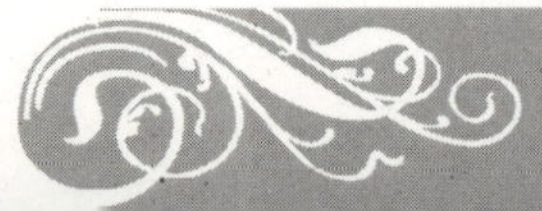

D-Day

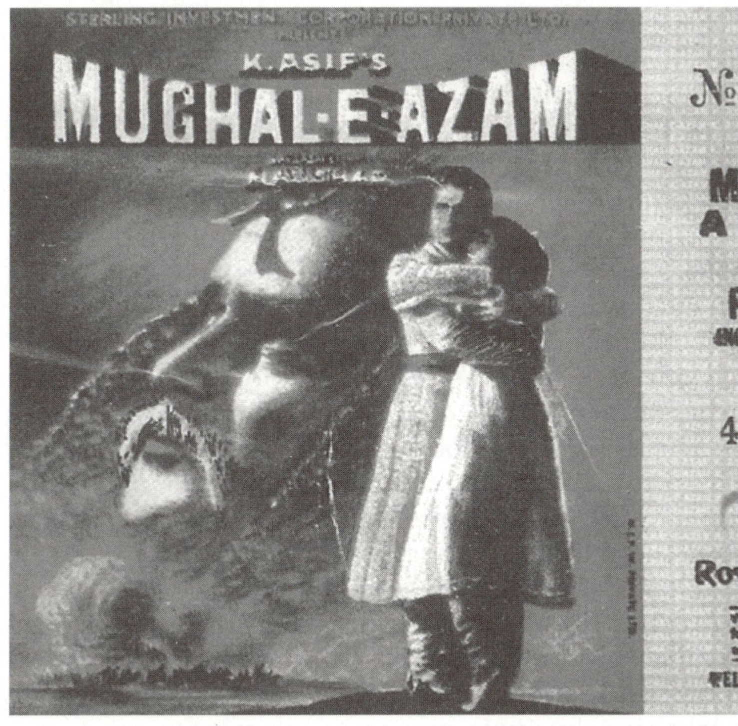

For the first hour, there were mocking whispers. And at the end of the nineteenth reel came the verdict — a complete disaster!

The publicity material for the film also set new standards. The images of dusty battlefields and Dilip Kumar, Madhubala and Prithviraj Kapoor in ornate costumes were mounted on lobby cards in large sizes varying from fifteen to twenty-three feet. The tickets, too, had an image of Madhubala and Dilip Kumar embracing each other, capturing a dramatic moment from the film. Booking opened ten weeks in advance and the tickets sold at fantastic prices. The stall price of Maratha Mandir those days was one rupee thirty paise, but for *Mughal-e-Azam* they were sold in the black market at a whopping one hundred rupees.

Such was the clamour for tickets that people came with their bedspreads to stay overnight in the queue outside the booking windows. Some enterprising fisherwomen endured the long hours of waiting in queues to sell them door-to-door for handsome profits. The army costumes of Prithviraj Kapoor and Dilip Kumar were kept in show windows on display for years after the release at Maratha Mandir.

Such was the clamour for tickets that people came with their bedspreads to stay overnight in the queue outside the booking windows.

Finally, the day everyone had waited for arrived. On 5 August 1960, K. Asif premiered his dream project at Bombay's Maratha Mandir. The theatre was decorated and lit with spotlights. The viewers were movie moghuls, celebrities, business magnates, glamorous stars and politicians. Raj Kapoor flew down from Czechoslovakia; Shammi Kapoor cut short a visit to the Far East. Swarnlata, Nazir and Shiraz Ali Hakeem came from Pakistan.

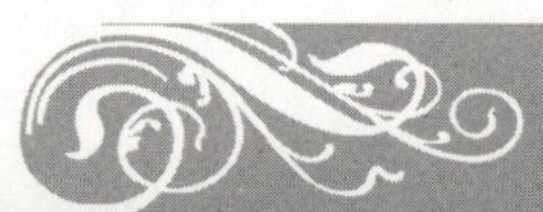

Saira Bano, who was then a great fan of Dilip Kumar, recounted to NDTV her experience at the premiere. She had attended it at Maratha Mandir with her mother, Naseem Bano, only to have a look at her favourite actor. She apparently took six days to prepare herself for the grand occasion, but was disappointed when Dilip Kumar failed to turn up because of his bitter relations with K. Asif over his sister's marriage.

The invitation cards were printed in a *shahi* (royal) manner with the title, 'Akbarnama' printed on them. According to cameraman Mathur, 'The release was a star-studded gathering with cars parked bumper to bumper, and only those who possessed the royal invitation with the seal of the Akbarnama were allowed entry.'

There was a huge forty-feet cut-out of Prithviraj Kapoor as Akbar outside the theatre. The absence of Dilip Kumar and Madhubala was sorely felt. Dilip Kumar did not attend it due to his tiff with Asif, while Madhubala never attended premieres on her father's instructions.

Cameraman R. D. Mathur brought the print of the film on a decorated and bedecked elephant, and at 9 p.m. sharp, the celebrity audience settled down in hushed silence to watch the greatest love story of all times unfold.

For the first hour, there were mocking whispers, '*boring hai*.' And, at the end of the nineteenth reel came the verdict — a complete disaster!

Shapoorji Pallonji recalled industrywalas' talk about his wealth being embezzled by K. Asif. Prithviraj Kapoor, who had devoted himself for the last ten years to bring Akbar alive on celluloid, was crushed. Everyone associated with the film was shocked and dejected. Only one man remained unmoved and disinterested: Asif himself.

Everyone associated with the film was shocked and dejected. Only one man remained unmoved and disinterested: Asif himself.

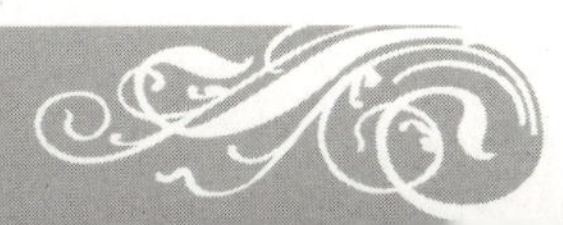

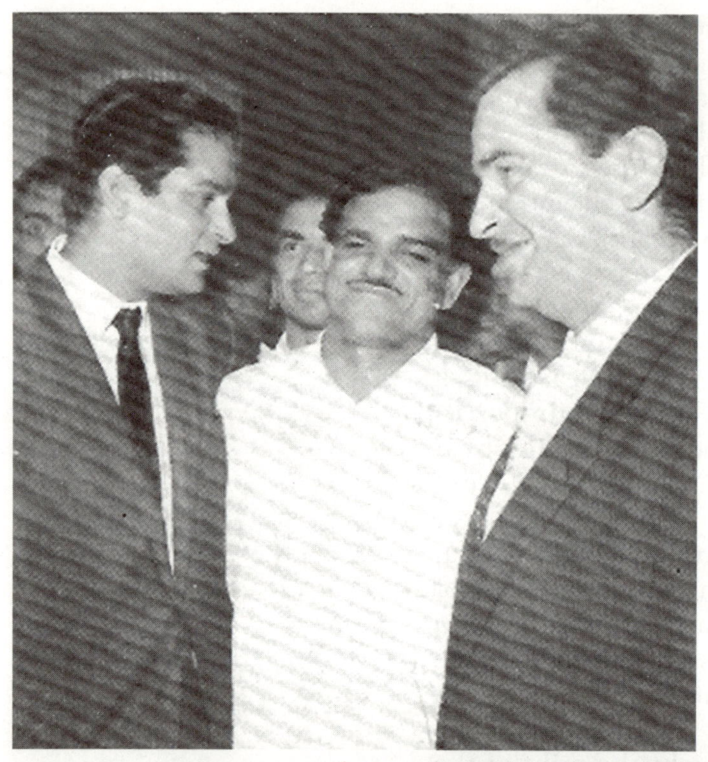

The viewers were movie moghuls, celebrities, business magnates, glamorous stars and politicians. Raj Kapoor flew down from Czechoslovakia; Shammi Kapoor cut short a visit to the Far East. Swarnlata, Nazir and Shiraz Ali Hakeem came from Pakistan.

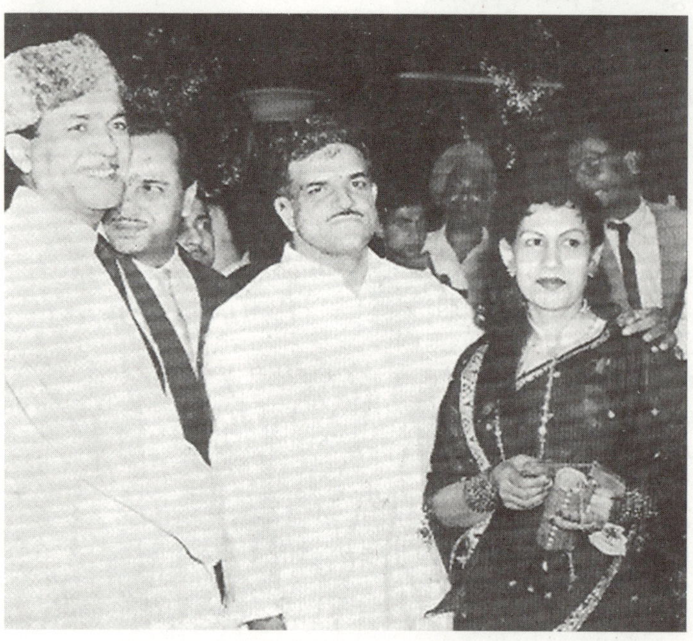

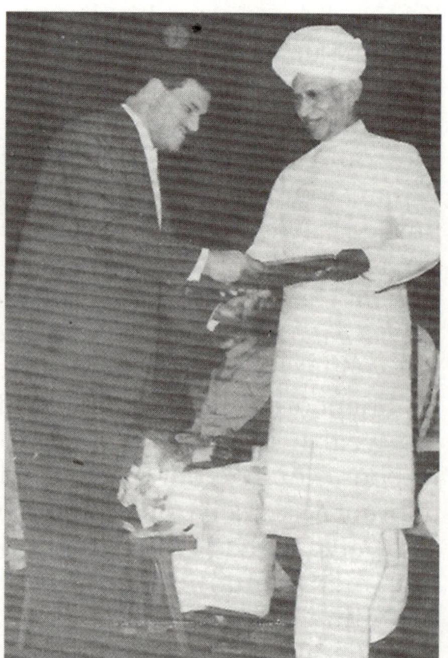

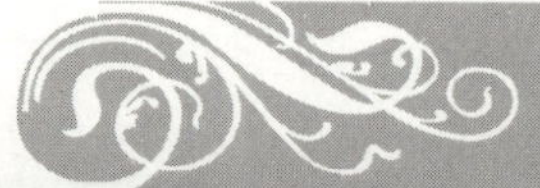

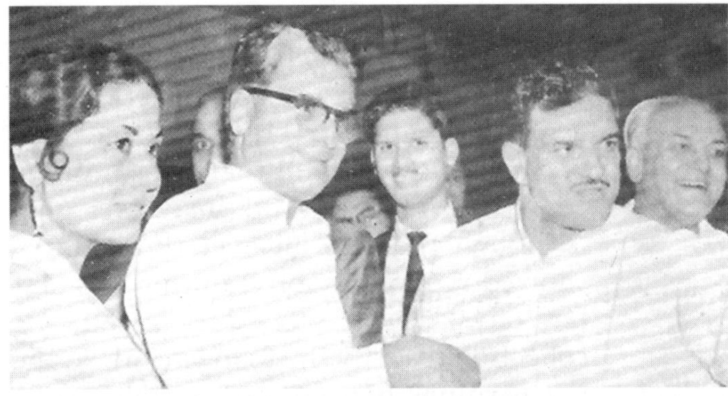

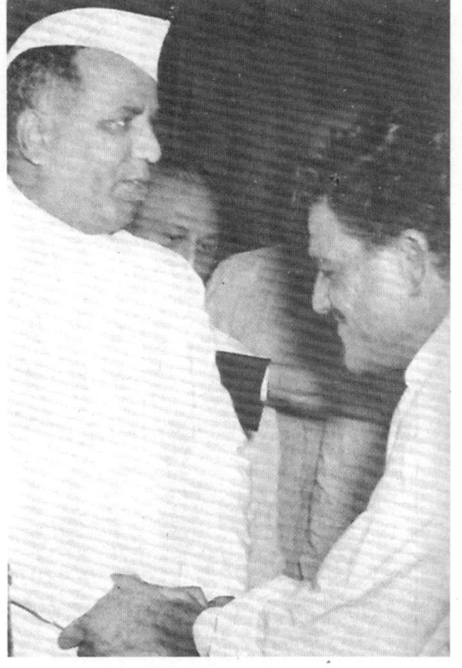

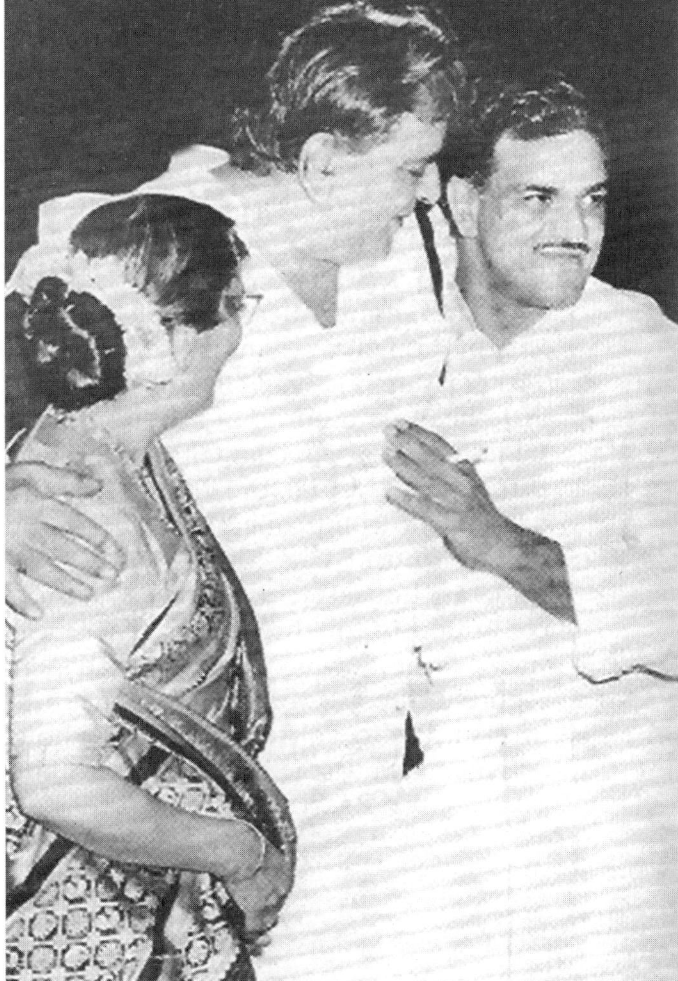

Clockwise from right:
V. B Chavan, the then chief minister of Maharashtra congratulated K. Asif; Prithviraj Kapoor with his wife and K. Asif; Meena Kumari, Kamal Amrohi and K. Asif.

Facing page clockwise from right:
K. Asif recieving president's Silver medal; Nazir, Pran, K. Asif and Nazir's wife Swarnlata at the premiere, 1960; Shammi Kapoor, K. Asif and Raj Kapoor at the premiere, 1960.

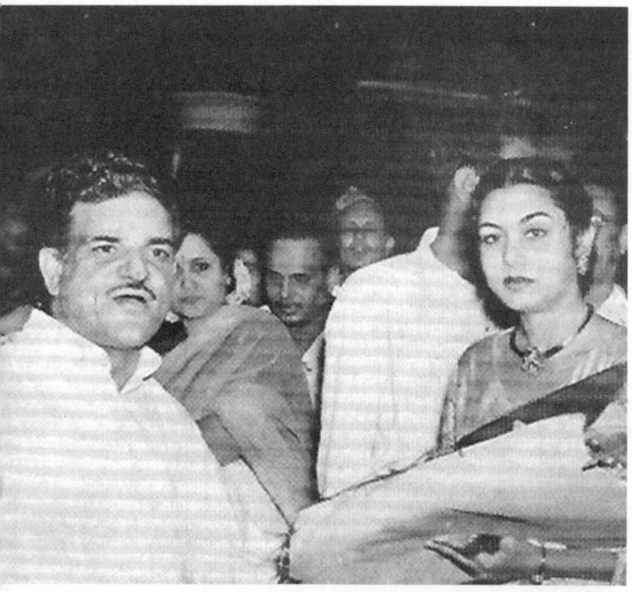

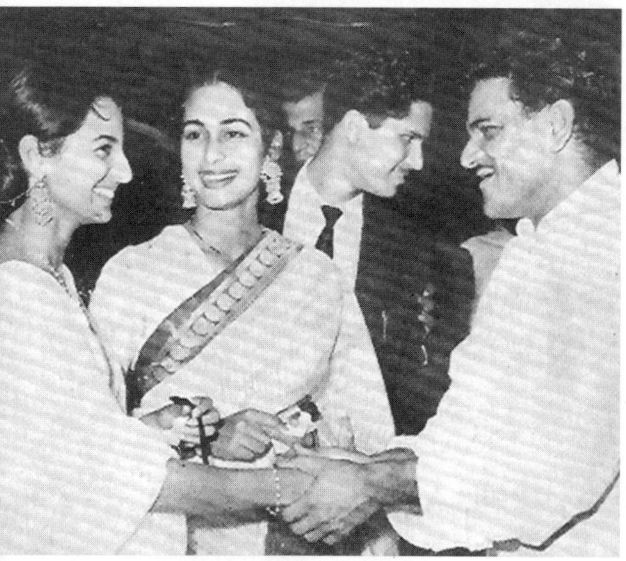

Top: *K. Asif and Nimmi.*
Above: *K. Asif, Nutan and Tanuja.*

He organised a party at his place after the show and urged his associates to give up their worries and anxieties. Asif assured them that the film would pick up within a week and there was nothing to worry about. And he was right! Although theatres all over the country showed a poor response during the first few days, as the week progressed, the collection rose. By the following week, the net earnings had crossed an impressive figure of Rs 40 lakh.

Finally, there was a smile on Shapoorji's face as the cash counters overflowed with collections amounting to three crore and fifty lakhs, which would be equal to more than three hundred and fifty crores today. *Mughal-e-Azam* proved to be the biggest blockbuster ever produced in India.

It ran houseful at Delhi's Golden Cinema for more than sixty-five weeks. Tickets were not available unless booked at least three months in advance. From Jama Masjid to Golcha Cinema, crowds thronged to watch the film. The only people who complained were the traffic police around the cinema halls. The film ran houseful in Maratha Mandir continuously for three years. There was such a fan-following that the newspapers reported the case of a man from the rural interiors who sold off his household belongings and reached Bombay to buy a ticket for Rs 200 in black. Another claimed he had seen the movie fifty-seven times and had memorised the dialogues from the first line, '*Main Hindustan Hoon*', to the last frame.

Such was the craze that many came from neighbouring countries to watch the magnum opus. After the war with Pakistan, as relations between the two countries worsened, there was also a ban on the export of Indian films. It is said that in 1976, on the day the movie was shown on Doordarshan television network, all the TV sets in Lahore, which could catch the signals beamed by Amritsar DD, were tuned to the film. Such was the fascination that all flights from Karachi to Lahore were booked in advance for eight days.

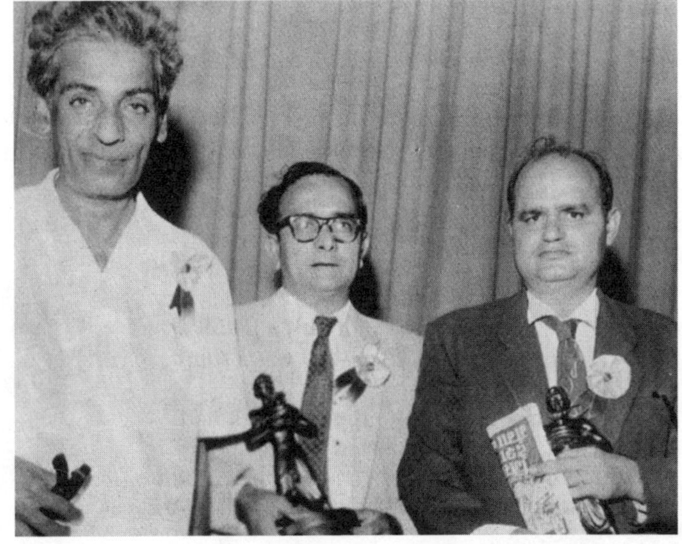

(l to r): Film editor Dharamveer, cameraman, R.D. Mathur and art director M.K. Sayyed.

Mughal-e-Azam bagged *Filmfare's* Best Film award for 1960, apart from a string of other awards that included Best Dialogue and Best Cinematography. The film also won the President's silver medal for the year 1960. *Filmfare* published a review that said:

'It is the work of a creative team drawn from different spheres of the art world. Mr Asif has utilised the best available talent, to give the Indian screen one of its most memorable and spectacular films .... a tribute to the imagination, hard work and lavishness of its maker... For its grandeur, its beauty, and the performance of the artists, it should be a landmark in Indian films.'

Reactions from the Film Industry

'...the intensity of love between Madhubala and Dilip Kumar came through beautifully. She was gorgeous, he was royal...'

Each scene in *Mughal-e-Azam* has lent itself to nostalgia. There are numerous fans of this landmark film, including politicians, scholars, professors, scientists, journalists and film stars. Opinions expressed by some of them on the love epic are reproduced here:

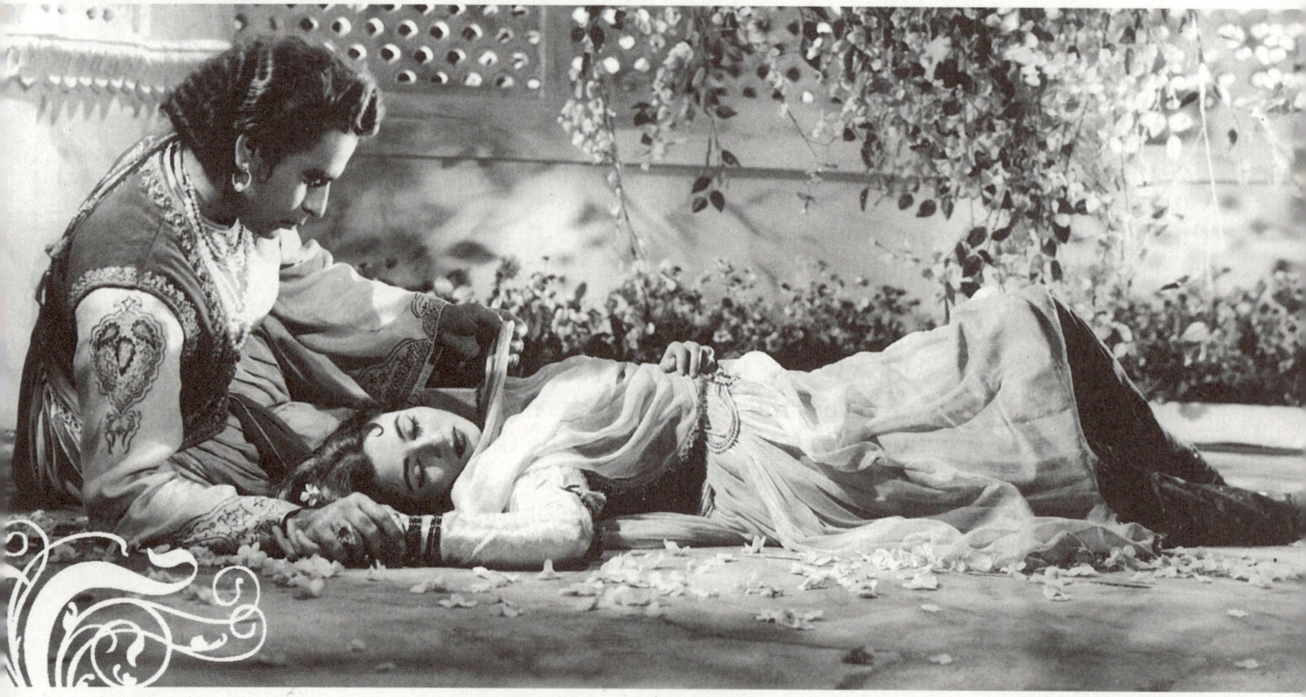

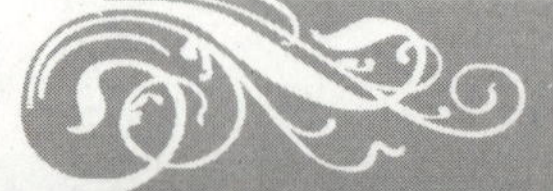

Saira Bano

I will never forget the scene when Jodhabai (played by Durga Khote) wants to set her eyes on her son Salim, who has come home after years of separation due to battles fought to expand his father's empire. That scene will always be quoted by film historians, it will be quoted for the way Salim walks towards Jodhabai, the way he kneels with respect and looks at his mother; here is a man of steel with the softness of silk in his eyes.

Shammi Kapoor

...And, there is one film, beyond words, beyond description, which defies imagination given the time span it took in the making, *Mughal-e-Azam* ... This magnum opus had some of the most powerful love scenes ever portrayed.

Asha Parekh

My favourite film is *Mughal-e-Azam*. Oof! What a film! The intensity of love between Madhubala and Dilip Kumar came through beautifully. She was gorgeous, he was royal.

Raj Kumar Santoshi

The brief war scene was amazing, and to think in those days there wasn't much technology available. Most films were shot with a single camera. Despite the limitations ... the scene was excellently mounted and shot in a desert. The coordination between so many people on such a wide scale could not have been easy, but K. Asif shot even the minutest detail with amazing precision.

Rakesh Roshan

Mughal-e-Azam is my all-time favourite. A film like that comes once in a lifetime. It brought to the screen the

poetry in romance, and generation after generation has been experiencing its impact. I think it is the perfect film where you can see the maker's thought process in every frame. Brilliant performances added to the depth of the film...

Naushad

My favourite film undoubtedly is *Mughal-e-Azam*. I don't think anybody can make a film like that again. It was fictionalised history presented with a literary flavour, which has become a reference point in Indian cinema ... a musical tribute to 'Love'.

Anu Malik

Naushad Saheb's genius came into full play in this historical romance, and of course, it starred the ultimate beauty Madhubala, who sent my heart into a tizzy. *Pyaar kiya to darna kya* shot in the Sheesh Mahal, *Mohe panghat pe Nandlal* and *Prem jogan ban ke,* which had the most erotic scene with Dilip Kumar caressing Madhubala's face with a feather ... nothing else could have captured the emotions of that song more succinctly.

Rekha

One of my favourite and eternal love scenes has for years been the one between Dilip Kumar and Madhubala in *Mughal-e-Azam*. The manner in which Dilip Kumar strokes and caresses his beloved's face with a feather has strong sensuous overtones. The music of Bade Ghulam Ali Khan travels through the long tresses of Madhubala and touches the audience. The scene is worth it for the melting expression in Madhubala's eyes. The serenity and peace the love scene exudes, despite the undercurrent of tension, is unbelievable. There is sensuality in the whole ambience ... the *mogra* flowers

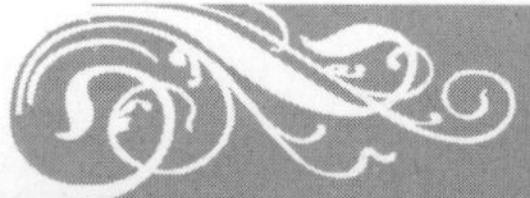

strewn all over, even though we know they are made of paper, somehow have a fragrance about them. The water fountain in the background has a system that is very suggestive...

N. Chandra

There might have been other films that had lovers rebelling against the establishment but none left an impact the way *Mughal-e-Azam* did. You can still experience that impact decades later. Perhaps this has as much to do with the extravagantly rich canvas as with the intense performance and the concept.

Anees Bazmee

I became a big K. Asif fan after watching the film more than one hundred and fifty times. Every time I watch the film, I learn something new from it. The last scene where there is a war over Anarkali is so well justified that you are convinced Madhubala is worth fighting for. The intensity of the romance between Dilip Kumar and Madhubala still touches me.

Urmila Matondkar

The best romantic scene I have ever seen is the legendary feather scene from *Mughal-e-Azam*. I am sure, it's the favourites of millions. The Dilip Kumar–Madhubala magic under the guidance of a maestro like K. Asif. Each time I see the film I see a different interpretation of the word romance.

Javed Akhtar

When I think of intense love scenes, only one actor comes to mind: Dilip Kumar. The scene like the one in *Mughal-e-Azam* where he and Madhubala spend a night together on the terrace...

Govind Nihalani

Mughal-e-Azam is the best film under the 'poetic romantic' genre which characterises the Mughal period and epitomises the extravagant style of that era. It brought to life a legend, contributing immensely to the concept of romance.

The Times of India, Bombay (after the release in 1960)

Never in the history of the Indian film industry has there been a motion picture, the release of which witnessed such mass hysteria. This fabulous production is a tribute to the patience, sincerity and almost religious fervour of its maker, the enigmatic K. Asif, whose weakness for splendour and spectacle, pomp and pageantry is no less than that of any Mughal emperor.

Sunday Standard, Bombay (in 1960)

Lyrical in its romance, patriotic in its purpose, enchanting in its entertainment value, panoramic in its photography, *Mughal-e-Azam* recaptures a glorious chapter from India's history.

Amrita Bazar Patrika, Calcutta (1960)

Asif's *Mughal-e-Azam* ... every bit a film worth one long wait, is an ideal marriage between spectacle and delicate drama.

The Hindu, Madras (1960)

Mounted on a lavish scale, with intense care to every detail, from the glass mirrors, stitched dresses of the dancing girls to the glass-studded Sheesh Mahal, the film is compellingly attractive.

'Alvida' Asif

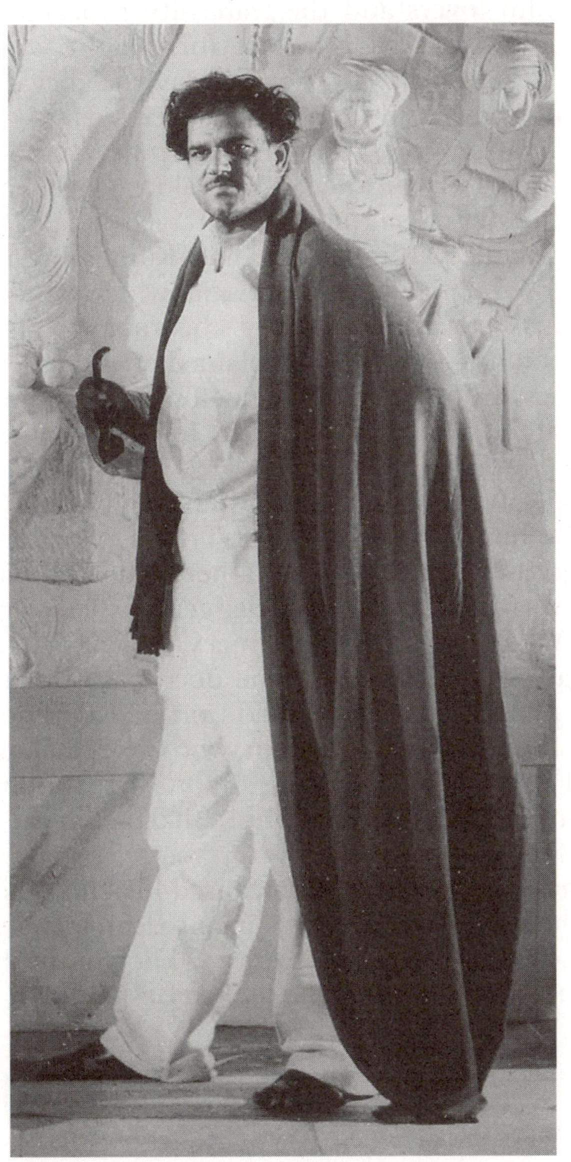

. . .turning to his wife,
he looked despairingly.
Even as death
stared at him,
'Love and God'
was on his mind.
'I leave behind
this film
for you to complete' . . .

K. Asif

It was on 9 March 1971 that K. Asif passed away, leaving film lovers and the fraternity shocked at his sudden demise. Asif was just forty-eight when he suffered a fatal heart attack on a day that began with his usual enthusiasm for a new project.

In the afternoon, at about 1.15 p.m., he had met Dilip Kumar, his brother-in-law, along with Sanjeev Kumar, the star of *Love and God*. After a couple of hours, Asif and Sanjeev Kumar left Dilip Kumar's residence and returned to Sanjeev Kumar's flat which was located close by. Asif retired to Sanjeev's bedroom to rest.

At about 3.45 p.m. he complained of uneasiness and a heaviness in his chest. Two doctors were summoned immediately. The pain subsided for some time, but worsened around 5 p.m.

As one of the doctors administered an injection, Asif turned to him and said, 'Doctor, I don't want to die in such a pathetic state. I prefer a heroic death.' Sanjeev Kumar was then at his bedside, gently massaging his chest. At about 5.30 pm. Sanjeev Kumar felt Asif's temperature gradually fall. The doctor was contacted on the phone, but Asif's condition had deteriorated rapidly. Producer Nasir Hussain, who was present there, phoned Asif's wife and others. Soon Mrs Akhtar Asif, her brother Nasir Khan, Abhi Bhattacharya, Asha Parekh, and Saira Bano arrived.

As moments passed, Asif realised his end was near. Feebly, he beckoned Sanjeev Kumar to lean forward and mustered enough strength to say, 'I know I am dying'. Then turning to his wife, he looked despairingly. Even

Facing Page:
Top left to right:
The mortal remains of K. Asif were brought down from his first floor flat. A shocked Johny Walker leads the way; Prithviraj Kapoor shoulders K. Asif in his last journey;

Below left to right:
A grief-stricken Dilip Kumar at the funeral; Namaz-e-Janaza (Prayer of Funeral).

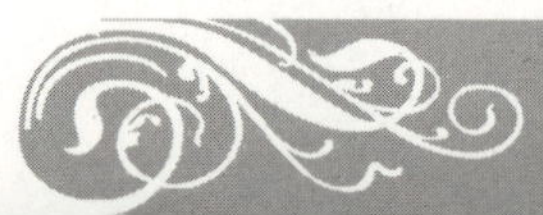

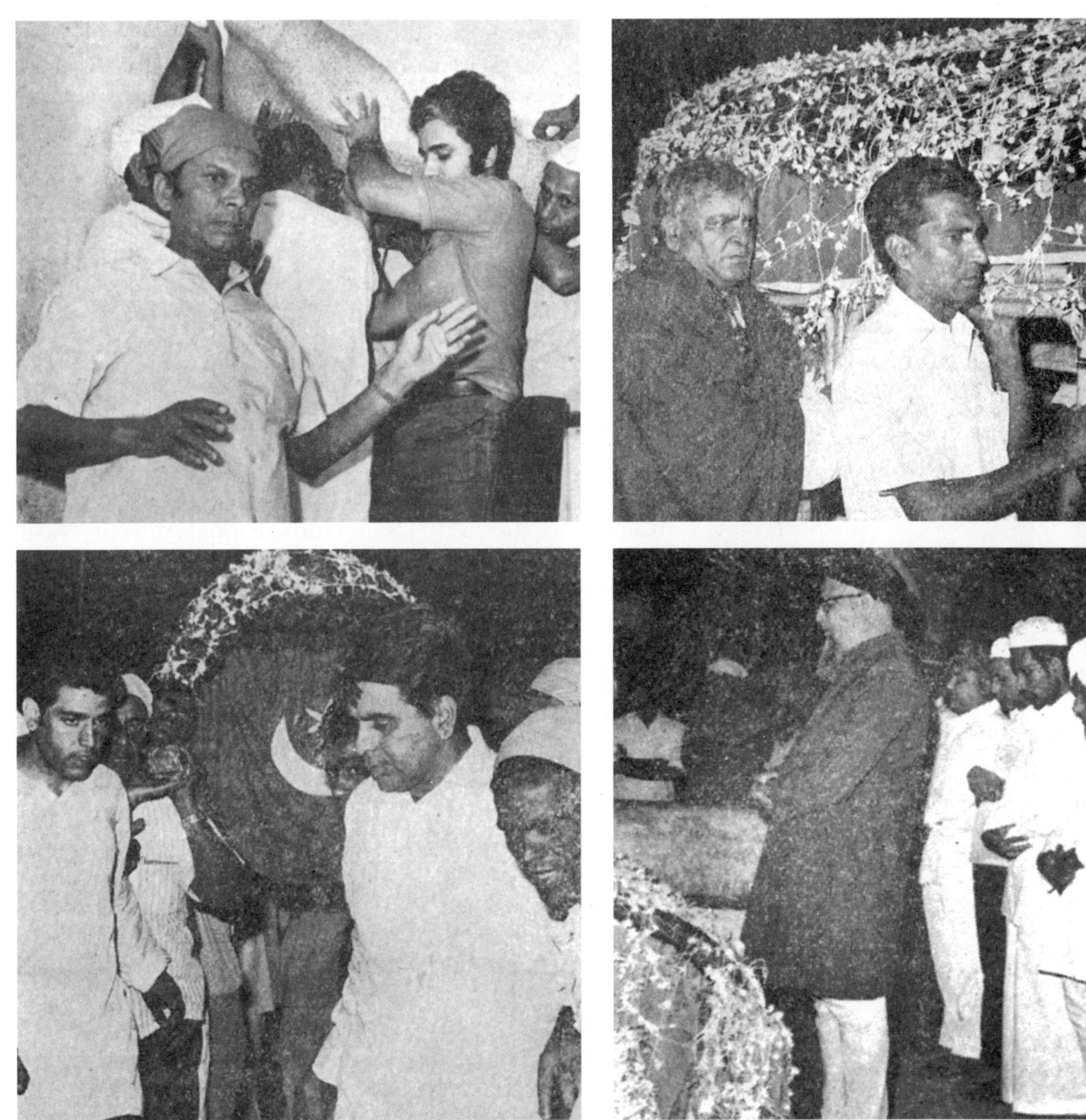

Asif was referred to as the Cecil B. DeMille of India, and his early death was an irreparable loss for Indian cinema.

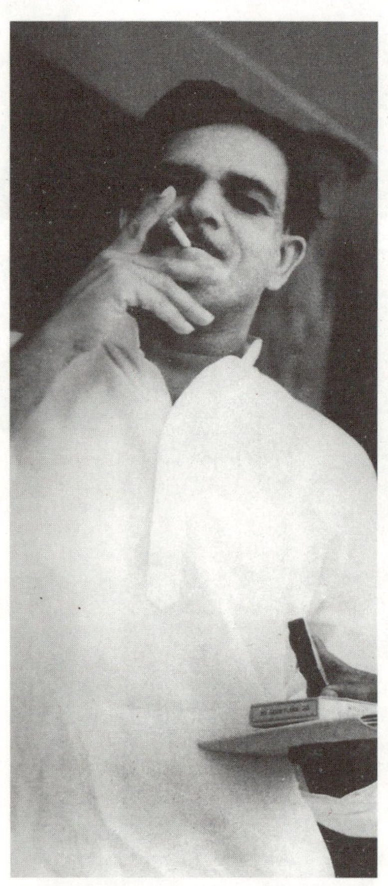

as death stared at him, the thought of *Love and God* was not out of his mind. 'I leave behind this film for you to complete...' These were Asif's last words after which he went into coma. At 6.25 p.m. the flame flickered out.

Dilip Kumar reached the place minutes afterwards. 'He was in such cheerful health only a few hours ago. I can't believe he is no more,' he said in a choked voice. At about 9 p.m., the mortal remains were shifted to his Juhu residence. By now the news had spread, and the film fraternity poured in to pay its homage to the departed soul. The funeral took place at the Muslim cemetery at Juhu. A congregation of over one thousand people, including prominent personalities of the film industry, attended it.

Among them were B.R. Chopra, G.P. Sippy, O.P. Ralhan, S. Mukherji, Dulal Guha, Kamal Amrohi, Nasir Hussain, Ramanand Sagar, K.A. Abbas, Kaifi Azmi, Majrooh Sultanpuri and Hasrat Jaipuri. There were others too – Prithviraj Kapoor, Dilip Kumar, Sanjeev Kumar, Raj Kumar, Sunil Dutt, Sanjay Khan, Firoz Khan, Sameer, Johny Walker, Mukri, Rehman, Pran, Vinod Khanna, Shammi Kapoor, Manmohan Krishna and Agha.

The burial took place at 3.15 a.m. As a mark of respect, the Bombay film industry remained closed on Wednesday, 10 March 1971. Shooting was called off at all film studios. Recording and processing laboratories, production and distribution offices remained closed to mourn the movie moghul. The premiere of *Anand,* scheduled for the next day, was cancelled. The Holi celebrations at R.K. Studios on 10 March were also cancelled.

On the tenth day, 'Fateha' was held at the late filmmaker's house in Juhu. The famous kathak dancer

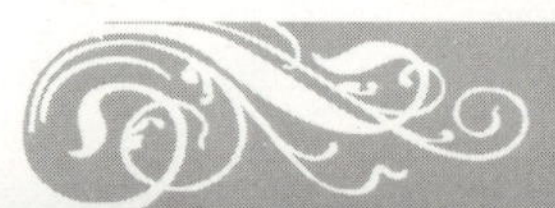

and ex-wife of Asif, Sitara Devi, had a shraadh feast on the thirteenth day (21 March), according to Hindu customs. A few close friends were invited; among them was Asif's second wife Nigar Sultana.

The genius of K. Asif died after him. No one from his family inherited his skill and passion for filmmaking.

Asif's sudden death jolted Akhtar as she was the person who had transformed a wayward man into an affectionate husband and a responsible father. She had written a poem just a few days before her husband's death. The last words were:

In its golden sands one day
When our bodies shall melt,
Dust to dust returneth
Then who shall say
You are not where I am
And I am where you are not
Till then I shall wait for you
Through the cycle of day and night.

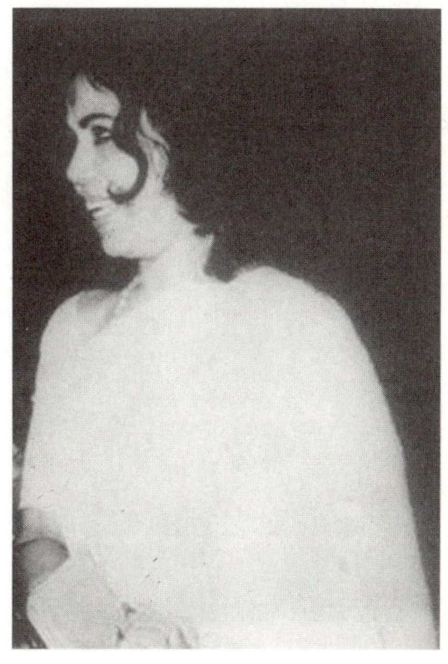

Sitara Devi in her youth.

Asif was referred to as the Cecil B. DeMille of India, and his early death was an irreparable loss for Indian cinema. He preferred an austere lifestyle but made the most ornate extravaganza of all times. The maker of *Mughal-e-Azam* lived in a two-bedroom flat throughout his life. Once Sanjeev Kumar, his close friend, asked him to buy a plot of land and build a bungalow for himself. Asif replied, 'I am here to make films, not bungalows.'

The resurrection

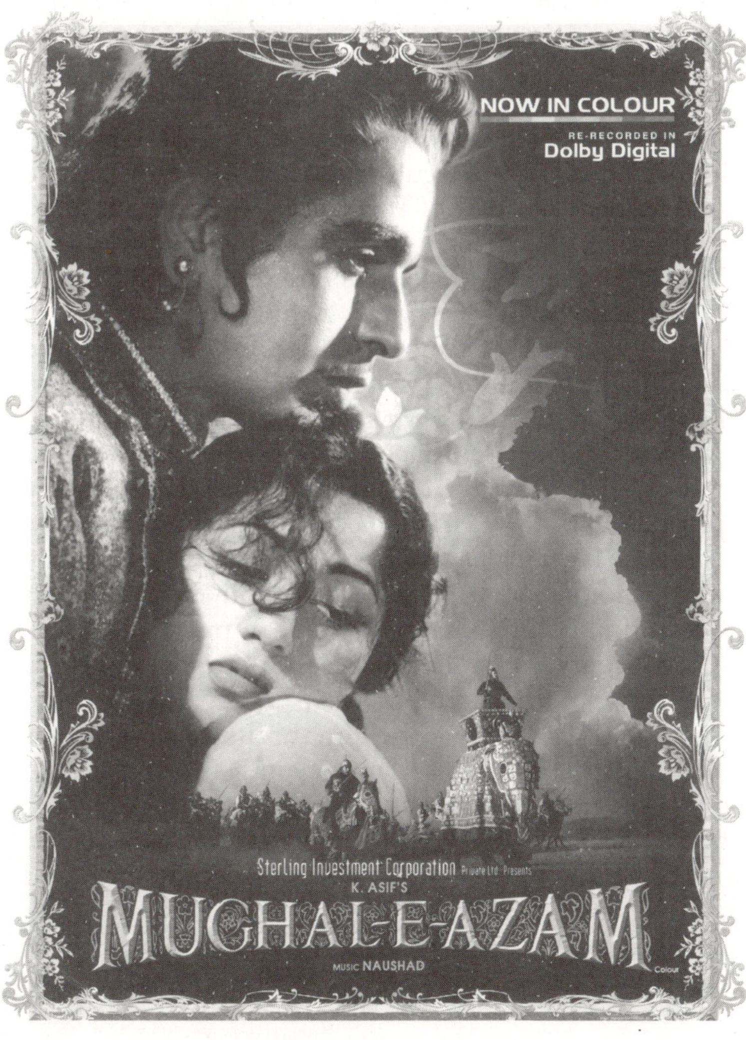

Computers were made intelligent enough to point out historical errors... One computer rejected a red rose simply because it had not been developed in the Mughal era!

Five decades have passed since the colour revolution hit Indian screens with Mehboob's *Aan* and Sohrab Modi's *Jhansi ki Rani* in the early 1950s. Asif himself wanted to shoot *Mughal-e-Azam* in colour, but had to content himself with using it only for two song sequences — '*Pyaar kiya to darna kya*' and '*Jab raat hai aise matwali*'. This amounted to thirty minutes of footage, which was processed in London.

It was the desire to acquaint a generation raised on colour images with the cult film that triggered off the digital metamorphosis of the epic, a rupees four-crore attempt to present the film in colour. And, the man behind it is a computer engineer, Umar Siddiqui, the managing director of Indian Academy of Arts and Animation (IAAA), Mumbai. Siddiqui and his associate Rajiv Dwiwedi designed special software for the job, which took more than two years to develop.

When the duo approached the owners of the film, Shapoorji Pallonji and Company, the idea was instantly appreciated; they were allowed to experiment with a ten-minute clipping as a trial. The results were amazing and Shapoorji Mistry, the grandson of Shapoorji Pallonji, immediately handed over the prints.

The twenty cans of negatives, Siddiqui says, were like decaying paint, smirched with fungus and scratches all over. They had to pass the film through several stages of digital processing. The scanning and cleaning of each frame was carried out using special and fully loaded 'Kodak' Scanner software. It was only after getting the film on hard disk that the final task of restoration and colourisation was taken up.

The mouse clicked on a palette of 24,000 million colour shades and each frame demanded the unfailing attention of several historians and researchers. For color grading, special software like, Digital Fusion (DFX), 'Flame' and 'Flint' were used. The colourisation process of *Mughal-e-Azam* was obviously different from a regular black and white film. There were thousands of details in each frame, like the period piece designs on jewellery and costumes of the Mughal era, chandeliers, curtains, carved walls, doors and arcs, the tents of armours (*zarra bakhtars*), indoor and outdoor settings, and the atmosphere on the battlefield. The technicians of IAAA faced enormous difficulties while managing the lighting effects of the film, as it was done as per the requirements of the black and white film. The background and foreground shades had to be merged with accurate and exact colours without diluting the impact of the scene. Computers were made intelligent enough to point out historical errors during the process. For instance, one computer rejected a red rose simply because the red rose had not been developed in the Mughal era!

Mughal-e-Azam is an unusually lengthy film and comprises approximately three lakh frames. Each frame (single photograph) normally consists of about thirty lakh pixels. When converted into a digital format, each frame had to be treated individually, taking care of lakhs of pixels and digital grains scattered all over. Thousands of shades of colours were used frame by frame, without overlapping and mingling them with each other, making the visual clear with the highest possible resolution available in non-linear technology.

The natural skin tone of the actors also needed precision while handling, without affecting the shades of their costumes and jewellery. Rajiv Dwiwedi, the technical director, said his team was at pains to colour

the outdoor scenes as well as the dissolve shots. They also faced problem in removing scratches, white streaks and video noises.

Hundreds of technicians were engaged, and it usually took twenty-four hours to convert one minute of black and white film into colour. There were some sequences, like the qawwali between Madhubala and Nigar Sultana (*Teri mehfil me kismat aazma ke)* which took three months to process. For continuity, even the coloured portion was re-coloured digitally.

The original soundtrack was also in a bad shape. IAAA sent it to US for cleaning and separation of the two tracks; the dialogue track and music track. The audio track went through digital cleaning and removal of a hissing sound without touching the dialogues. This was done by Chace Production, LA, US, a specialist in the job. The separation of the dialogue and music tracks was far more complicated because the track recorded originally was mono mixed.

The audio track was then converted into digital Dolby form to make the background score more effective in keeping with the new look of the film. Naushad supervised the recreation, assisted by his son Raju Naushad and Uttam Singh. Time, Naushad added more instruments in recomposing the music; it was done to enhance the impact of the situation without tampering with the lyrical value or melody of the song, he said. About 120 musicians were called in to play Hindustani classical instruments, and about sixty chorus singers were employed to give the desired effect. A special team of musicians was called in from Chennai for the string section. The final task of mixing the recomposed music with the voices of Bade Ghulam Ali Khan, Mohammad Rafi, Lata Mangeshkar and Shamshad Begum from the old track was carried out at Fiesta Studio, Mumbai.

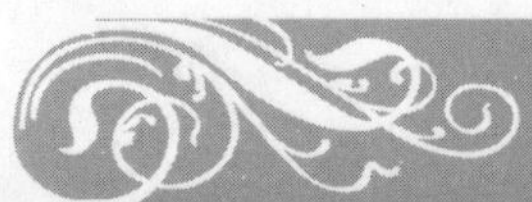

The colour and digital Dolby sound is in fact a tribute to Asif's dream of making the film in colour. 'IAAA has performed the job, which is a first of its kind in the world, with full mastery,' says Umar Siddiqui. According to Siddiqui, while Hollywood had earlier attempted the colourisation of a video film in 1982, India today has the honour of converting the world's first full-length black and white feature film into a coloured version.

Asif's son, Akbar Asif, felt overwhelmed as he expressed his gratitude to the Pallonjis. Describing the painstaking work undertaken by the whiz kids, he said, 'The emotional depth of the narrative was retained, taking care that the gloss did not overtake the content.' He then gifted a sum of one crore and eleven lakh rupees to be shared by the technical team in acknowledgement of the monumental effort.

He expressed this in a letter to Shapoorji Mistry:

Dear Shapoorji Saab,
Even if I write on all the papers in the world, it would not be enough...I cannot, now or ever, do justice to what I feel for you. My prayers, my appreciation and my admiration will always be with you for making my father's dream a reality.

The coloured version was released on 12 November 2004. Akbar Asif moved a step ahead to pay tribute to his father's labour of love. He set up a private museum in his penthouse in London and commissioned M.F. Hussain to create paintings of more than fifty immortal visuals from the film. He resides in the same penthouse and has converted the grand living room into his workshop, seeking inspiration from the original as he watches the film over and over again on a giant plasma screen. Hussain says he feels delighted and proud to interpret this great film on huge canvasses.

The re-release

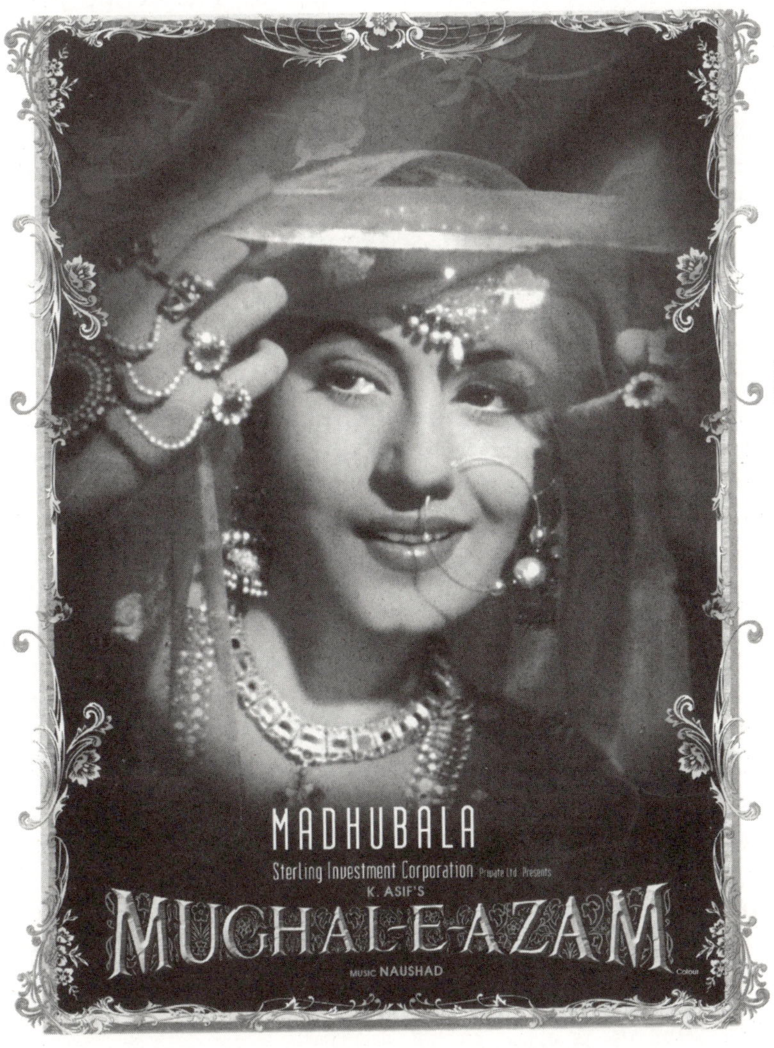

There were wolf whistles at the entry of Prithviraj Kapoor, Dilip Kumar and Madhubala!

The day was 10 November 2004 when the prints of *Mughal-e-Azam* were brought on a *palki* (palanquin) set on the back of a decorated elephant. The venue was Eros Cinema, in Mumbai and the occasion was the re-release of *Mughal-e-Azam* in a digitally improved and coloured format. There were other premieres in the city the same week. The Abhishek Bachchan starrer *Naach* and Kareena Kapoor's *Aitraaz* were due for release. But all eyes were on Eros.

Men and women dressed in royal uniforms stood in a row outside the hall to symbolise the splendour of Akbar's darbar. The theatre was done up lavishly. Palace doorways were studded with ornamental work and adorned with crimson curtains. Statues of Dilip Kumar as Prince Salim, Madhubala as Anarkali and Prithviraj Kapoor as Akbar were lined up. The palanquin carrying the prints of the film made straight for the projection room. A galaxy of stars, including Dilip Kumar, Saira Bano, Rekha, Sridevi, Boney Kapoor, Anil Kapoor, Sanjay Kapoor, Govinda, Tabu, Rani Mukherjee, Aishwarya Rai, Raza Murad, Akshay Kumar and other eminent personalities such as Samajwadi Party leader Amar Singh, Shapoorji Mistry, the grandson of Shapoorji Pallonji, Sitara Devi, and Akhtar Asif were among those present. Eros Cinema reminded one of 5 August 1960 when the grand epic was first released at Maratha Mandir.

Dilip Kumar said, 'I feel choked by the sheer emotion and significance of this occasion.' He thought the coloured version had vastly enhanced the movie's

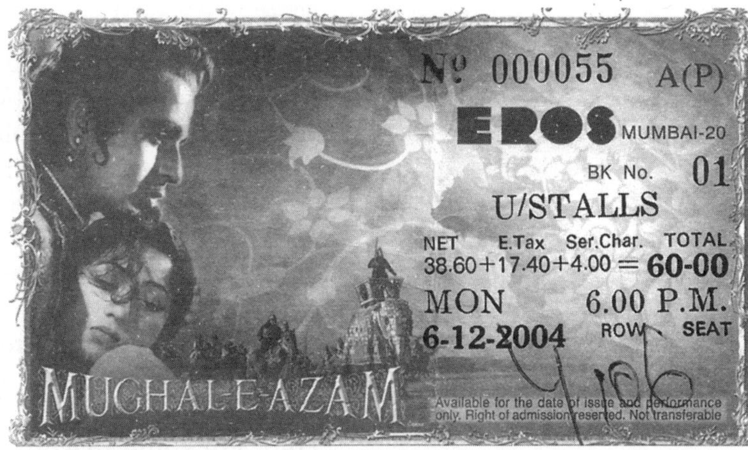

appeal. Saira Bano said the colourisation and digital conversion of the film was like '*Sone pe suhaga*'. She was lucky to have been able to attend both the premieres. Tabu said she had been waiting impatiently for the release. Aishwarya Rai said the movie was a classic, the charm of Madhubala was exquisite and eternal; in colour it was a totally different experience. Anil Kapoor said it was very special as his father, Surender Kapoor, had worked as an assistant director on it. Surender Kapoor was a young bachelor when Asif started the project. By the time the film was released, he was not only married and established but also a father of three children, including Boney and Anil Kapoor. Interestingly, Boney Kapoor has now bought the distribution rights of the film. Actor Raza Murad, who claimed to have seen the film 400-500 times, was waiting eagerly to see it in the new version. He said he had the privilege of attending the 1960 premiere of the film with his father when he was only eight!

The film recreated box office history once again! As weeks passed by, people flocked to the cinema halls to watch the magic unfold! A classic made over fifty years ago was competing gracefully with the contemporary films. Month after month, theatres put up the 'houseful' boards, which posed a threat to many other big budget movies released in the same period. According to a report in *Screen,* dated 26 November 2004, more prints of *Mughal-e-Azam* were soon ordered to meet the demand.

The audience comprised all ages, from teenagers to middle-aged couples and senior citizens in the age group of seventy and eighty. While the nostalgia of elderly viewers is understandable, the clamour of teenagers was certainly a pleasant surprise. There were wolf whistles at the entry of Prithviraj Kapoor, Dilip Kumar and Madhubala. The spontaneous applause for scenes and dialogues is clearly a proof of the timeless appeal of the epic.

Reviewing a film already regarded as a masterpiece is a tricky task. The *Times of India* in its issue of 15 November 2004, had a write-up by Jitesh Pillai: 'Here are some reasons why *Mughal-e-Azam* is a must-see ... for its sheer canvas, its majestic framing and not for being a gaudy costume drama ... for the somewhat subdued reference to Akbar's religious tolerance ... for Dilip Kumar, who runs a feather across Indian cinema's most beautiful face and time stops absolutely still ... for the glorious Sheesh Mahal where Madhubala defiantly dances.....Our filmmakers ... cannot think beyond Manhattan ... they don't make them like this anymore.'

M.J. Akbar, former editor-in-chief of the *Asian Age* discussed the film's philosophy of love, as propounded through the famous song '*Pyar kiya toh darna kya*': 'It was an age when virginal love was considered scandalous ... fantasy had a wonderful time ... *pyar kiya toh darna kya, pyar kiya koi chori nahin ki, chup chup aahen bharna kya* (why should I fear when I love. It is not a theft ... why should I sigh from behind a curtain?) It would need a social historian better than I to convey how powerful, even revolutionary, the idea was that love transcended fear. For every father was an emperor then, demanding the destruction of love in the name of some high social principles.'

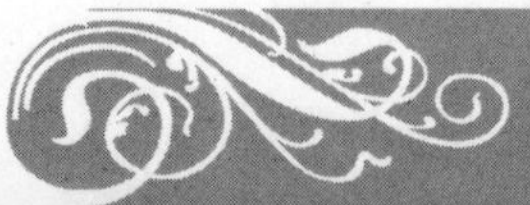

Akbar further mentions how the spirit of religious tolerance is woven into the script of *Mughal-e-Azam*. Madhubala prays in her namaz for the life of Durjan Singh, son of Man Singh, who has just rescued her at the cost of his own life. The emperor prays to Allah, through the Sufi saint Salim Chisti, for a son and accepts prasad from his Hindu wife Jodhabai after she has worshipped Lord Krishna on Janmashtami. A moulvi ties taweez on the right arm of the emperor with the famous victory words of the Holy Quran *Nasrumminallah-e-fateh-un-quareeb*. Then, a Hindu priest blesses the emperor with a saffron mark on the forehead. '*Arrey,*' asked a curious voice in the auditorium, '*Ye Hindu hai ki Mussalman*?'

Taran Adarsh, the editor of the most reputed film trade magazine, *Trade Guide*, expressed his thoughts on the movie in the following words: '*Mughal-e-Azam* is a must for every moviegoer. Here is a prime example of pure, unadulterated cinema ... the grand look, the haunting musical score, the breathtaking battle scenes, the splendid performances, the heartrending emotions, the legendary romance between Salim and Anarkali, and of course the confrontation scenes between Akbar and Salim ... *Mughal-e-Azam* will always remain a benchmark.'

Following are some of the press reviews published in leading newspapers of the country.

> 'In comparison to today's Bollywood pathetic and banal blockbusters *Mughal-e-Azam* towers tall in its scale and sweep in having viewers raptly engrossed in its ensemble, heart-wrenching drama of pathos and passion.'
> (*Deccan Herald,* Bangalore)

'It was a tantalising prospect to witness the eternal glory of *Mughal-e-Azam* in the flesh and blood of colour. The colourisation has added to the spell of what is the most evocative drama in the history of Indian Cinema'.
(*Pioneer,* New Delhi)

'*Mughal-e-Azam* in colour is a great experiment. It is about revisiting something that can be easily ranked among the best Indian films ever. One is reminded of Hollywood greats such as *Benhur* and *Gone with the Wind.'*
(Asian Age, New Delhi)

'After forty-four years the movie fills colour in Salim and Anarkali's love. It's a treat to one's eye'.
(*Danik Jagran,* National)

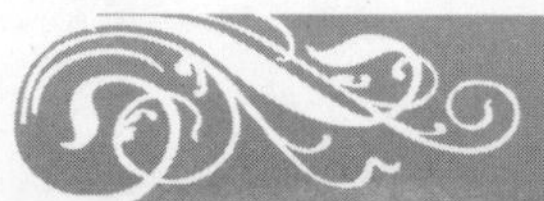

Songs of Mughal-e-Azam

Shubh din aayo:
Ustad Bade Ghulam Ali Khan

Mohe panghat pe Nand lal ched gayo re:
Lata Mangeshkar and chorus.

Teri mehfil mein qismat aazmakar:
Lata Mangashkar, Shamshad Begum & chorus.

Ai ishq ye sab duniyawalein bekar ki batein:
Lata Mangeshkar

Prem jogan ban ke sunder pee ki oar chali:
Bade Ghulam Ali Khan

Mohabbat ki jhooti kahani pe roye:
Lata Mangeshkar

Hamein kash tum se mohabbat na hoti:
Lata Mangeshkar

Pyar kiya toh darna kiya:
Lata Mangeshkar

Bekas pe karam kijiye:
Lata Mangeshkar

Zindabad ai mohabbat zindabad:
Mohammad Rafi

Ye dil ki lagi.... jab raat hai aisi matwali:
Lata Mangeshkar and chorus

Wo aayi....khuda nigehbaan ho tumahara
Lata Mangeshkar

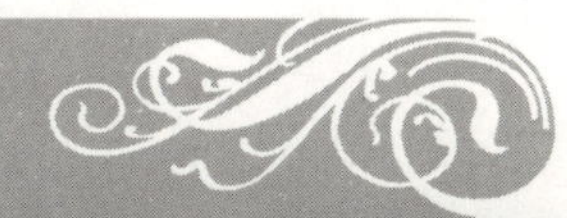

Cast and Credits

Director: K. Asif

Music: Naushad

Cast: Prithviraj Kapoor, Dilip Kumar, Madhubala, Nigar Sultana, Ajit, Kumar, Murad, Zillu Bai, Sheela Deloy

Guest Artistes: Surender, Gopi Krishna, Jalal Agha, Tabassum and Johnnie Walker

Screenplay: K. Asif, Aman

Dialogues: Kamal Amrohi, Vajahat Mirza, Ehsan Rizvi and Aman

Lyrics: Shakeel Badayuni

Photography: R.D. Mathur (W.I.C.A.)

Art Director: M.K. Sayyed

Dance Director: Lachhu Maharaj

Sound: Akram Sheikh

Editing: Dharam Veer

Associate Director: S.T. Zaidi

Chief Asst. Director: Khalid Akhtar

Assistant Directors: H.R. Riyaaz, Rasheed Abbasi, Rafique Arabi, Surender Kapoor, Mohd. Anwar, K. Manohar

Additional Cameramen for Outdoors:

M.W. Mukadam, Shaffan, Suleman, Karve

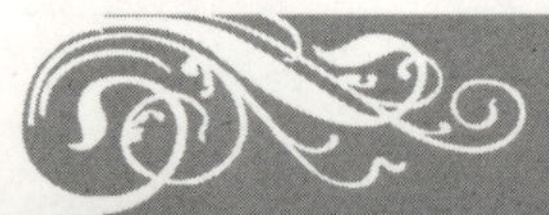

Bibliography

Books

The One and Lonely (Autobiography): Kidar Sharma

Indian Filmography: Firoz Rangoonwala

The Life And Times Of Nargis: T.J.S. George

So Many Cinemas: B.D. Garga

Madhubala, Magic & Masti: Alpna Choudhry

Filmfare (1952, 1953, 1954)

Film India (1942 to 1960)

Cine Advance

Notes of Naushad: Shashikant Kiniskar

Bollywood Encyclopedia of Indian Cinema: Ashish Rajadhyaksha and Paul Willemen

Mee Durga Khote: An autobiography of Durga Khote

Filmography: Dr. R.K. Verma, Silent Cinema, 1913 to 1934

Madhubala: Mohan Deep

Dilip Kumar: Star Legend of Indian Cinema: Bunny Reuben

Articles

'K. Asif's Mughal-e-Azam: An Obsession': Roshmala Bhattacharya, (*Zee Premier*, June 1999)

'Dilip Kumar: Portrait of an Actor': Hamidduddin Mahmood (*Star & Style*, December 1973)

'I Found the Key to Film Music': Naushad Ali (*Filmfare*, 27 June 1952)

'Bade Ghulam Ali Saw Ragas in Nature': Nilakhsha Gupta (*Asian Age*, 8 August 2005)

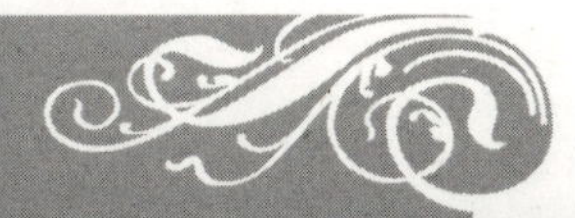

Photo Credits

Indian Academy of Arts & Animation (IAAA)
Rajkamal Academy of Cinematic Excellence
Design Intervention India Pvt. Ltd.
Film India journal 1942 to 1950
Noor Merchant: librarian of old film journals;
Abid Husain and Hussaini: collector of old films' memorabilia.

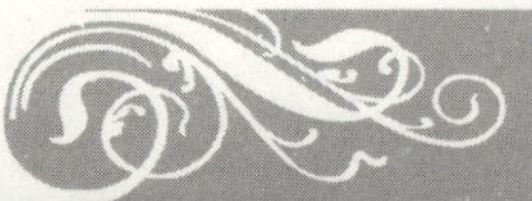